Trafficking Women in Korea

Based on in-depth ethnographic work, this book presents a study of Filipinas trafficked to South Korea, focusing on women who entered South Korea as migrant entertainers and subsequently became deployed in exploitative work environments around US military bases there. It contributes to the extension of our knowledge about human trafficking in the Asian region through an exploration of the experiences of more than 100 women who took part in the study. The book challenges many of the accepted understandings about 'trafficking victims' and unravels the implications of these narrow understandings for the women themselves. It explores the ways women negotiate trafficking largely outside of the emerging formal anti-trafficking framework, and explains how new community formations and social networks emerge crafted by the women themselves to manage and overcome their vulnerabilities in migration.

Sallie Yea is Assistant Professor in the Department of Humanities and Social Science Education at the Nanyang Technological University, Singapore.

Asian Studies Association of Australia Women in Asia Series

Editor: Louise Edwards (University of New South Wales)
Editorial Board:
Susan Blackburn (Monash University)
Hyaeweol Choi (The Australian National University)
Michele Ford (The University of Sydney)
Trude Jacobsen (Northern Illinois University)
Vera Mackie (University of Wollongong)
Anne McLaren (The University of Melbourne)
Mina Roces (University of New South Wales)
Dina Siddiqi (The City University of New York)
Andrea Whittaker (The University of Queensland)

Mukkuvar Women
Gender, hegemony and capitalist transformation in a south Indian fishing community
by Kalpana Ram 1991

A World of Difference
Islam and gender hierarchy in Turkey
by Julie Marcus 1992

Purity and Communal Boundaries
Women and social change in a Bangladeshi village
by Santi Rozario 1992

Madonnas and Martyrs
Militarism and violence in the Philippines
by Anne-Marie Hilsdon 1995

Masters and Managers
A study of gender relations in urban Java
by Norma Sullivan 1995

Matriliny and Modernity
Sexual politics and social change in rural Malaysia
by Maila Stivens 1995

Intimate Knowledge
Women and their health in north-east Thailand
by Andrea Whittaker 2000

Women in Asia
Tradition, modernity and globalisation
by Louise Edwards and Mina Roces (eds) 2000

Violence against Women in Asian Societies
Gender inequality and technologies of violence
by Lenore Manderson and Linda Rae Bennett (eds) 2003

Women's Employment in Japan
The experience of part-time workers
by Kaye Broadbent 2003

Chinese Women Living and Working
by Anne McLaren (ed) 2004

Abortion, Sin and the State in Thailand
by Andrea Whittaker 2004

Sexual Violence and the Law in Japan
by Catherine Burns 2004

Women, Islam and Modernity
Single women, sexuality and reproductive health in contemporary Indonesia
by Linda Rae Bennett 2005

The Women's Movement in Post-Colonial Indonesia
by Elizabeth Martyn 2005

Women and Work in Indonesia
by Michele Ford and Lyn Parker (eds) 2008

Women and Union Activism in Asia
by Kaye Broadbent and Michele Ford (eds) 2008

Gender, Islam, and Democracy in Indonesia
by Kathryn Robinson 2008

Sex, Love and Feminism in the Asia Pacific
A cross-cultural study of young people's attitudes
by Chilla Bulbeck 2008

Gender, State and Social Power
Divorce in contemporary Indonesia
by Kate O'Shaughnessy 2008

Gender, Household, and State in Post-Revolutionary Vietnam
by Jayne Werner 2008

Young Women in Japan
Transitions to adulthood
by Kaori Okano 2009

Women, Islam and Everyday Life
Renegotiating polygamy in Indonesia
by Nina Nurmila 2009

Feminist Movements in Contemporary Japan
by Laura Dales 2009

Gender and Labour in Korea and Japan
Sexing class
by Ruth Barraclough and Elyssa Faison (eds) 2009

Gender Diversity in Indonesia
Sexuality, Islam and queer selves
by Sharyn Graham Davies 2010

New Women in Colonial Korea
A sourcebook
by Hyaeweol Choi 2012

Women Writers in Postsocialist China
by Kay Schaffer and Xianlin Song 2013

Domestic Violence in Asia
Globalization, gender and Islam in the Maldives
by Emma Fulu 2014

Gender and Power in Indonesian Islam
Leaders, feminists, sufis and pesantren selves
edited by Bianca J. Smith and Mark Woodward 2014

Practicing Feminism in South Korea
The women's movement against sexual violence
by Kyungja Jung 2014

The Korean Women's Movement and the State
Bargaining for change
by Seung-kyung Kim 2014

Gender, Nation and State in Modern Japan
edited by Andrea Germer, Vera Mackie and Ulrike Wöhr 2014

Women and Sex Work in Cambodia
Blood, sweat and tears
by Larissa Sandy 2015

Growing up Female in Multi-Ethnic Malaysia
by Cynthia Joseph 2015

Women, Sexual Violence and the Indonesian Killings of 1965–66
by Annie Pohlman 2015

Love and Marriage in Globalising China
by Wang Pan 2015

Women and Climate Change in Bangladesh
by Margaret Alston 2015

Women and Politics in Contemporary Japan
by Emma Dalton 2015

Trafficking Women in Korea
Filipina migrant entertainers
by Sallie Yea 2015

Women and Sharia Law in Northern Indonesia
by Dina Afrianty 2015

China's Leftover Women
Late marriage among professional women and its consequences
by Sandy To 2015

Trafficking Women in Korea
Filipina migrant entertainers

Sallie Yea

LONDON AND NEW YORK

First published 2015
by Routledge
2 Park Square, Milton Park, Abingdon, Oxon, OX14 4RN

and by Routledge
711 Third Avenue, New York, NY 10017

*Routledge is an imprint of the Taylor & Francis Group,
an informa business*

© 2015 Sallie Yea

The right of Sallie Yea to be identified as author of this work has been asserted by her in accordance with the Copyright, Designs and Patent Act 1988.

All rights reserved. No part of this book may be reprinted or reproduced or utilised in any form or by any electronic, mechanical, or other means, now known or hereafter invented, including photocopying and recording, or in any information storage or retrieval system, without permission in writing from the publishers.

Trademark notice: Product or corporate names may be trademarks or registered trademarks, and are used only for identification and explanation without intent to infringe.

British Library Cataloguing in Publication Data
A catalogue record for this book is available from the British Library

Library of Congress Cataloging-in-Publication Data
Yea, Sallie, author.
  Trafficking women in Korea : Filipina migrant entertainers / Sallie Yea.
    pages cm — (Women in Asia series / Asian Studies Association of Australia)
  Includes bibliographical references and index.
  1. Human trafficking—Korea (South) 2. Filipinos—Employment—Korea (South) 3. Women foreign workers—Korea (South) I. Title. II. Series: ASAA women in Asia series.
  HQ418.Y43 2015
  306.3′62082—dc23
  2014034880

ISBN: 978-0-415-85530-3 (hbk)
ISBN: 978-0-203-73693-7 (ebk)

Typeset in Times New Roman
by Apex CoVantage, LLC

Printed and bound in the United States of America by Publishers Graphics, LLC on sustainably sourced paper.

In memory of my mother, Margaret McCormack Yea
(8.3.32–28.12.03)
—the bravest woman I've known

It is . . . necessary to focus on the subject situated at the periphery, as she has the power to bring about normative disruptions.
—Ratna Kapur, *The Tragedy of Victimisation Rhetoric*, 2002: 30–31

Contents

Illustrations		xi
Series editor's foreword		xiii
Acknowledgements		xv
Acronyms		xvii
1	Introduction	1
2	'Sex trafficking' comes to Korea's *gijich'on*	19
3	Re-thinking trafficking in *gijich'on*	38
4	Health in trafficking	68
5	Romancing (in) the club	87
6	Running to the future	107
7	Anti-trafficking by NGOs and entertainers	130
8	Home is where the hurt is	148
9	Conclusion	162
	References	165
	Index	175

Illustrations

Figures

1.1	Map of the Korean Peninsula showing major US military camp towns	2
3.1	Copy of Nikki's promissory note	45
3.2	Copy of a woman's contract	54
5.1	Excerpt from bar fine and ladies drink record for May 31–August 31, 2002, for Cherry-Lyn	95

Table

5.1	Excerpt from bar fine and ladies drink record for May 31–August 31, 2002, for Cherry-Lyn	94

Series editor's foreword

The contributions of women to the social, political and economic transformations occurring in the Asian region are legion. Women have served as leaders of nations, communities, workplaces, activist groups and families. Asian women have joined with others to participate in fomenting change at micro and macro levels. They have been both agents and targets of national and international interventions in social policy. In the performance of these myriad roles women have forged new and modern gendered identities that are recognisably global and local. Their experiences are rich, diverse and instructive. The books in this series testify to the central role women play in creating the new Asia and re-creating Asian womanhood. Moreover, these books reveal the resilience and inventiveness of women around the Asian region in the face of entrenched and evolving patriarchal social norms.

Scholars publishing in this series demonstrate a commitment to promoting the productive conversation between Gender Studies and Asian Studies. The need to understand the diversity of experiences of femininity and womanhood around the world increases inexorably as globalisation proceeds apace. Lessons from the experiences of Asian women present us with fresh opportunities for building new possibilities for women's progress the world over.

The Asian Studies Association of Australia (ASAA) sponsors this publication series as part of its ongoing commitment to promoting knowledge about women in Asia. In particular, the ASAA Women's Forum provides the intellectual vigour and enthusiasm that maintains the Women in Asia Series (WIAS). The aim of the series, since its inception in 1990, is to promote knowledge about women in Asia to both academic and general audiences. To this end, WIAS books draw on a wide range of disciplines including anthropology, sociology, political science, cultural studies, media studies, literature and history. The series prides itself on being an outlet for cutting-edge research conducted by recent PhD graduates and postdoctoral fellows from throughout the region.

The Series could not function without the generous professional advice provided by many anonymous readers. Moreover, the wise counsel provided by Peter Sowden at Routledge is invaluable. WIAS, its authors and the ASAA are very grateful to these people for their expert work.

Lenore Lyons (The University of Sydney)
Series Editor

Acknowledgements

This book has been a long time in the making. After returning to Australia from eighteen months of ethnographic fieldwork in South Korea in late 2003 I was hit with the shock of my mother's rapidly deteriorating health and, a few weeks later, her death. Writing the book was put on hold, and inevitably my initial thoughts about the meaning of the experiences of the many women I met in Korea changed with time, reflection and ongoing email and telephone exchanges with some of these women. When I finally put pen to paper again in 2008 it was with the encouragement of colleagues from the Department of Geography at the National University of Singapore, particularly Shirlena Huang and Tracey Skelton. Routledge editor Helena Hurd took an immediate interest in the manuscript, and I began to feel that perhaps I did have something novel to say about the much debated and written-about topic of trafficking in the commercial sex and nightlife entertainment industry. I wish to thank Helena, Shirlena and Tracey for their encouragement to re-visit and ultimately realise the book project. Lenore Lyons also deserves thanks for her meticulous editing of the manuscript. It is a far more robust treatise with her insights and extensive knowledge of gendered migration and labour regimes in Asia. Some of my arguments in the book benefited from rich discussions with Kathleen Maltzahn.

This was not easy fieldwork, and I am ever grateful to Sister Theresa Oh, Kim Eun Mee, Father Glenn Jaron and the staff of the Philippines Embassy in Seoul for their insights into migrant worker and gender issues in Korea. But I reserve my most heartfelt thanks to Cherry, Lisa and Grace, three dear friends who opened their lives, houses and hearts to me during my fieldwork. For allowing me to stay at their apartments, for accompanying me to clubs, for sharing food and inviting me to parties and outings and for so many other small gestures I can never thank them enough.

I thank the following publishers for permission to reprint sections of 'Runaway Brides' (Wiley, *Singapore Journal of Tropical Geography*) and 'Labour of Love' (Elsevier, *Women's Studies International Forum*).

Finally, I wish to thank my husband, Ariel Ellao, for supporting me in so many ways to pursue this research. He has always been a steadfast source of support for my work with both migrant women and contentious social issues in the Philippines. My son, Jericho, and daughter, Lylah, were both born whilst the manuscript was in preparation, and I hope one day they will read it and appreciate the hardships, trials and resilience of the migrants whose lives I hope to portray.

Acronyms

ARB	Artist's Record Book
AST	Academic and Skills Test
CATW	Coalition Against Trafficking of Women
CPs	Courtesy Patrols (US military)
DOLE	Department of Labour and Employment (Philippines)
EPS	Employment Permit System
IOM	International Organisation for Migration
KATUSA	Korean Augmentee to the United States Army
MPs	Military Police (US military)
NGOs	nongovernmental organizations
NIEs	newly industrialising economies
OFWs	overseas Filipino workers
PMRW	Philippine Migrants Rights Watch
POEA	Philippines Overseas Employment Administration
R&R	rest and recreation
ROK	Republic of Korea
SOFA	Status of Forces Agreement
STIs	sexually transmitted infections
TDC	Tongducheon (slang term)
TIP	Trafficking in Persons
TVPA	Trafficking Victims Protection Act
US DoD	United States Department of Defense
US DoS	United States Department of State
USFK	US Forces Korea

1 Introduction

Rosie and I sat at a quiet corner table of a tiny coffee shop in a backstreet of Seoul's trendy youth district of Hyehwa-dong and chatted about her life and how she had ended up in South Korea. Rosie arrived in 2001 to take up a job as an entertainer in a bar in the town of Tongducheon (known as TDC by the migrant entertainers and US military personnel who live there), which is located on the edge of Camp Casey, the largest US military base in South Korea, forty kilometres south of the North Korean border (see Figure 1.1). Rosie, who was sixteen at the time, had no intention of migrating abroad until she was awoken one evening by a knock on the door of her boarding house in Manila. The woman at the door was a recruiter for an entertainer's promotion agency. She asked Rosie if she would like to earn a lot of money by working overseas. Rosie was told that everything could be arranged very quickly through the agency. When Rosie showed up at the agency in Santa Cruz, Manila, two days later, she was asked by a Korean woman to strip, put on a see-through negligee and dance (turning around slowly and shaking her hips). Rosie informed the woman that she didn't know how to 'slow dance'. Nonetheless, of the thirty or so young women who were at the agency for an audition that day, Rosie was amongst the five chosen to go to Korea. She signed a contract which said she would entertain customers by serving them drinks, sitting with them and chatting. She was also told she would dance on the stage, 'like a star'. The work appeared to combine dancing with hostessing for a promised wage of USD 450 (KRW 500,000) per month.

In Korea, Rosie was deployed in Y Club. Her Korean boss owned two other clubs in nearby Toka-ri – the infamous M Club and NBC Club. She was sent to M Club to learn how to dance before being transferred to Y Club, where she had a six-month contract to work as an entertainer, renewable for a second period of six months. With the assistance of her American soldier boyfriend Rosie ran away from the club on her fourth attempt to do so. Some of the reasons that Rosie gave for running away from the club meet the United Nations definition of her as a 'trafficked person'. First, Rosie discovered that hostessing meant much more than dancing, chatting with customers and serving them drinks. Within one week of being at Club Y she was sent to one of the two VIP rooms at the rear of the club for 'VIP sex' (ten to fifteen minutes) with a customer. She had to take a condom and a tissue with her whenever she went into one of these rooms. Sex was also

2 *Introduction*

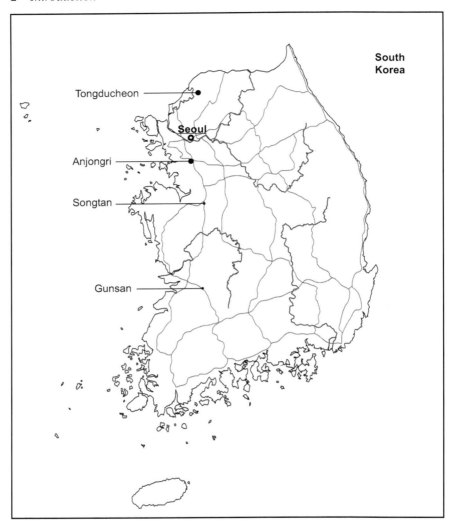

Figure 1.1 Map of the Korean Peninsula showing major US military camp towns

performed in the club as 'short time' (thirty minutes) and 'long time' (six to seven hours overnight upstairs in private rooms). Rosie serviced on average two or three customers this way each night during the three months she was there.

Y Club did indeed have dancing, but not exactly the kind of dancing Rosie was expecting. Nightly strip shows started at 9 p.m, and each woman had a song she would perform to. Each woman was required to strip completely naked before the completion of her song. A woman was required to get on stage when her song began to play, even if she was having sex with a customer at the time – the mama-san would knock on the door to tell her to go to the stage. "We have to run quickly, otherwise we would be punished", Rosie said. The DJ played the music loud enough to be heard anywhere in the club. Rosie said, "We would get so cold in winter and we would all go to the heater before the customers arrived. But when the mama-san sees this she would turn the heater off and tell us to get up on stage and practice our dancing. Because, you know, none of us knew how to dance when we came to Korea". The women would usually dance for three hours a night between the hours of 9 p.m. and 12 midnight. On average Rosie said she would get no more than five hours of sleep a night and even less on weekends, when the working hours were 2 p.m. to 5 a.m. At night all the women in Y Club were confined upstairs in their sleeping quarters.

The club instituted a points system to regulate the women's work. One 'ladies drink' (at USD 20) equalled two points. Twenty minutes after the drink was bought the woman had to stand up and ask the customer to buy her another drink or she would move to another table. The mama-san advised:

> When you sit with a GI you have to sit on his lap facing him [straddled over his legs] and dance – even before he buys you a drink. If after one minute he doesn't buy you a drink, you have to go to another customer and do the same thing until a GI buys you a drink.

For each ladies drink sold in a week, the woman would receive KRW 2,000 (USD 1.50), and this money would be given to her every weekend. If a woman earned 200 points (that is, 100 drinks) in a month, she was allowed one day off. Any less and she had no days off.

Rosie did not receive any of her promised USD 450 a month salary in the three months she was in Y Club, only tips from customers and the commission generated through her drink sales. All the salary was supposedly deposited in a bank account of which the mama-san was the signatory, so only the mama-san could sign withdrawal slips. After Rosie ran away and checked the bank account she discovered that only half a month's salary had ever been deposited into her account and not the USD 1,350 she was expecting.

For Rosie it was the arbitrarily imposed punishments that she and the other women were routinely subjected to that cemented her decision to run away from Y Club. The woman who sold the lowest number of drinks per week was punished by having to do the cooking, cleaning and laundry for all the women for that entire week. This meant getting up at 7 a.m., even if she had worked until 5 a.m. the night before. The week before Rosie ran away she sold the lowest number of drinks and had this punishment imposed. The other form of punishment Rosie described was being locked in a closet with the light switched off for up to half a day. Rosie received this punishment three times in the three months she was at the club. The first time was when the MPs (United States Army Military Police) came to the VIP room, as they routinely undertook inspections of all the clubs near US military bases looking for infringements, including evidence of prostitution involving US military personnel. She was in the VIP room with a customer and an MP asked her what was going on in there. She replied, "This is part of my job. That is why I'm here doing this". The mama-san was so mad at her for saying it was part of her job that she locked her in the closet for punishment. The closet contained the used condoms and tissues from the women's sexual encounters, and there was no room to stand up or a bucket to relieve oneself.

A few days after I met Rosie in 2002, she told this same story, as well as other dimensions of her migration experience, to a reporter from *Time Magazine* (see McIntyre 2002). The story was widely circulated in the United States and Korea, as well as other parts of Asia, and even provoked a reaction from the US government (see Goldman 2002). But because I knew Rosie, I knew what the *Time Magazine* reporter had omitted from her story as well as what he had chosen to include in the article that was published. McIntyre employed a 'politics of sex trafficking storytelling' that requires victims to be presented in a particular way or according to a particular framing of the problem. Much of the information that circulates publicly as knowledge about trafficking into the sex and nightlife entertainment sector produces selective truths that incite some form of political action or, more accurately, reaction. Nicolas Lainez (2010) has elsewhere called this "the victim staged".

I knew what Rosie had told this reporter, what he had chosen to omit and what I thought were the equally important aspects of her experiences in Korea and in Manila. What was still unknown about Rosie's experience from McIntyre's story, for instance, was how exactly she executed her departure from the club and what happened to her afterwards. There was a fifteen-month gap between the time Rosie ran away and her return home to Manila. What had happened to Rosie in the interim period between running away and telling her story to *Time Magazine*? How had she overcome her experiences in Y Club and attempted to forge a more positive migration experience during this time? How had Rosie, in other words, moved on from her experience of trafficking?

After running away Rosie had in fact gone to the Archdiocesan Pastoral Centre for Filipino Migrants in Seoul (hereafter, the Centre) for advice and assistance. While she was sheltering at the Centre, the staff found her a job at a nearby factory. Rosie worked six days a week, twelve hours a day for a year at the factory as an undocumented migrant. During this time she kept in contact with her American soldier boyfriend, who had assisted her in running away from the club. After a year she decided to return to Manila because she was tired of having to remit all her monthly salary each month to pay for her mother's expenses and medical costs. Remitting all her salary from the factory meant she had to continue to rely on her boyfriend in Korea for money for her own living costs. Once back in Manila Rosie returned to the impoverished squatter district of Tondo where she lived with her mother and two younger siblings. She soon met and fell in love with a Filipino man to whom she became pregnant. They planned to marry and rent a house together not far from Rosie's mother in Tondo, but her mother had other ideas. After she returned to Manila, Rosie's American soldier boyfriend regularly sent her money. Rosie's mother was hopeful that this American boyfriend would eventually marry Rosie, so she sent her back to Korea to become engaged. Rosie was naturally reluctant to go given her new romance in Tondo. When she arrived at the apartment in TDC that her ex-boyfriend had rented for her and revealed that she was three months pregnant with another man's child, he tried to strangle her. Although she was badly beaten, Rosie managed to kick him and run from the apartment without her clothes, passport or any money. She made her way back to the Centre for a second time and sought their assistance to recover her passport so she could go home. Although Rosie told this story to the *Time Magazine* reporter he decided not to include this information because, as he later told me, it diluted Rosie's positioning as a "pure victim" and was thus not in the best interests of the story. Now pregnant at eighteen years of age, unmarried, subject to abuse by a former American boyfriend, employed as an irregular migrant worker in a factory in Seoul . . . these were, I was told by the reporter at the time of the story's publication, unnecessary complications to an unambiguous story of sex slavery involving a minor.

Two years after Rosie first migrated to Korea as an entertainer she returned to Manila to marry her Filipino boyfriend and have her baby. She resumed her life as a survivor of trafficking in ways I had never seen reference to in the burgeoning literature on human trafficking, where victims are commonly understood to be in need of rescuing, rehabilitating in shelters and subsequently reintegrating into their home communities, or in ways that were reflected in *Time Magazine's* reporting of Rosie's story. This disjuncture between the 'victim staged', which privileges a particular discourse of sexual servitude, and the lived experience of trafficking and post-trafficking for women like Rosie, with its silences, absences and anxieties, forms the basis of this book.

Points of contention: trafficking, post-trafficking and moving on

This book has two aims. The first is to examine exactly how some migrant Filipinas who come to South Korea on entertainer's visas are 'trafficked'. In the context of current academic literature on human trafficking understanding exactly how a group of migrant women is trafficked is a contentious exercise because of an increasingly influential body of scholarship eschewing a trafficking framework in interpreting women's experiences of marginal migration into the sex and nightlife entertainment sectors. To elaborate, we might divide human trafficking research into two broad categories: those which attempt to document the experience of sex trafficking, as in the *Time Magazine* story, and those which attempt to refute claims of trafficking through alternative interpretations of women's experiences of vulnerable migration and precarious work in the sex and nightlife entertainment sectors. The latter studies make various arguments to the effect that a trafficking framework is not useful in interpreting women's experiences because the women concerned knowingly and willing participate in pub and bar work, including where they perform sexual labour, and because current anti-trafficking interventions often act to further marginalise women and compromise their human and labour rights. Thus, even though women may operate under "constrained choices" (Sandy 2007) when they agree to migrate for sexual and erotic labour, they nonetheless exercise agency in their migration and work decisions. This argument has been made in relation to many groups of migrant sexual labourers and specifically in relation to Filipina migrant entertainers in Japan (Parrenas 2011) and in Korea (Cheng 2010).

Yet in reflecting on the experiences of women like Rosie in TDC it seems clear that trafficking does supply an important frame for understanding these Filipinas' employment situations. And it is here that the 'either/or' dyad of sex trafficked or not trafficked is ultimately unhelpful in understanding experiences of women like Rosie and why I wish to advance a different trafficking interpretation of these women's experiences in this book. My argument is that women like Rosie *are* trafficked but that their trafficking experience cannot be reduced to the types of sensationalist platitudes or superficial interpretations supplied in media accounts of sexual servitude or 'thin' research which emphasises extreme sexual exploitation as the key site through which their trafficking emerges. The opening vignette describing Rosie's experiences illustrates that sexual exploitation is one element of a broader pattern of exploitative practices and labour relations in Club Y and that it was *labour* issues – non-payment of salary, arbitrary deductions and fines, humiliation and physical punishment and so on – that Rosie chose to emphasise in recounting her situation both to me and to the *Times Magazine* reporter. Rosie had three GI boyfriends and strategically deployed her sexuality and sexual intimacy to recover and advance her own goals in migration, so I find it difficult to endorse any suggestion that she was a 'sex slave' or victim of sex trafficking, even if she may have preferred a job where sexual labour was absent or less starkly performed. As I will demonstrate in this book, 'labour exploitation' more accurately describes the most significant realm through which women understand themselves as exploited and bonded labourers in Korea. Adopting such an understanding has implications for the ways we view various aspects of exploitative situations in *gijich'on* (lit. US military camp towns, in Korean) pubs and other sites where sex trafficking is supposedly rife.

The second aim of the book is to explore the trajectories of migrant Filipina entertainers after they leave the clubs to which they are deployed in Korea. I examine how vulnerable and exploited migrants like Rosie manoeuvre and work towards overcoming situations of marginality and exploitation in their migration through their own agentic expressions that emerge outside responses to them as sex trafficking victims. How, in other words, do women like Rosie enact transnational possibilities of 'moving on' in ways that sit almost entirely outside a framework of anti-trafficking interventions? Despite a growing body of research on the migration of Filipinas as entertainers very little attention has focused on post-club lives of women, especially where they remain in the migrant destination, often as undocumented or irregular migrants. Despite their book-length treatment of the personal and working lives of Filipina entertainers in Korea and Japan respectively, neither Cheng (2010) nor Parrenas (2011) give more than passing treatment to post-club manoeuvrings of women who run away from the clubs and remain in the migration destination, with Cheng focusing principally on what happens to women only after they return home to the Philippines. Lieba Faier's (2008) study of Filipina wives in rural Japan is an important exception to this omission in its ethnographic treatment of former Filipina migrant entertainers who marry Japanese men – often ex-customers in the bars where they previously worked – and remain as wives in Japan. Following Faier, I also found that women's post-club lives are fraught with the challenges of breaking away from the club and the stigma attached to club work. In their romances, in other types of work and in relations with 'home' in the Philippines, as well as with service providers and support workers for exploited migrants, these women must continually negotiate, manoeuvre and resist the impositions of the club. This book focuses on the lives of women who run away and remain in Korea.

Points of contact: methodology

The silences and absences in the re-telling of Rosie's and other women's experiences are replicated in the vast majority of accounts of trafficking for commercial sexual exploitation.[1] Many researchers who study human trafficking interview victims in shelters or rehabilitation facilities because these places provide a convenient source of potential research participants. This has led Brunovskis and Surtees (2010) to identify the problems with current approaches to research with women trafficked into sex industries globally as "selection effects", where biases in who gets to tell their story, how and in what context (usually a shelter) result in narratives of many trafficked persons outside this narrow purview remaining untold. The overwhelming majority of accounts of any form of trafficking – by researchers, nongovernmental organisations (NGOs) and the media – are indeed based on a small number of identified and assisted victims, located predominantly within and through NGOs and shelters. This bias reflects one of the key issues facing researchers in this field – namely, the difficulty of finding and then accessing "hidden populations" of trafficked people (Laczko 2005). Researchers either access victims' accounts first-hand from the women who use the services of NGOs (for example, Crawford 2010) or they interview NGO staff and obtain selectively drawn accounts based on NGO records (for example, Samarasinghe 2008). When researchers do manage to meet trafficked persons the line of questioning often pertains to a narrow range of topics, such as how many men the victim was forced to have sex with, if she was deprived of food and/or freedom, if she was abused and so on. This line of questioning, which also appears in media accounts like the *Time Magazine* story mentioned earlier, reveals only absences and reinforces only stereotypes of what is known and what is expected to be known about the 'global problem of sex trafficking'.

Apart from selective and partial encounters between researchers or media and trafficked persons, much existing research on human trafficking does not actually *aim* to include the voices of trafficked persons. As Long (2004: 8) laments,

> contemporary sexual trafficking experiences remain largely invisible, reflecting in large part the particular interests and agendas of those defining trafficking for sexual exploitation rather than the lived experiences and perceptions of those who are trafficked. Thus, despite the current preoccupation

and popularity of this issue, such experiences are largely the contemporary hidden histories.

This has prompted Laura Agustin (2002) to call for approaches to research with women and men in global sex and nightlife entertainment industries that are "undertaken by people who are very close to sex workers' lives . . . will above all commit themselves to honestly recording all the different and conflicting points of view and stories they run into during the research". Viewed this way, the silences and complexities in Rosie's story become equally, if not more, important than the sex slave narrative to 'honestly record'.

Thus, the principal problem with the "selection effects" identified by Brunovskis and Surtees (2010) is that important issues remain unaddressed. Some of these include the following questions: Why do exploited individuals decide not to come forward, even if they are aware that they have been subject to exploitation and/or abuse during their migration experiences? How might these women manoeuvre their situations and express agency within them in ways difficult to gauge when looking for 'victim profiles' within shelters? How are the experiences of exit and moving on negotiated outside an anti-trafficking framework? And with what outcomes? Last, how do these people who remain otherwise 'hidden' from our analytical purview advance our own understandings of what trafficking is and is not, and how it should, or should not, be responded to? In order to address these issues, this book uses a different point of contact with participants than in an institution in which their trafficking status is subject to measures to rehabilitate them and their experiences subject to prior interpretation by those charged with supporting them. Central to this approach is something all too rarely seem in trafficking research – namely, ethnography.

Starting points: ethnography and human trafficking

This book is an ethnography of migrant Filipina entertainers deployed in US military 'camp towns', or *gijich'on*, in Korea. I conducted fieldwork in Korea for eighteen months during 2002 and 2003. I returned again in mid-2005 for a further two months, mainly to see what, if any, impact Korea's new anti-trafficking law (developed in late 2003) was having on the lives of women like those I encountered during my initial fieldwork. I met more than 100 women during my two fieldwork stints, and whilst many of the women narrated their experiences to me in a single encounter, around one-third of these women continued to meet with me informally over the course of my fieldwork, engaging in casual conversations, shared outings, meals and parties at their homes or in their workplaces and living with some of the women in their rooms and apartments after they had run away. I also assisted them in navigating a range of problems they encountered as they sought to improve their positions in/through Korea. The fieldwork took place primarily in TDC (where Rosie was deployed) and Songtan, which is located thirty kilometres south of Seoul and is home to the largest US Air Force base in Korea. I also spent a shorter amount of time in Kunsan, North Cholla province, and Anjong-li, in Kyunggi province, a twenty-minute bus ride away from Songtan. All of these places have a significant US military presence.

I commuted from Seoul to TDC by suburban train and then provincial bus once a week and stayed in the apartments of one of three different women – Cherry, Grace and Lisa. These three women were all 'runaway brides', meaning they had run away from the clubs where they were deployed in order to marry (or at least with the hope of marrying) a former customer-cum-boyfriend. Although I spent time with several women who were still working in the clubs, the club was a space that was prohibitive to deep interactions and not conducive to building trust and rapport because club bosses were generally opposed to their entertainers spending time with anyone in the club who was not associated with the generation of profits for the club and because club bosses were often suspicious of me and my reasons for wanting to talk to their entertainers. Gregory (2005) encountered similar problems studying the everyday lives of sex workers in the Netherlands, where she reflected that she felt like an intruder in their places of work and perhaps was interrupting business. I also found that because women in some clubs were often not allowed to go out unaccompanied during their time off, or if they did, were only allowed out for an hour or two, it was sometimes difficult to meet outside the clubs, especially those where the movement of their entertainers was curtailed by club bosses. By only cultivating interactions with women still working in the clubs, my research was thus biased to women who worked in 'better' clubs where they had relative freedom of movement and were able to go out to the local market or to dine at one of the restaurants that catered to Filipina entertainers. I knew many clubs in *gijich'on* that did not allow women to go out in such a capacity.

Sometimes I stayed with either Cherry or Lisa or Grace for a whole week, but on other occasions I moved between their apartments and did not return to Seoul at all. Often we would go into the clubs together and talk with the women working there. Going as a group was far less intrusive than if I went alone because I was in the company of Filipinas. I met all three women at the Filipino Centre for Migrant Workers. Their stories, and those of their friends with whom they had previously worked in the clubs, form a central part of this book.

Nine months into my fieldwork I had the opportunity to go to a meeting in Songtan at the behest of Father Glenn Jaron, the Filipino priest who ran the Centre. Songtan, like TDC, was renowned for its 'base problem', and during the period of my fieldwork media reports increasingly claimed that large-scale trafficking of Filipina and Russian 'sex slaves' was taking place there (Jhoty 2001, Demick 2002). At that point in my research I felt it would be good to consider a second research site. Unlike TDC, which is a depressingly poor and highly stigmatised place in Korea (see Yea 2007), Songtan was beginning to attract other expatriates besides US military personnel and had largely evaded the marginal status of TDC. English teachers, backpackers and other foreign workers based in Seoul would often find their way to Songtan for shopping and clubbing. I felt much less conspicuous and far more relaxed there.

The meeting Father Glenn invited me to was an extraordinary performance of anti-trafficking. The then chief of police in Seoul, a feisty woman named Kim Kang Ja, had mobilised the clubs to send all their foreign entertainers to a public hall in the centre of Songtan for a lecture on human trafficking and their rights as possible victims of trafficking. The women were encouraged to report to the police if they felt they were 'victims'. Russian women sat on one side of the hall and Filipinas on the other. I sat towards the back of the hall in a spare seat next to one of the Filipinas. At the meeting I met Maricel, Eva, AJ and Sandra. These four women were still working in a club in Songtan, so their situations were in some ways different from women like Cherry, Lisa and Grace in TDC who had already run away. Most significantly, although these four women in Songtan all had boyfriends, they were still working in VIP Club with little intention of running away to get married. Further, the mama-san of VIP Club seemed quite happy for me to hang around in the evenings in the club and sit with these four women when they were not occupied with either customers or performing erotic dances on stage. Every second week I travelled to Songtan by bus and spent time with these four women, who lived in a second-floor apartment two doors down from the club where they worked. Ten Russian women employed in another club owned by the same Korean couple lived on the first floor of the same apartment building. I was able to access the Filipinas' apartment – which is not an easy task because of the constant surveillance women are under in their living and working places – because, if I lowered my head, I could pass under the security camera as one of the Russian women who lived on the floor below, much to the amusement of Maricel. I spent time with these women in the club where they worked, in restaurants in Songtan and in their apartment. I met three of them in the Philippines after their contracts finished a few months after I first met them.

My aim in both TDC and Songtan was to centre the voices and experiences of the women who participated in the research in ways that did not advance any particular agenda about human trafficking, or indeed about prostitution and sex work, and that started from the reality of the women themselves, rather than the intractable problem of sex trafficking. In focusing on sex tourism workers in the Philippines, Law (2000: 11), for example, also disagrees with the totalising potential of the victim identity, which

> neglect[s] the worldviews and everyday experiences of Southeast Asian sex workers, who rarely consider themselves victims of the political economy or part of global sex traffic. Instead, their lives are framed by issues of employment opportunities, family responsibilities and dreams of a better life – at home or abroad. Furthermore, their relationships with foreign tourists are often understood in romantic or benign terms, where paid sexual encounters are meshed with exit from the industry.

At times centring women's own narratives was difficult because different actors wished my research to reflect or give credence to their agendas, a situation which Marcus (2005) has dubbed the "anthropologist as witness". Montgomery (1998:

240) reflected on a similar dilemma when she conducted ethnographic research with child prostitutes in Thailand; "To study child prostitution in developing countries . . . is extremely difficult because there is a great deal of pressure to examine it as a prelude to stopping it", such that the research subject "must always be cast in terms of being a problem needing a solution". Far too often in trafficking research the everyday is sacrificed at the expense of the episodic. My research in Korea was thus inspired by some recent studies that focus on Asian migrant women, including entertainers, that reject constructions of these women through singular and essentialist identities, which reduce them to victims of multiple and overlapping forms of oppression, including that exercised by customers and traffickers. I privileged the everyday and intimate lives (Gregory 2005) and everyday spaces (Hubbard 1998, Law 2000) of women working as entertainers in Korea's *gijich'on*. The everyday in this context means the nuanced micro-processes (see also Faier 2008, 2009) in which women negotiate, resist, manoeuvre and (attempt to) overcome their marginal positions in Korea.

Some feminist academics have rightly cautioned against research which posits to reveal the voices of third-world marginal women (hooks 1990, Mohanty 1987) or expose "subjugated knowledges" (cf. Foucault 1990), especially where the researcher is a white, Western woman who may inadvertently perpetuate an essentialised and universal victim through a moralist, colonising gaze. Reflecting on positionality thus becomes extremely important. Thus, respectfully and appropriately positioning myself in relation to the women in my research was utterly pivotal to maintaining an open relationship with them and came in two unexpected and serendipitous ways. First, Lisa had arranged a blind date for me with one of her fiancé's workmates, a GI named Kevin also based at Camp Casey in TDC. To the satisfaction of Lisa, we hit it off and within weeks had developed a serious relationship, thus allowing me to engage with every one of my participants – and their boyfriends – in ways that involved common – and for them paramount – preoccupations of dating a GI, love and romance within the club and beyond it and the centrality of marriage within future migration and livelihood trajectories. Julie Cupples (2002: 383) has argued for recognising the importance of sexual subjectivities in the field since "the subjective experience of sexuality in the field can challenge distance between us and them . . . getting around the inadequacies of the insider/ outsider debate". Whilst GI boyfriends and the 'discourse of love' became a site for positioning myself in relation to my participants, the topics of discussion it generated yielded important insights into women's sense of selfhood and about their desires to move on from their experiences in the clubs through lively, empathetic exchanges about romance, fidelity and, always interwoven through this, money.

Second, through the course of interviews and informal encounters many stories of violent and abusive domestic situations within the Philippines – and sometimes Korea – emerged from my participants (see Yea 2004). I had not expected that some of these stories would relate quite so powerfully to my own past with an abusive and drug-addicted partner and my eventual disclosure of elements of my own experience to some of my closest informants and friends in TDC and

Songtan. These "analogous life issues" (Cloke et al 2000: 144) opened the way for a reconsideration and dilution of the power dynamics between my participants and myself as researcher. These, then, became key sites of empathy in which my informants became my friends and in which the research became reciprocal in quite unexpected ways.

At the same time, the power differentials between my research participants and I were reinforced through my position as someone who could always leave the *gijich'on* and Korea; my legal migration status as a researcher in Korea; my local knowledge of important local geographies of Seoul/Korea; and my ability to speak Korean. It took weeks to build trusting relationships with many of the women, and this often happened in the context of supporting women's needs, whatever these may be. As someone perceived to be associated with the Centre and Father Glenn in particular (considered a heroic figure in defending the rights of Filipino migrant workers in Korea) I was seen initially as someone who could help women with certain problems they faced. I soon learnt how I was able to support them. I navigated the Seoul subway system with them, accompanied them to the Philippines Embassy in southern Seoul, translated Korean into English (to the best of my ability) for women who needed health checks and devised compensation claims for women that enabled them to break the key aspect of their vulnerability, namely a lack of money.[2] This work strengthened the insights I was to gain about the situations, needs and aspirations of the women who were trafficked to Korea's *gijich'on* and allowed a more nuanced interpretation of the meaning of 'protection' of victims of trafficking and 'prevention' of trafficking in that context.

Points of departure: critiquing and re-framing (anti)trafficking

Many recent feminist and post-structural studies of anti-trafficking interventions and ideology eschew human trafficking as an inaccurate characterisation of migrant sex workers' experiences and denial of women's agency. Critical perspectives on anti-trafficking policies and interventions have focused on the negative impacts of anti-trafficking policies and practices on the welfare of both trafficked and non-trafficked persons, especially migrants (Kempadoo et al. 2005, GAATW 2007, Ford et al. 2012). This work generally makes two arguments: the rights and freedoms of trafficked persons are often compromised, rather than enhanced, by anti-trafficking interventions; and anti-trafficking policies and projects can often reduce the ability of non-trafficked persons to migrate freely and legally, especially if they are sex workers. Anti-trafficking can thus force many people within the global South, both those who are trafficked and those who are not, into positions of greater, rather than reduced, vulnerability and exploitation.

This book builds on this work by recognising the need to attend to the everyday lives and transnational geographies of migrant entertainers in research. However, I depart from the main thrust of these critiques, which focuses largely on anti-trafficking frameworks, and instead return to one of the prior concerns of much of the earlier research on human trafficking – namely, what exactly are the circumstances of trafficked persons? This question has previously been dealt with remarkably poorly because much research supports particular ideological or institutional agendas – for example, to close borders to certain migrants or to admonish sexual labour as legitimate work – and remains uninterested or unable to reveal anything particularly insightful about trafficked persons' broader lives, anxieties, resistances or desires (Agustin 2002). A few exceptions are worthy of note including Lisborg and Plembech's (2009) study of Filipino and Thai women who returned home after experiences of trafficking; Brunovskis and Surtees's (2007) study of trafficked women's decisions to decline assistance in Europe; Caouette and Saito's (1999) study of Thai sex workers in Japan; and Parrenas's (2011) study of Filipina hostesses in Japan. These studies share in common a focus on asking questions about women's support needs, how trafficking intersects with social identity and moral and legal/territorial regimes and how trafficking is actually expressed and experienced by women. These studies also focus to a greater or lesser degree on 'undetected' or 'unidentified' trafficked persons. Although women in *gijich'on* clubs were widely rumoured to be sex trafficked, none were subject to interventions associated with trafficking until my fieldwork was close to concluding. This offered an interesting site in which to explore women's lives in the context of trafficking but not necessarily *anti*-trafficking.

This book examines the experiences and voices of the subjects of trafficking themselves, who may also be said to offer an everyday critique – what Kapur (2002) calls "normative disruptions" – of these frameworks through their own manoeuvrings, re-workings and mobility projects. It explores the ways women who are exploited abroad negotiate and overcome such positions largely outside the purview of the any anti-trafficking interventions. I therefore find it useful to distinguish between a 'victim of trafficking', by which I refer to a person who is subject to anti-trafficking interventions, and a 'trafficked person', by which I refer to a person who is affected by the experience of trafficking but is not defined by anti-trafficking stakeholders as a victim, and I focus avowedly on the latter. Rosie, Cherry, Lisa, Grace and the four VIP Club women in Songtan, like many of my other participants, all wanted to leave their club work because they were ultimately deceived about the conditions attached to their work (primarily their salary, living conditions and freedom of movement and association) and, for some of the women, about what the work itself involved. They were trafficked, but not 'sex trafficked', and their migrations to Korea were fraught, precarious and uncertain. These aspects of their lives deserve to be documented and understood.

Terminology troubles

Trafficking is an academic subject where confusion and imprecision around terminology abounds. It is necessary to define key terms associated with human trafficking at the outset of this book since there is a politics to the current human trafficking discourse that can act to unwittingly position researchers. This is particularly the case with terms used to describe sex work/prostitution that underscore positions within debates around the legitimacy of commercial sexual labour as a form of work (Doezema 2000, Peach 2005). In this book I refer to women who are deployed in *gijich'on* as entertainers, since this is the visa they entered Korea with and this is the term the women normally use to refer to themselves. None of the women in this study identified themselves as either sex workers or prostitutes, and I doubt any of them would have distinguished between these two terms in any case. The term 'entertainer' therefore is far more important to understand in this context. Women also used the term 'migrant' or 'migrant worker', but hostessing in the context of an entertainer's visa seems most appropriate to describe the majority of my participants' work.

The term 'sex trafficking' is deliberately avoided in this book since it has no reference point within the United Nations definition of human trafficking as laid out in the Protocol to Prevent, Protect and Suppress Trafficking in Persons, Especially Women and Children (hereafter the Protocol) (2000). According to the United Nations (2000) definition human trafficking involves

> the recruitment, transportation, transfer, harbouring or receipt of persons, by means of threat, use of force or other forms of coercion, abduction, fraud, deception, the abuse of power, a position of vulnerability, the giving or receiving of payments, or benefits to achieve the consent of a person having control over another person for the purpose of exploitation. Exploitation shall include the exploitation of the sex service, other forms of sexual exploitation, forced labour or services, slavery or practices similar to slavery, servitude or the removal of organs.

Trafficking involves a range of *different* forms of sexual exploitation that are specifically named and distinguished within the Protocol. The term 'sex trafficking' – and equally 'sex slavery' – usually collapses these important distinctions into the fold of trafficking for prostitution, thus largely blindsiding the other manifestations of sexual exploitation in trafficking, including outside the sex industry (within transacted marriages or within the context of forced labour, for example), and other forms of sexual exploitation within the realm of erotic labour, such as strip dancing, pole dancing, oral sex, lap dancing and so on where penetrative intercourse may not be present or may not be the most common form of sexual labouring. Further, trafficking in the context of being an entertainer can involve forced labour, which means that sexual exploitation may be one element of a trafficking experience that straddles different categories laid out in the Protocol or, indeed, may not be a concern at all. Currently virtually all human trafficking research continues to maintain the rigid distinctions between one type of trafficking and another, as though they are somehow competing for prominence (recent attempts to foreground the hitherto neglected issue of labour trafficking, especially amongst men, may in part be read this way). Parrenas's (2011) study of Filipina hostesses in Japan, for example, recognises that exploitation occurs in the migration process and working conditions as much as, or more than, in prostitution, even though the issue here is framed by the United States and Japanese government as a 'sex trafficking problem'. This is a finding echoed in this book (see chapter 2).

The UN definition of human trafficking is the most comprehensive and the most commonly invoked definition in national anti-trafficking legislation globally – including in the Philippines and Korea. I describe my participants as having been trafficked according to the definition contained in the Protocol, namely that there was deception in recruitment and facilitated transportation and transfer, as well as exploitation at the destination. However, beyond this what appeared important in the situations of women in *gijich'on* clubs were issues of freedom/control and agency. One of the key characteristics of human trafficking is a loss of freedom and control. This might include freedom of movement, freedom of association or, more broadly, freedom to take control of one's situation, including the ability to leave that situation. The opposite of removal of freedom and loss of control in trafficking situations is empowerment, which, in a trafficking context, we might take to mean "a process through which an individual can develop her/his ability to stand independently, make decisions and show control over her/his life" (Lisborg and Plambech 2009: xii).

A focus on freedom and control leads to a consideration of the notion of agency and how it is constrained and expressed over time. It is generally assumed, thanks largely to unhelpful stereotypes produced in the media and some academic research (as in Brown 2000), that trafficked persons exercise no agency in their situations of exploitation—an assumption which is largely contested in this book. Sex worker rights advocates tend to take the opposite view: that migrant sex workers express agency in their decisions to migrate abroad to work in sex industries globally. The experiences of participants in this book reveal that considerations of agency need to be unfettered from debates about prostitution and sex work. In order to move on from exploitative labouring experiences in the clubs where they were deployed the women whose stories are narrated in this book exercised considerable agency and resilience, both whilst still in the clubs and after they had run away from them.

There is also considerable controversy around the use of the term 'victim' amongst feminist scholars to describe women who have been trafficked into the commercial sex industry. Criticism centres on the implied passivity and lack of agency ascribed to women by this term. However, Brunovskis and Surtees (2007: 26) use the term 'victim' to describe the status of trafficked persons employing an understanding of the term where,

> from a human rights framework, the term 'victim' is important as it designates the violation experienced and the necessity of responsibility and redress ... 'victim' denotes someone who has been the victim of a crime and does not refer to the person's agency or any other characteristics.

In line with this understanding I also posit that victims of trafficking may exercise agency in a range of ways – such as in the decision to migrate or in working to reduce their exploitation in ways that may not necessarily be tied to their exit from the clubs and so on – but that they are still subject to exploitation. There is no inherent reason why the Filipinas in this book cannot exercise agency in these situations, albeit often in limited or hidden ways. Although I recognise the importance of locating the term 'victim' in a human rights discourse, I nonetheless avoid using the term in the book for a different reason than that laid out by feminist geographers and sex worker rights advocates. I wish instead to make a distinction between a victim of trafficking and a trafficked person. This distinction revolves around one key characteristic – namely, where a trafficked person has been officially defined or named as a victim and thus has been subject to supports and other interventions by the state or other actors such as anti-trafficking NGOs. This is a crucial distinction in this book since I wish to make a case for understanding the lives of trafficked persons who are not victims in the sense that they are not subject to interventions under an emerging architecture of anti-trafficking.

The question of how Filipinas are trafficked to Korea's *gijich'on* is an important one taken up by this book, especially in chapters 3 and 4. But I also ask another, equally important, but far less well-considered question: how does a person move on from the experience of trafficking from outside the gaze of the anti-trafficking framework? Chapters 5, 6 and 7 attempt to provide at least some inroads into answering this question, which is always bound to be contingent and contextual. The everyday lives and narratives of migrant entertainers labouring under exploitative and often degrading conditions around US military bases in Korea must necessarily be taken as the starting point for such a project.

Overview of chapters

Chapter 2 describes the politics of US military presence in South Korea, drawing particularly on the key role ascribed to camp towns in fuelling anti-American sentiment. The ongoing tensions created by the presence of Korean women working as prostitutes around US military bases in Korea arguably produced the need to find another source of women to 'entertain' US soldiers. Women from the Philippines were logical choices given their widespread presence as entertainers in Japan and domestically in the Philippines around former US military bases in Subic and Angeles. The chapter describes the emergence of the anti-trafficking paradigm in South Korea during the period of my fieldwork and the ways in which trafficked women's experiences were accounted for within this framework. The location of these Filipinas as 'modern-day comfort women' by both academic and media accounts is given particular attention in the chapter for its discursive potential to name and mark Filipina entertainers in ways that foreclose other questions about their trafficking experiences.

In chapter 3 I turn to the experiences of the women themselves. I look at their migration to Korea as entertainers and the conditions they encounter upon their arrival and deployment. I critically evaluate *how exactly* their experiences constitute trafficking. I found that whilst a few of the women are subject to sexual exploitation, for most women the main problem they face in their workplaces concerns debt, fines and punishments and the removal of freedom, thus paralleling findings of Parrenas (2011) concerning Filipina hostesses in Japan. The migration process, including recruitment, contracts and the role of promotion agencies, is the key to understanding the main problems women subsequently encounter upon their deployment in Korea.

In chapter 4 I continue my focus on the circumstances of trafficking. If chapter 3 reveals how women's experiences of trafficking need critical deconstruction according to the ways in which exploitation occurs, then this chapter further extends this critique to the site of health. Although the health impacts of trafficking are generally considered an under-researched dimension of the trafficking experience, most of the limited attention has been directed at the health effects of trafficking for commercial sexual exploitation. The limits of existing studies that privilege sexual health problems, such as HIV/AIDs and other sexually transmitted infections (STIs), are made evident through women's narratives about experiences of health in and beyond *gijich'on* clubs.

In chapter 5 I explore Filipina entertainers' micro-geographies of resistance (cf. Pile and Keith 1997) within trafficking situations, which are usually much more constrained and circumscribed than those of other migrants. This is because they have their freedom (of movement and association) removed or curtailed and because they are subject to heightened surveillance. In addition, for these women threats of punishments, abuse and arbitrarily imposed fines act to 'keep them in their place', both literally and figuratively. In the chapter I wish to explore the ways these women also exercise agency by inserting fun, pleasure and romance within these highly constrained contexts, thus unsettling stereotypical notions about trafficked women as unable to play a role in shaping their migration experiences, as if their victim status is a totalising effect. I also look at the ways that developing romantic associations with customers can provide various forms of support for the women and often can help precipitate their complete departure from the clubs and bars where they are deployed. I invoke the concept of strategic intimacy to frame these encounters.

In chapter 6 I focus on the ways women leave the clubs and negotiate their post-club futures by either attempting to marry an ex-customer-cum-boyfriend or taking a job in a factory as an irregular migrant worker. In this chapter I contest the increasingly invoked idea of the "rescue industry" (Agustin 2007), asserting instead that women by and large craft their own exit strategies from the clubs that are executed without the intervention of well-meaning NGOs or the police. This is both the case before and after anti-trafficking interventions arrived in Korea. I also discuss the emerging communities of 'runaway brides' that are coming to mark the re-inscription of places around many US military bases in South Korea. I focus on the ways these communities are constitutive of broader transformations in women's migration trajectories, focusing in particular on the concept of 'transnational platforms', which allow women to retain their transnational positions and attempt to craft future mobilities. I discuss the volatility of such efforts, which can equally result in failures and further immobility and thus unravelling of some of the women's post-club strategies for regaining some control over their lives.

In chapter 7 I explore how women also articulate strategies to move on from trafficking at a community level. I explore the ways women use social networks and creative projects to re-work the situations of not only themselves, but also other women in *gijich'on* who are still in the clubs. I argue that these strategies sit outside commonly instituted anti-trafficking responses, such as rescue and rehabilitation of women, and are often deliberatively against its impulses. The chapter also briefly discusses some of the ways NGOs in Korea are responding to the situations of migrant women in *gijich'on* clubs and how these often are not driven by the self-identified needs of the women, but by the needs of the organisations to count and manage 'clients'.

In the final substantive chapter I focus on what happens to women who return to the Philippines after their trafficking. I document some of the ways in which they negotiate the complex subjectivities conferred as part of being trafficked once they return home. In particular these women rely on and constructively re-worked friendship networks established during their experiences abroad for the purposes of support, empathy and, in some cases, attempting to craft livelihood strategies anew. These negotiations and alternative support arrangements both explain and are tied to their decisions not to self-identify as 'victims of trafficking'.

Notes

1 I avoid using the term 'sex trafficking' because it is a value-loaded, vague term. It has become a catch-phrase for sensationalist media accounts of sexual slavery. It excludes elements of trafficking for commercial sexual exploitation and prostitution that do not fit the sex slave persona, including labour exploitation. It also fails to recognise that sexual exploitation takes place in a range of forms of human trafficking outside the commercial sex sector, including in servile marriages and for some individuals who are trafficked for forced labour.
2 In Tongducheon, Lisa and Cherry, and another Filipina participant named Beth, took on some of these roles and extended them in new ways. Once Lisa learnt the Seoul subway system, for example, she began taking other Filipinas to the Embassy. Beth and Cherry also both offered refuge at their apartments for women who ran away from clubs in Tongducheon.

2 'Sex trafficking' comes to Korea's *gijich'on*

Harley's Club in the main strip of TDC – which the GIs refer to as 'downrange' – does not have a stage for its Filipina entertainers to perform erotic dances. It plays music and has tables and chairs where the Filipina entertainers sit with customers for drinks and a bar where customers can hang out if they don't have money to buy a drink for one of the entertainers. Hae Mee is the only Korean women working in the club. She is twenty-six years old and is separated from her American GI husband, who is now based in Yongsan Army Base in Seoul, and to whom she has a six-year-old daughter. She has a new GI boyfriend now, Jason, who is twenty-two and also recently divorced. Jason is based at Camp Casey in TDC and told me he used to be a skinhead back in Denver, Colorado, where he dealt drugs and "shot at people for fun" until his grandparents sent him to Texas to live with his dad and stepmother. He enlisted in the army to get his life together and to escape the US for a while. Jason tells me he loves Hae Mee but that it's hard to predict what the future will hold for the two of them. As for Hae Mee, she is figuratively and literally stuck in TDC because it's hard for a Korean bar woman who is a single mother to a daughter who is a *pan saram* (lit. half person, meaning half Korean, half American) to enter normative spaces of Korean society and morality. She tells me she will remain in TDC for the rest of her life working in the clubs and making her way up the club hierarchy to manager unless she can marry Jason and move with her daughter to the United States. She does not have any Korean friends in the clubs, apart from Sunny, who is the current bar manager and also engaged to a GI based at Camp Casey.

Hae Mee attends Tabitha's House (*Tabithaui jip*), an unusual little church located at the end of TDC's main strip. Intensely emotive nightly services are conducted in Korean. Tabitha's House also offers women working in the clubs of TDC and nearby Toka-ri after-school care for a few hours while the women go to work. Tabitha's House has performed dozens of weddings between GIs and Korean women over the years. Since 2000, however, the priest tells me, there are fewer Korean women working in the clubs. The tiny church, with room to seat only around thirty people at a squeeze, hardly fills to capacity anymore – maybe just five or ten parishioners a night and only a few more on Sundays. Filipinas do not attend Tabitha's Church because they don't speak Korean. If they want to marry a GI they go to Father Glenn in Seoul.

My friend Kyung Hee was a volunteer at Tabitha's House when I began my research. She introduced me to Sunny and Hae Mee in Harley's Club, as well as the three Filipinas and some of the regular clientele at Players Club on the main strip of TDC, eight doors down from Harley's Club. Players Club is what is known as a *heulk in* club (lit. dark man's club, in Korean) as generally only African-American GIs patronise the venue.[1] Amongst the regular clientele is Bobby, a former GI who now works as a civilian contractor at Camp Stanley, just outside Uijongbu some forty kilometres from TDC. Bobby has been in TDC for more than twenty years. He stayed because he married a Korean bar woman, whom he later divorced. He now has a new Korean partner, also a former bar worker in TDC. His current partner owns Foxwood Club in Toka-ri. Foxwood is one of the clubs that does not let their entertainers out and pushes them to have sex with customers. Bobby is in trouble with his partner because he has been having sex with some of the Filipinas in exchange for benefits such as money, extra food and alcohol. I question Bobby about his indiscretions and he simply shrugs and tells me he has "an Asian persuasion". Intensely jealous, Bobby's partner punishes all the Filipinas in Foxwood because of their liaisons with Bobby.

Two of the Filipinas at Players Club, Alma and Fhem, go out with me to eat and shop, and they tell me they don't like Jane, the other Filipina, because since five Filipinas ran away from the club a few months earlier to work in factories, Jane acts like the mama-san, or female boss. Fhem and Alma are due to go back to the Philippines in two weeks. Unlike Jane, they do not want to renew their contracts. Fhem is hoping her GI boyfriend will sponsor her to the United States as his fiancé, and Alma wants to go back to her home province of Batangas in Southern Luzon because she is worried about her ailing father whose health has been steadily declining whilst she has been on contract in Korea. Alma also has a boyfriend whom she met in Players Club, but, according to Alma, he cheats on Alma regularly. Fhem does not think there will be any future for Alma and her boyfriend after she leaves Korea, except hopefully an occasional cash remittance from him.

Fhem, Alma and I lunch at a café in American Alley called Maruha's Place, owned by a former Filipina entertainer who also ended up marrying her GI boyfriend. After lunch we walk through a backstreet of American Alley and pass the office of Saewoomt'uh, an NGO dedicated to supporting the rights and needs of bar women working in *gijich'on*. Fhem and Alma reveal that they would never consider going to Saewoomt'uh if they needed help; they perceive it to be a refuge for Korean bar women, many of whom are now much older and no longer able to work in clubs. We drift back to the main strip, and I leave Fhem and Alma to return to Players Club before the owner notices they have been out longer than their allotted two hours free time. They spend the rest of the afternoon showering, dressing, putting on their make-up and getting ready for the night to come.

The dynamics of TDC, Toka-ri and the other *gijich'on* are both changing and enduring in the early to mid-2000s when I conducted my fieldwork. Places like

Tabitha's House and Saewoomt'uh are becoming less significant because the Korean bar women they supported no longer constitute the mainstay of the clubs' female entertainers. The rise in the numbers of foreign women in the clubs is creating tension between the new arrivals and their Korean predecessors.[2] Women like Hae Mee and Sunny, who are bound to TDC because of the discrimination they face outside the *gijich'on*, attempt to craft their futures abroad, whilst they are still able. If they cannot secure a fiancé visa to the United States, they are likely to become recipients of the support offered by Saewoomt'uh, where *harmonimui* (lit. grandmothers, in Korean) sit and chat, weaving and sewing to fill in their days.

The three Filipinas in Players Club show that the circumstances and aspirations of the foreign women in the clubs are not necessarily the same as the Korean women before them or the same as each other. Jane wants to renew her contract because she has found a way to make the club system work for her by becoming the bartender and not having to go with customers. Fhem and Alma, much like Hae Mee and Sunny, look for transnational routes to mobile futures through their relationships with customers. Maruha has achieved what many of the women aspire to – marriage to her GI boyfriend and ownership of a thriving small business that gives her financial stability and a degree of economic and social independence. Eventually Maruha will also 'make it' to the United States once her husband's tour of duty in Korea ends.

But these changes and continuities in *gijich'on* are not the subjects of recent public attention. 'Sex trafficking' as an imaginative project for political (and moral) intervention has come to (re)define the *gijich'on*, as well as the relations between foreign entertainers, their clientele and their bosses. The "spectacle of trafficking" (Shah 2006) and the "fantasy of the innocent victim" (Lainez 2010) have come to obscure the everyday relations described in the opening vignette and simplify the complex and nuanced social relations and gendered and racialised power topographies of *gijich'on* life. In this chapter I draw on ideas put forward in recent social science scholarship which seeks to understand sex trafficking as an arena for the production of spectacle and fantasy (see Andrijasevic 2007, Hoijer 2004, Lainez 2010, Lindquist 2010). Svati Shah (2006) has examined the way prostitution is produced and functions as spectacle in Mumbai's main red light district, which itself is framed by discourses of trafficking, as well as local dialectics of shame and stigma. Like Mumbai's red light district, Korea's *gijich'on* have become the figurative and actual location of sex trafficking in Korea.[3]

I look at the particular ways *gijich'on* have become a key site in which sex trafficking occurs and in which migrant entertainers emerge as the penultimate victims of sex trafficking in Korea. I focus on two already widely circulated emotive registers which have been central to such a production – the sex slave subject as symbolised by the 'original' comfort women of World War Two and masculinist-military formations, particularly the US military and global peacekeeping forces. Before moving to this discussion, I first provide some background about the political-economic positioning of Korea and the Philippines and the ways this has created opportunities for the labour migration of Filipina entertainers to Korea in recent times.

Peripheral Korea and global Philippines

This study was undertaken at a time when Korea was undergoing dramatic change in which the consequences of intensive state-led development were materialising and where contemporary social life was becoming largely urban and consumerist in nature. A global modernity was on the horizon and was being played out in the glittering shopping malls of Seoul's trendy suburb of Apkujong, the high-rise apartments of Seoul's southern Kangnam area, and the bars and clubs of the youth district of Sinsadong. The Korean wave (*hanryu*) was taking first China and then other parts of Asia by storm and with it demonstrating that non-Western modernity could produce different cultural and social forms that embedded, rather than erased, social and cultural difference, albeit markedly hybridised in its motility. Concurrently, Korean capital was rapidly advancing into Southeast Asia, including the Philippines, where it has produced an array of expressions including retirement tourists, sex tourists, garment and electronic factories and transacted marriages to Korean men, amongst other effects.

Yet at the same time as the core of Korea's economy, society and culture was setting the stage for a new global role, the peripheries of the country were also transforming in less auspicious and arguably far more contested ways. Rural areas were suffering a hitherto unseen crisis of reproduction. Korean women, attracted by the lure of modernity in the nation's large cities, were abandoning rural and regional lives en masse, leaving in their wake thousands of Korean farmers and small town labourers who were unable to find a wife and so threatening the ultimate embodiment of the physical reproduction of the countryside, namely the male offspring.

While the Korean countryside grapples with the possibility of extinction, other peripheries in the Korean landscape were enduring, despite popular opposition to them. US military bases remain central to the security of the nation, with tensions between the North and South constantly fluctuating but never entirely abating. Yet for Koreans the continued presence of the US military in Korea presents an ongoing compromise to Korea's global aspirations, symbolising the continued colonial presence of the nation by the powerful hegemonic force of the United States. Whilst anti-American sentiment within Korea has largely dissipated within the general public it has found renewed potency in the base issue, leading to the formation of organisations such as the National Campaign for the Eradication of Crime by the US Troops in Korea in 2000.

New peripheries are also emerging in line with Korea's economic ascendency. Migrant workers performing low-skilled jobs have been imported into Korea for employment in small factories performing a range of mundane tasks and, more recently, servicing American military and civilian personnel around the US military bases and in prostitution districts catering largely to Korean men. With the regularisation of migrant workers in certain sectors in 2003 and 2004 and their growing legitimacy and legality within Korean society, districts like Seocho in southern Seoul have become celebrated migrant worker spaces, and indeed Korea now proudly calls itself a multicultural nation. But places associated with the

US military, like my research sites of TDC, Toka-ri and perhaps to a lesser extent Songtan, were conversely to be avoided and labelled as foreign, dangerous and deviant spaces in the national imaginary (Yea 2007).

Meanwhile in the Philippines the promise of 'second tiger' status, following on from the success of Korea and the other NIEs (newly industrialising economies) and anticipated for the countries of Thailand, Vietnam and the Philippines, has largely failed to materialise. Plagued by ongoing corruption and nepotism, the Philippines embarked on a different strategy for development, capitalising on its English-speaking and comparatively highly educated population to supply low-skilled and semi-skilled labour to the households, factories and ships of advanced nations. As part of this state-managed labour export program, a much less understood category of workers also crystallised: Filipina entertainers. As Parrenas (2006) points out, despite their large numbers and potentially high levels of remittances, Filipina entertainers have been relatively neglected in the burgeoning scholarship on migrant Filipinas, which has focused almost entirely on domestics (for example, Yeoh and Huang 2000) and increasingly marriage migrants.[4]

In these circumstances the government began to revisit the strategy of overseas employment for Filipinos that was first introduced in the mid-1970s. In 1974 overseas employment became an official program of the Philippines government with the signing of the Labor Code (known as Presidential Decree No. 442). This program was introduced by President Marcos to curb high unemployment and the economic slowdown caused by the oil crisis. President Marcos had declared martial law throughout the Philippines in 1972 to control the massive popular protests in Manila against the corruption, widespread poverty, wealth concentration and inflation that emerged under his presidency. During the period immediately after the introduction of this policy the majority of Filipino migrant workers were men migrating to the Middle East for opportunities in the construction industry. The initial success of this migration strategy lent it further momentum in the 1980s, where it became an important component of the government's debt management policy. In 1988 the Overseas Investment Fund Act was introduced and became law in 1991. With this act, workers' remittances became part of a foreign debt reduction strategy. In 1985 the Migrant Workers and Overseas Filipinos Act (Republic Act No. 8042) was passed for the protection of Filipino migrant workers and promotion of their welfare. This act and the establishment of the Philippines Overseas Employment Administration (POEA) under the Department of Labour and Employment (DOLE) effectively heralded an official change of attitude towards migrant workers from an interim strategy during times of economic downturn in the Philippines towards a long-term strategy for national economic development with incumbent legal and bureaucratic infrastructure to bolster it. President Corry Aquino (1986–1992) continued to support the out-migration of Filipino workers during her presidential term, as have successive governments in the 1990s and 2000s. These administrations have all projected the image of Filipinos overseas as "new hero(ines)" (Tadiar 1997), with the previous president Gloria Macapagal-Arroyo also calling these men and women "overseas Filipino investors" (Suzuki

2000b). The positive spin given to Filipino labour migration abroad and the continuing economic problems in the domestic economy in the Philippines, as well as evidence of the wealth and substantial financial benefits of many returnees, continues to provide powerful incentives for Filipinos to go abroad to work.

The legacy of the Philippines government's pursuit of overseas employment as a development strategy has meant that, out of a population of 76.5 million in 2000 just prior to when this research was conducted, there were over 7 million Filipino women and men employed overseas, with approximately 2,300 nationals leaving for work abroad every day, making the Philippines one of the top ten countries globally from where migrant workers originate. The remittances of these workers constitute a major source of foreign revenue for the Philippines economy, with workers remitting around USD 7 billion per year. Philippines nationals live and work in over 170 countries globally, with the largest number of workers residing in Saudi Arabia (190,732), Hong Kong (113,583) and Japan (74,093) respectively. While Saudi Arabia and other Middle Eastern countries constitute important employment destinations for both men and women, with men working mainly in construction and women as domestics, the vast majority of Filipinos in Hong Kong and Japan are female workers. In 1999 in Japan there were approximately 27,000 Filipina entertainers, comprising 23.4 per cent of the total number of Filipinas there (the other major categories of Filipinas in Japan are spouses of Japanese men) (Suzuki 2000b: 102).

Korea does not currently figure amongst the top ten destinations for Filipino workers generally but already ranks amongst the top five destinations for Filipina entertainers (the other four being Japan, Hong Kong, Saipan (US) and Malaysia). In 1999 entertainers constituted 28.4 per cent, or 43,092, of the total number of new hires of Filipinas abroad and is steadily growing as a category of overseas employment for Filipinas. According to Korean Ministry of Justice figures the number of Filipinas entering Korea on entertainer's (E-6) visas has steadily increased since 1995. For both males and females Korea also constitutes the highest absolute number of E-6 visa arrivals of any Asian country, and in fact the Russian Federation is the only country with higher numbers of female E-6 visa holder entries.

The feminization of Filipino overseas migration and the increasing importance of Asia as a destination were two trends that became more evident in the 1990s. The number of female migrants began to outweigh that of men in the 1990s so that in 1999 women accounted for 64 per cent of the total legal migrant workers for that year (earlier figures were 12 per cent in 1975, 47 per cent in 1987 and 58 per cent in 1995). The main reason for this was the government's deliberate promotion of traditionally feminized work abroad, including employment as domestics, nannies and entertainers. This was combined with the pre-existing lack of opportunities for many women of lower socio-economic status and education in the Philippines itself and gender stereotyping of women that relegates them to commodified roles in traditional arenas of domestic and sexual labour.

As several Asian economies, including Japan, Hong Kong, Singapore, Taiwan, Malaysia and South Korea, achieved development levels commensurate with middle income countries in the 1990s, and as women in these countries began to re-enter the labour force (either voluntarily or as a result of formal government policy and incentives), the demand for foreign women to fulfil traditional feminised roles increased. At the same time unrest in the Middle East, and the 1991 Gulf War in particular, led to a reduction of Filipino workers there. Battistella and Asis (1999: 20) state that during the Gulf War 30,000 Filipinos were repatriated from the Middle East. By the late 1990s the effect of this unrest began to be felt in the dramatic increase of migrant workers to Asian destinations, and in 1997 for the first time the number of Filipino migrant workers in Asia outnumbered those in the Middle East.

As a result of the combination of these circumstances a large network of promotion and talent agencies has emerged to capitalize on Filipinas' desires to work abroad in Asia, thus complimenting the official, governmental apparatus that has developed to send Filipinas abroad. Work as an entertainer is often appealing to young women who do not have a professional qualification or who are unable to pay the often exorbitant fees (often paid to intermediaries to facilitate migration) associated with work as a domestic or in a factory. These promotion and talent agencies capitalize on women's desires to go abroad for work by providing them with an easy and normally highly attractive avenue through which to migrate (further discussed in chapter 3). The vast majority of these agencies also send women to Japan and other destinations where entertainers are sought (including most prominently Malaysia, Singapore, Hong Kong and Macau). In fact, many of the participants in this research stated that the promotion or talent agency responsible for their migration also sent women to Japan and/or was originally planning to send them to Japan.

In addition, the presence of US bases in the Philippines until 1992 provided a domestic bar and club sector in the city of Angeles and Subic Bay/Olongapo – locations of the Clark Air Base and Subic Navy Base, respectively – oriented to the R&R (rest and recreation) needs of the US military personnel stationed there. It is estimated that there were up to 55,000 Filipinas employed in bars in these two locations during the US base era (Sturdevant and Stolzfus 1993: 47), complimenting the 68,000 Filipinos who were employed on the bases themselves (Enloe 1989: 86). Today many of the bars and clubs around Subic and Angeles continue to operate, and the Coalition Against Trafficking of Women (CATW), Manila office has reported that these two sites constitute one of the biggest destinations for the domestic sex trafficking of Filipinas. As often happens when the US military is present in a location, a sex tourism sector oriented to civilians, both local and foreign, springs up. Capitalising on the large numbers of Filipinas continuing to work in bars and clubs in these locations, a host of promotion and talent agencies promising women work abroad as entertainers has also emerged.

The migration of Filipinas for employment as entertainers has a particular stigma attached to it, as there is a common perception within the Philippines that such work "alludes to some kind of 'prostitute', working in bars or marrying . . . men for convenience" (Suzuki 2000b: 101). The fact remains that the visa category of entertainer both valorises and falsely represents the nature of the work of migrant Filipina entertainers. The E-6 visa is in fact for professional singers, dancers and cultural performers. According to Korean Ministry of Justice Regulations (2001), an E-6 visa

> is available to foreigners who, for the good of profit-making, wish to be engaged in art activities such as music, art, literature and so on, and such activities as entertainment, performance, play, sports, advertisement, fashion modelling, and other occupations corresponding to those above. The maximum period of stay is six months and might be extended.

Filipina entertainers have thus ended up in Korea for a number of reasons that have to do with the collusion of the present moments of modernity and nation-building in Korea and economic crisis and labour export in the Philippines.

Apart from the US military camp towns, the other major destination for migrant entertainers in Korea is Korean-oriented bars and pubs, particularly karaoke and hostess clubs. Here there are no Filipinas or GIs, only Russian and Korean women servicing Korean men. There has, to date, been virtually no research with Russian women in Korean entertainment districts. Despite their dramatic increase in Korean-oriented and *gijich'on* clubs, little systematic attention has so far been paid to their experiences, the conditions in the clubs where they work and modes of migration and recruitment. To date only two empirical studies (Korea Church Women United [KCWU] 1999 and 2002) and two background reports (Saewoomt'uh 2002, International Organisation for Migration 2002) have appeared on the issue.

Base instincts: the US Department of Defense and *gijich'on* trafficking

International recognition of trafficking involving Korea as a sending or source country in the early 2000s first prompted wider scrutiny of Korea as a context in which trafficking was apparently occurring. In 2001, following evidence of the trafficking of Korean women primarily to the United States, the US Department of State (US DoS) gave Korea a Tier Three ranking in its Annual Trafficking in Persons (TIP) report.[5] In the report Korea was said to be "a country of origin and transit for trafficking in persons", with "young female Koreans ... trafficked primarily for sexual exploitation, mainly to the United States, but also to other Western countries and Japan" (US DoS 2001). Korea was also described as a transit country for Chinese women being trafficked to Western countries for commercial sexual exploitation. The report criticised Korea for failing to have a specific law to address trafficking and not supporting NGOs that assist women who may be trafficked. The 2001 report failed to recognise the vulnerabilities of foreign women in Korea's *gijich'on*, most of whom apparently met the international definition of trafficking put forward by the United Nations (see also McMichael 2002a and 2002b).

One, albeit belated, response to the embarrassment caused by the 2001 TIP ranking was the 2004 drafting by the Korean government of a new law entitled the "Sex Trade Prevention Act" (known also as the Anti-Prostitution Law), aimed explicitly at curbing trafficking for commercial sexual exploitation and prostitution involving Korea as a source and transit country. The act has come under criticism from various sex workers rights groups in Korea and abroad (see Cheng 2010) and is increasingly seen as an abolitionist tool to eradicate Korea's prolific sex industry, which, in early 2002 when my fieldwork began, accounted for just over 4 per cent of Korea's GDP. The politics of the lawmaking process were central to the way the final act appeared. As Yun Won-ho, a lawmaker for the Uri Party, claimed, "the anti-prostitution law was put into effect by the so-called 'wives troika', of assemblywoman Cho Bae-sook; Ji Eun-hee, the former Minister of Gender Equality and Family; and Kang Geum-sil, who was Minister for Justice when the bill was enacted. Their involvement made the bill into a 'women's issue' " (*Joongang Daily* 2007). The main provisions of the act were to criminalise all actors in the sex industry, apart from the sex workers themselves, who were to be given the status of 'victim' and receive related supports, such as counselling and alternative livelihoods training. Clients and pimps were to be punished with heavy fines and/or jail terms. In 2006, just a year after the act came into force, 35,000 clients were prosecuted under its provisions.

The act dealt a devastating blow to Korean women in the country's multifarious sex sector since it failed to distinguish between women who chose to be sex workers and those who were trafficked into prostitution. As Cheng (2004) rightly points out,

> The underlying assumption of the law . . . is wrong. Not all women in the sex trade are 'victims' who want to be rescued from the brothels. That they want to be free from exploitation and abuse does not mean that they want to be out of a job.

An additional problem for sex workers is that, unless they can prove their victimisation – meaning that they were forced or coerced into the sex trade – they will not be defined as victims and therefore are not eligible for the support services offered. At worst, they may also be charged with violating the new act and subsequently penalised. The most dramatic expression of disaffect with the new act was a hunger strike by sex workers in front of the National Assembly building in central Seoul for six weeks during October and November 2004, which followed two public protests involving more than 2,000 sex workers. The women stated that the act simply pushed their work further underground, exposing them to further harm and exploitation, rather than reducing it.

The act has created what I call 'unintended fallout geographies', defined principally by the off-shoring of major segments of Korea's sex industry. These geographies have led to a higher prevalence of Korean sex tourists and child sex tourists operating in Southeast Asia, with reports from the Philippines and Cambodia suggesting that Korean men constitute the most numerically significant group buying sex in those countries (Chung 2005). In 2007 a special law was passed in Korea's parliament which gave authorities the power to deny the issuance or renewal of passports to men who had a track record of buying sex, with the fear that these men would exploit women and children abroad if given the opportunity (Associated Federated Press [AFP] 2007). These fallout geographies have also included the movement of Korean sex workers abroad, particularly to the United States, Japan and Australia. Because of their greatly reduced ability to perform sex work in Korea, these women are arguably vulnerable to abuse in the migration process as well, thus possibly leading them to enter exploitative sex work arrangements in these destination countries. One key aspect of this has been the emergence of agents or brokers who offer Korean women the service of facilitating their migration abroad for sex work (Lim 2008). There is some evidence that this service perpetuates the vulnerabilities of migrant sex workers (see chapter 3).

Sitting alongside this conundrum for Korean sex workers created by the new act were the responses trafficking generated in relation to Filipina and Russian women in the *gijich'on*, which unfolded largely as a US military 'problem' rather than a Korean prostitution issue. In fact it was a feature story run by US media giant Fox Television which was the catalyst for putting *gijich'on* on the global trafficking map. Spurred by the inclusion of Korea in the 2001 TIP report and the apparent connections between US military prostitution areas in Korea and the trafficking of Korean women to the United States, in March 2002 – just after I commenced my fieldwork in TDC – Fox News reporter Tom Merriman, along with a team from Fox 8 News, went to TDC in order to disclose the situation of Korean women serving US GIs in the *gijich'on* hoping to make connections with Korean women trafficked to the United States. Much to Merriman's surprise as evidenced in the program aired by Fox Television, when he reached TDC's clubs it was not Korean women he saw serving the GIs, but Filipinas and Russians. Merriman amended the focus of his exposé and 'interviewed' (or rather, fleetingly spoke) to a few Filipinas in some of the clubs, all of whom stated that they were not free to leave, had their passports taken away and had to service debts through selling drinks and other duties not agreed to. Merriman's exposé had two particularly significant follow-on effects. First, conservative Republican US congressman Chris Smith,[6] along with twelve other members of Congress, penned a letter to the then US secretary of defense, Donald Rumsfeld, stating,

> My colleagues and I remain very concerned that military personnel may not understand that millions of women each year are trafficked against their will *for the purpose of working as sex slaves*. The US military – which fights for freedom worldwide – must lead by example and make no allowances for activities that keep people – in this case women – in bondage. (Smith 2002, my emphasis)

The letter called for an immediate investigation by the Pentagon into the allegations made in the Fox exposé.[7]

With Chris Smith's damaging letter to the US Department of Defense (US DoD), the US military needed to respond to accusations that US GIs were buying the sexual services of trafficked women in Korea. In early 2004 it introduced what became known as the 'zero tolerance policy' where any military personnel caught visiting a commercial sex establishment could be subject to court martial. Bars and clubs were to have regular inspections by US Military Police and any establishment that was considered to be violating this policy was placed off limits to US military personnel. Simultaneously the Korean government exempted areas around US military bases from its anti-trafficking responses (Kloer 2010). Instead the *gijich'on* were to be policed by the US MPs, which is consistent with provisions under the controversial Status of Forces Agreement (SOFA), where governance and policing of US military personnel in Korea – including prosecuting crimes committed by US servicemen and civil contractors – is undertaken by the US Forces Korea (USFK) and US DoD, rather than according to Korean legal provisions.

The second follow-on effect of the Fox Television report was further local and international reporting, all of which appeared to confirm Merriman's initial assessment. The first whiff of the production of the spectacle of sexual slavery in *gijich'on* and migrant entertainers as sex slaves was now undeniably in the air.

Space-time geographies: circulating comfort women/mobilising military masculinities

In the aftermath of Merriman's report and Congressman Chris Smith's letters to Donald Rumsfeld, the term 'sex slave' began to be increasingly applied to a range of women in Korea, including Korean *gijich'on* entertainers (as well as former Korean *gijich'on* women who subsequently entered the United States as brides of US servicemen), their Filipina and Russian counterparts and former comfort women. The distinctions between the experiences of these various groups of Korean and migrant women have been further collapsed under a global military-masculinist project of gendered exploitation and violence where the US military and international peacekeeping forces are seen to create particular effects (gendered violence, encouraging local prostitution and so on) in all countries they occupy, including Korea, Japan and the Philippines. Establishing equivalence in this way through time and space locates Filipina and Russian women as hapless sex slaves who are unable to influence or alter their situations and simultaneously positions US military customers exclusively as violent exploiters of women's sexual labour through forced prostitution.[8] These locations mean that understandings of foreign entertainers' (and GI customers') situations are already neatly packaged for anti-trafficking consumption.

The comfort women: equivalence through time

A frenzy of local and international media reporting followed Tom Merriman's original exposé of the plight of migrant entertainers in *gijich'on* clubs. These media reports (McIntyre 2002, Capdevila 2002, Jhoty 2001, McMichael 2002a and 2002b) mobilised the original comfort woman of the Second World War as the emotive register for their reporting of the status of foreign women trafficked to *gijich'on* as sex slaves. Some of these reports picked up on the International Organisation for Migration (IOM)'s (2002) report on trafficking of foreign women into Korea for prostitution. The report claimed that more than 5,000 women, mostly from the Philippines and Russia, were used as 'comfort women' in prostitution in Korea.[9] Drawing on the report, Capdevila (2002) subsequently wrote in his *Asia Times* article titled "Korea's new 'comfort women'" that "the reports called to mind Japan's use of 'comfort women,' mostly Korean, for its soldiers entertainment from 1910–45".

These media constructions were not without their academic counterparts. A decade before foreign women became visible in Korea's *gijich'on*, Kim (1997) attempted to make an even more direct connection between the former comfort women and Korean *gijich'on* bar women, claiming that some of the original comfort women were subsequently used by the US military in peacekeeping operations in Korea following Japan's defeat in the Second World War. In a similar vein, Donna Hughes, former president of the anti-prostitution organisation Coalition Against Trafficking of Women, teamed up with the anti-trafficking organisation Polaris Project to undertake a joint data-gathering exercise in 2002 which claimed evidence that connected no less than *three* different types of trafficking: domestic trafficking of Korean women to US military camp town clubs in Korea, transnational trafficking of foreign women to US military camp town clubs in Korea and transnational trafficking of Korean women to the United States – with the damaging accusation that US military personnel may be directly involved in the latter by using sham marriages to bring women into the United States (or sometimes through bona fide marriages that have later failed). The study (Coalition Against Trafficking of Women–Asia Pacific 2002: 903, my emphasis), like Kim's study before it, labelled these Korean and foreign women as 'modern-day comfort women':

> The abuse and exploitation of Korean women for 'rest and relaxation' by soldiers preceded the arrival of U.S. troops. The Japanese army used Korean women for sexual slavery during World War Two . . . At that time, the women were euphemistically referred to as 'comfort women', and although that term is no longer used, a number of Asian women's NGOs characterised the ongoing trafficking and sexual exploitation of Korean and Philippine women by U.S. troops as a *continuation of the same practice*.

The evidence collected by Hughes and the Polaris Project is highly suspect, drawing only on second-hand accounts (including the media reports listed earlier) and an anonymous email from one American soldier. In a direct response to Hughes and the Polaris Project, Sealing Cheng (2008) noted the limitations of the study since it was not informed by a solid empirical research base, but simply reiterated unsubstantiated claims made by sensationalist media reporting.[10]

The nature of the comfort women system and the history of prostitution around US military bases involving Korean women are important to consider in understanding the specific ways the *gijich'on's* foreign entertainers became established as the 'new sex slaves' within this broader history. Research on the extent and characteristics of the Japanese system of militarised prostitution in the 1930s and 1940s (for example, Hicks 1995) points to the existence of a Japanese government policy of recruiting somewhere between 200,000 and 300,000 women to work as prostitutes for Japanese military personnel. The policy began in the early 1930s and lasted until the conclusion of the Second World War. Whilst these women were drawn from a range of countries within the Asia-Pacific region, Korean women were estimated to comprise 80 to 90 per cent of all comfort women. The vast majority of the women drawn into this system did so unwillingly, with most being told that they would be engaged in paid employment in Japanese factories or as domestic servants. Hicks (1995: 19) estimates that the average overall ratio of soldiers to comfort women was fifty to one, indicating the extremely exploitative conditions of performing prostitution and the negative health consequences for the women. Most of the women were held against their will, and many suffered enormous and long-term physical and psychological damage as well as social discrimination. They were ostracised in their own countries when (and if) they managed to return. As a result of personal testimonies of a small number of former comfort women, as well as testimonies from some Japanese soldiers and doctors, it has been revealed that, unless seriously ill or pregnant (and sometimes notwithstanding this), women were forced to serve between ten and forty men per day, seven days a week. There was no respite during menstruation or illness. Many of the women who became pregnant or contracted serious sexually transmitted diseases were abandoned and left to die or killed. When Japan lost the Second World War, many of the comfort women were executed by the Japanese soldiers.[11] The suggestion that the migrant (and Korean) entertainers around US military bases in Korea were the same as comfort women thus seems an extreme characterisation in light of these characteristics of the comfort women system.

During the period of militarised peace in Korea following the Second World War a permanent US military presence was established. At this time, the highly derogatory slang term *yanggongju* (lit. foreign princess, in Korean) was commonly used by Koreans to describe Korean prostitutes in *gijich'on*. The term emerged in the context of the Korean War when US soldiers reportedly raped young Korean women and girls by forcing their way into their homes (Halliday and Cumings 1988). Shortly thereafter, the term was applied to Korean women who sold sex to US GIs in the *gijich'on*, and the label has remained ever since. These women in camp town prostitution have tended to experience extreme discrimination by other Koreans who see them as a symbol of the US occupation of the Korean peninsula. The same applies to their Amerasian children who are seen as 'bastards of Western princesses' (lit. *yanggongju saekki*, in Korean*)*. These women have been vilified by Korean society and once 'used up' find it almost impossible to re-enter mainstream society (as in the *harmonimui* in Saewoomt'uh's shelter described in the opening vignette of this chapter). Many of these Korean women are now in their fifties and sixties. They are no longer desired as prostitutes but are too young to be eligible to receive a modest government pension. They tend to end up in one of three situations: they join an income-generating project offered by an NGO such as Saewoomt'uh and make a little money to buy food; they remain in prostitution, selling themselves on the streets (or in 'special clubs') for intercourse or oral sex for five US dollars or less; or they re-enter the clubs as overseers or managers and, in turn, come to control the sexual labour of the foreign women who have more recently been deployed there.

Korea's post–Korean War history is littered with incidents of violence involving American GIs as perpetrators of various crimes against Korean prostitutes living in camp town areas. The most infamous of these was the brutal murder of prostitute Yoon Geun Mi in October 1992 by US serviceman Kenneth Markle, stationed at Camp Casey in TDC – my main field site. She was found with an umbrella inserted in her rectum and other signs of severe physical abuse prior to her death. When found her dead body was covered in laundry detergent. In May 1993, a fifty-year-old woman who operated a bar in TDC was found unconscious after being beaten and kicked in the head and face by a US corporal who was apparently trying to rape her. On January 30, 1999, also in TDC, a Korean woman was found strangled in her rented room in American Alley. Also in 1999 an American sailor was suspected of killing his Korean wife and their adopted son in their home outside Yongsan Army Base in Seoul. Petty Officer 1st Class James W. Furhman was investigated and later arrested on suspicion of killing the two after dumping their bodies a mile from their home in the Seoul suburb of Hannam Village and then setting fire to them. The violence of these tragedies notably has made its way into nationalist/anti-American movements centred on the US military presence within Korea. Whilst it is clear that some Korean camp town prostitutes and hostesses experience high levels of abuse and violence, women like Sunny and Hae Mee unsettle claims that this was or still is the general situation facing these women and that it can be applied to characterise the experiences of Filipinas in *gijich'on*.

Masculinist military formations: equivalence through space

Globally, one of the hallmarks of the current era is the geographical reach of the US military and international peacekeeping forces as a masculinist-military formation. In Korea the sex slave subject is also locatable within the recent history of such a formation, specifically where Korea is part of the US military 'empire'. This is exemplified by both academic accounts and reports from international organisations. Geographer Vidymali Samarasinghe, in her book *Female Sex Trafficking in Asia* (2008: 21, my emphasis), articulates this spatial equivalence in the following way:

> Wherever there are military bases, the sex industry seems to flourish. Filipino women are conspicuous around the American military base in Okinawa in Japan and in South Korea in proximity to the Demilitarised Zone, most of the Filipino women who work there fall into the category of Overseas Filipino Worker (OFW), who are on limited term work contracts or undocumented workers, in an illegal industry.[12] *The work routines of women in the sex industry near the American military bases in South Korea and Okinawa are very*

similar to that experienced by women in Olangapo and Angeles City in the Philippines.

The similarity she refers to remains unclear, which is unsurprising since she did not conduct empirical research with women in either location as a basis to understanding their similar – or perhaps different – experiences. It is apparently enough that Filipinas and the US military are involved in all three locations to be able to equate the experiences of women in one place with the other. Other academic accounts mirror this interpretation. Agathangelou and Ling (2003) suggest that the South Korean government negotiated militarised prostitution as a foreign policy enticement for US troops on the peninsula and that, in doing so, "the US effectively institutionalised what Japan's imperial army tried to coerce during World War II – *a geographically diverse distribution of Comfort Women*" (Agathangelou and Ling 2003: 138, my emphasis).

Perhaps the most pertinent example of this emerges not from academic sources, but from a 2003 investigation by the US DoD which examined the involvement of US military and peacekeepers in human trafficking in several international locations. The investigation was ordered by Donald Rumsfeld, then secretary of defense. With the logistical difficulty of conducting investigations in all commands around the world, the initial assessment was to involve the two media 'hotspots' of Korea and the Balkans. Sarah Mendelson from the Washington DC–based Centre for Strategic and International Studies wrote a report in 2005, *Barracks and Brothels*, which examined the relationships between UN and US peacekeepers and human trafficking and the efficacy with which the investigation was conducted in the Balkans. She concluded that despite the US DoD, NATO and the UN all taking dramatic steps to stop human trafficking where US military and peacekeepers are involved, the pre-existing attitudes of "indifference, denial, misperception, and even acceptance" continue to prevail (2005: ix). These findings were generalised to the Korean context, despite no similar evaluation of the DoD's investigation taking place there (see Mendelson 2005: 40).

An interpretation of Filipina entertainers' situations in *gijich'on* clubs that is grounded in the rhetoric of sexual slavery (the comfort women) and militaristic violence (the US military's R&R needs) serves the agendas of international organisations like CATW–AP (Coalition Against Trafficking of Women–Asia Pacific), as well as some Korean NGOs working on camp town prostitution issues. During my fieldwork in 2002 through 2003 and again in 2005 the then deputy director of CATW–AP, Jean Enriquez, based in Manila, visited Seoul to assess the situation of Filipinas there. Two years prior to this, and following the publication of a report on the situation of foreign women in camp town entertainment venues (KCWU 1999), she penned an article for CATW–AP entitled *Filipinas in Prostitution around US Military Bases in Korea: A Recurring Nightmare* (Enriquez 1999). This article also drew comparisons with the presence of the US Navy in Subic Bay:

> During the stay of military forces in the Philippines, around 17,000 women have been prostituted in Olongapo City alone, which is site of the largest US

military base outside the US itself . . . the construction and maintenance of prostitution is integral to the US military's strategies for keeping the male soldiers content.

Although she spent time at the Filipino Catholic Centre in Seoul and visited local women's organisations in Seoul on her return visit, she did not once venture to TDC to spend time with the women there.

In a similar fashion to the Filipina entertainers around Korea's US military bases, both *yanggongju* and the original comfort women, have become objects of politicisation and intervention. Yet, as Moon (1999) discovered, the comfort women of the Second World War clearly articulated their displeasure at having their experiences equated with those of *yanggongju* in the feminist-nationalist movement of the 1990s in Korea, so unsettling this universalising advocacy project. *Yanggongju* occupy an ambivalent space within the Korean imaginary, at once the object of discrimination and marginalisation and increasingly the invoked symbolic embodiment of the foreign occupation of Korea by a colonial power, namely the United States. Whilst in the first four decades following the Korean War *yanggongju* were largely either ignored or vilified by Korean society, in the mid-1990s they became subject to activist construction as both symbolic and "material evidence of imperialist violence against the bodies of Korean women" (Kim 1998: 189). *Yanggongju* have consequently been implicated in debates about national security and national interest such that they have been described as "a body sequestered in camp town ghettos but in service of national security" (Cho 2006: 314). Like Kim's (1998) discussion of the representations of *yanggongju*, Sarah Soh (2000 and 2001) has also argued that the ways the comfort women have been represented – as either prostitutes or sex slaves – serve particular political and ideological agendas. Importantly, Soh (2000: 59) recognises that both labels are "partial truths deriving from narrative frames that not only reveal the ideological stances of the opposing camps but also serve there partisan interests in the global post-Cold War politics of women's rights as human rights". There is no doubt that "prostitution can [also] serve the national security interests of the sovereign state", as Zimelis (2009: 52) has suggested in his focus on the sex industry in Korea, Japan and the Philippines. Arguably, trafficking has now also emerged as the key platform for the advancement of such an agenda.

NGOs – such as CATW and the Polaris Project – and the governments of both Korea and the Philippines have been quick to endorse these constructions of sexual slavery as accurate depictions of the situations of foreign women in the *gijich'on*, even though it is quite clear that very little of their 'research' is grounded in, or informed by, interactions with people who live and work in *gijich'on*. In the realm of human trafficking the presumed problem of access to these 'hidden populations' is often cited as a reason to avoid direct encounters with the subjects of trafficking themselves, in which case media accounts and highly selective victim testimonies substitute for – or indeed take on a role as – legitimate knowledge and authoritative voice (Zhang 2010).

Conclusion: the (geo)political bar 'girl'

I began this chapter by describing the way Korea first emerged on the map of global trafficking since this attention directed the media's gaze towards the *gijich'on* areas and led to both concrete responses by the US DoD and to a flurry of media interest in *gijich'on* entertainers and their clientele. In the main part of the chapter I focused on these media representations as well as a small number of (moralising) academic accounts that draw on these media constructs to substantiate their own claims and agendas. Because of the history of systematised military prostitution involving Korea and/or Korean women that began with the comfort women during the Second World War, the comfort women trope was – and continues to be – routinely invoked in these media and academic narratives as a reference point to locate foreign entertainers in a broader history of sexual exploitation of women by military forces in Korea. Other accounts focus more centrally on locating *gijich'on*-based entertainers as victims of contemporary military and peacekeeping operations around the globe. In doing so the discourse of militarised sexual slavery historically and presently establishes equivalence between migrant entertainers and comfort women through time and space, denies difference between and amongst these groups of women and collapses them all into a single sex slave object. Put simply, this sex slave rhetoric cannot accommodate the agency and aspirations of the women at their centre, nor the types of nuanced relationships and subtle practices that characterise the everyday spaces and practices of *gijich'on*. Further, it enables outsiders (NGOs, state actors, researchers, media) to presume they can understand these women's lives and experiences without ever needing to speak, or indeed listen, to them.

Sexual slavery has thus become a mobile, circulating discourse, globally and within Korea. As Manzo (2008) argues, central to discursive formations with politically provocative and emotive intent – such as advocacy and awareness raising – is the invocation of equivalence between the sexual slavery subject in various places around the globe and throughout history. In the process of creating such equivalence the great diversity of women's experiences disappears and in their place a single object of politicisation and intervention emerges – namely the female sex slave. In Korea this discursive strategy has been applied to the comfort women of the Second World War, the Korean prostitutes and hostesses serving US military personnel in the post-war period (*yanggongju*) and, finally, the foreign women currently deployed as entertainers in *gijich'on*. Despite what these historically different groups of women – and discrepant voices within each – might themselves have to say about being located within the sex slave discourse, a single unified subject has nonetheless emerged as an enduring and repeated focus of political action serving both feminist-nationalist and humanitarian/anti-trafficking agendas. *Yanggongju*, and in turn Filipina and Russian entertainers, have, in short, been collapsed within the comfort women paradigm. Locating migrant entertainers in Korea's *gijich'on* as part of a broader project of US military occupation of women's bodies in host countries establishes these women within a broader discourse of trafficked sex slaves in other conflict zones across the globe, including, as demonstrated earlier, in the Balkans.

A common thread of exploitative sexual servitude involving a hegemonic military power runs through and even directly connects the comfort women, the Korean women serving the US military in Korean *gijich'on* and the foreign entertainers in the *gijich'on* today. These contemporary sexual/geopolitical histories are linked by masculinist-military formations that operate globally and reproduce particular patriarchal formations that exploit and subjugate local women as sexual objects, often with abusive and violent outcomes. This interpretation, which is productive of a type of sexual slavery discourse that is imagined through the lens of militaristic violence, physical entrapment, lack of remuneration for sexual labour performed and sometimes death, is extrapolated from a diverse array of historical subjects and contemporary formations and universalised, producing a particular "will to knowledge" (Foucault 1980). Consequently, subject positions such as 'sex slave' produced by those other than the women they seek to describe ascribe no agency and no voice to the women who are their object. Ratna Kapur (2002: 30–31) summarises it aptly when she suggests that "it is . . . necessary to focus on the subject situated at the periphery, as she has the power to bring about normative disruptions". Failing to "focus on the subject at the periphery" leads to interpretations of women's experiences from outsiders and, we should note, from those with political interests in representing these subjects in highly circumscribed ways that promote particular agendas and interventions concerning prostitution, nationalism, anti-Americanism and the US military empire. These representations are couched in the language of human rights abuses, gendered violence, nationalism and, ultimately, sex trafficking. Unfortunately, as I have suggested, very little of this label derives from women's own self-understandings, nor are their accounts generally sought or included in the sex slave narrative.

In the chapters that follow I attempt to re-centre the subjects marginalised in these accounts to answer the question of how and in what ways these women are (and are not) trafficked and how they move on from these situations. Such disclosures reveal the limits of the 'new comfort women' label and its location within the broader mobile discourse of sexual slavery. In the next chapter I turn to the task of exploring the complexities of migrant entertainers' situations in Korea's *gijich'on*. Money, debt and coerced labour are writ large in this account.

Notes

1 The DMZ (De-Militarised Zone) is also used colloquially by GIs in TDC to refer to a specific alley at the back of the main strip where most of the clubs are oriented to African-American patrons; here DMZ substitutes as Dark Man's Zone.
2 As KCWU (1999) note, in 1997 there was a large protest in 'America Town', the US military camp town outside Kunsan, North Cholla province. This protest involved Korean camp town hostesses and prostitutes rallying against the increasing numbers of foreign women working in the clubs who were taking over their customers.
3 In an overview of *gijich'on* fiction, Bruce Fulton (1998) demonstrated that *gijich'on* – like *yanggongju* ('foreign princess') – have figured prominently in the nationalist imaginary of Korea since the end of the Korean War, thus revealing the historicity of the current spectacle.

4 For important exceptions see Hildson and Giridharan 2008, Parranas 2011, Yea 2004 and 2005, Cheng 2010, Faier 2009.
5 The US DoS assesses countries globally according to their efforts to reduce and eradicate human trafficking. Tier One ranked countries are those that have made concerted efforts to counter human trafficking; Tier Two countries are those that have made some effort but still have a substantial (and possibly growing) human trafficking problem. Tier Three countries are classified as those that have both a substantial human trafficking problem and have made minimal efforts to either recognise or reduce it. The collective rankings and country reports are available in the annual Trafficking in Persons (TIP) report released each July.
6 Congressman Chris Smith is a conservative Republican who was responsible for forming the working party that developed the United States' first anti-trafficking legislation, the Victims of Trafficking and Violence Protection Act. He has tirelessly lobbied the US DoD to implement stricter provisions to control the use of trafficked and prostituted women for sexual gratification by US military forces globally. He currently serves as the co-chair of the Congressional Caucus on Human Trafficking.
7 As a response to this letter, an assessment project was designed to examine commands around the globe, not just in Korea, focusing on the extent of complicity in human trafficking. Korea and the Balkans were selected by senior management within the inspector general's office as two foci for the investigation. The Korean part of the investigation began in August 2003, three months before the conclusion of my main fieldwork period in Korea. Unfortunately, there was no prior investigation called for to assess the precise nature and extent of human trafficking involving foreign women in camp town areas, leaving Merriman's claims largely accepted at face value.
8 Indeed, Soh (2001) has also contested this sex slave image in relation to the comfort women themselves because it denies their "powerful human agency and their personal strength in overcoming hardships of both their life and during and after the war".
9 The IOM (2002) report did not conduct direct interviews with anyone in camp town areas themselves. The researcher for this report, June Lee, relied on the testimony of one group of eleven Filipinas who had sought the assistance of the Philippines Embassy in Seoul. The report extrapolated their case to make more general conclusions about the situations of all migrant entertainers in Korea's *gijichon*. As has been noted by Meg McLagan *(2003)*, in the absence of more comprehensive evidence and with the ability to ignite public emotions, the role of victim testimony has become central to accounts of sex trafficking.
10 For Donna Hughes's response see Hughes (2008).
11 This issue came to public attention in South Korea in November 1990 when the Korean Council for Women Drafted for Military Sexual Slavery by Japan was formed with the purpose of "recovering the human rights of the comfort women". Since the first public testimony by a former comfort woman, Kim Han Soon, was given in August 1991, over 150 victims have come forward to testify about their experiences. Most, however, are unwilling to face the shame and public humiliation they expect would result from declaring their histories as comfort women, since, as Hicks suggests, "Given the high moral value attached to chastity, the comfort women invariably emerged from their wartime experiences defiled, yet unable to accuse their abusers. They had everything to gain by keeping silent and everything to lose by making accusations" (1995: 21).
12 Factually, this statement is incorrect; the bars and clubs around the US military bases in Korea are all licensed, and the women employed there are on employment contracts as entertainers. Just because conditions of work may not be adhered to does not then make the entire industry 'illegal'.

3 Re-thinking trafficking in *gijich'on*

On December 22, 2001, Cherry-Lyn arrived at Inchon International Airport on the outskirts of Seoul, where she was picked up by her Korean promotion agent, whom she called her manager. She was driven for an hour and a half through the cold December snow to Top Hat Club in Anjong-ri, about fifty kilometres south of Seoul, where she was employed to work for one year as a singer and hostess. She only stayed there for two and a half months because, as she recalled, "We have to dance [pole dance]. No food. No salary. No hot water. And we have to go with customers. That's why we all run away from Top Hat". After running away Cherry-Lyn and her five Filipina co-workers found work in a factory about thirty kilometres away, but the shifts were thirteen to fifteen hours per day, six and sometimes seven days a week, and the work was exhausting. So she decided to try her luck in a different club. She called her manager and laughed as she recalled how she begged him, "I want to come back. Don't put me in jail". Cherry-Lyn's manager decided to place her in Olympia Club in Anjong-ri, but it was only one week before she again requested to change clubs because Olympia also had pole dancing. From April to early November Cherry-Lyn worked at Yes Club in Song-tan, which she thought she could handle because it was "only a karaoke club, and no dancing".

Cherry-Lyn didn't receive any salary from any of the Korean clubs she worked in, and her thoughts started turning back to the Philippines and the son and daughter she had left behind in the care of her mother. She had not remitted any money to them in the six months she had been in Korea. Yes Club's owner had started forwarding Cherry-Lyn's salary to her manager after the debts incurred for her migration costs were paid out, but when she questioned her manager about the salary he told her, "You don't need any salary – you have free food and a place". Cherry-Lyn knew the owner of Yes Club paid USD 1,000 per month to her manager for Cherry-Lyn's continued placement in the club, USD 400 of which was supposed to be paid to Cherry-Lyn as salary. When she persisted with questions about her salary her manager again chided, "You don't need to have salary because you're illegal". In fact Cherry-Lyn's manager was punishing her because her entire group had run away from Top Hat Club several months earlier to work in factories. Because Cherry-Lyn was the oldest in the group at age twenty-seven, her manager held her personally responsible for his losses with the other five women, despite having misled the women with regard to keys aspect of their work, namely having to perform pole dancing, having to go out with customers and not receiving salary or food.

Cherry-Lyn's irregular status resulted from the failure of her manager to extend her E-6 (entertainer's) visa in Korea. After six months in Korea migrant entertainers are supposed to have their visas extended for a further six months, which is always done by a woman's Korean manager. On May 20, 2002, Cherry-Lyn's original visa expired, but her manager did not extend it for the second six months. That May there was a one-month amnesty period for irregular migrant workers to leave Korea without penalty, and Cherry-Lyn decided that she would apply under the amnesty to go back to the Philippines. But the owner of Yes Club would not let her go, so she decided to take matters into her own hands a month later and went to Immigration with her manager to see what she needed to do to return to Manila. The Immigration officer told her she could not leave Korea unless she paid USD 400 for having no alien card[1] and an additional penalty for the one month she had overstayed on her visa, since the amnesty period had already ended. She told the officer that it was not her fault that she overstayed or indeed that she did not possess an alien card, as her manager had not arranged these things on her behalf and the club owner would not allow her to visit Immigration during the amnesty period. Anticipating trouble, Cherry-Lyn's anxious manager jumped in and told the officer he was just a neighbour who wanted to help Cherry-Lyn go back to Manila.

With no other option immediately discernible to her, Cherry-Lyn started working in Yes Club once again so she could earn money to pay her Immigration fines in order to leave Korea. The club owner wanted her to start going on bar fines, which entailed a customer buying a woman's time to take her outside the club on a 'date'. The owner of Yes Club told Cherry-Lyn, "You're in Korea to earn money, right? So make the most of your chance and go out with customers". Her manager also told her that if someone paid out her contract – meaning the remainder of the debt incurred for migration fees owed to the Korean and Philippines promotion agencies – which was vaguely determined to be USD 1,000, he would give her the USD 400 required by Immigration to pay her fine. One of Cherry-Lyn's regular customers *did* in fact pay the contract out, and yet her manager still failed to provide her with the promised USD 400. Cherry-Lyn was furious: "How can my customer be asked to pay out my contract when I don't even have a contract?" It was, indeed, also the question on my lips.

Like Rosie, Cherry-Lyn's story was also the subject of the media's sex trafficking narrative. Cherry-Lyn was interviewed by a reporter from one of Seoul's leading progressive newspapers, *Hangyure Sinmun*. When I read the article I found fragments of Cherry-Lyn's narrative re-told in an almost unrecognisable form. If I had not known her I would have concluded that her trafficking experience was one of repeated and forced prostitution. And yet this was not something she ever mentioned to me in the conversations that form this vignette.

I met Cherry-Lyn at the Centre in Seoul in early November 2002. At the time she had been in Korea for just under a year. She had arrived at the Centre the previous day after Father Glenn went to Songtan to take her out of Yes Club. Cherry-Lyn had a pen pal, an American woman whose husband was based in Okinawa but was previously at Osan Air Base in Songtan. The pair had been emailing when Cherry-Lyn told her friend that she was in trouble in her job in Korea. Her friend said she would see if she could find someone to help. Her friend searched the Internet and found a newspaper article mentioning the work Father Glenn did supporting migrant Filipinos in Korea, and so she contacted Father Glenn and asked if he could help Cherry-Lyn. Father Glenn went to Songtan the next day and took Cherry-Lyn out of the club and back to the Centre in Seoul. Cherry-Lyn and I talked over the course of two days, during which she recounted the multiple sites through which control over her body, labour and migration status in Korea were continually diluted in the context of her work.

The experiences of many migrant entertainers in Korea – both in *gijich'on* and elsewhere – contain elements of trafficking, but the ways they are and are not trafficked depart markedly from those interpretations put forward in the sex slave accounts discussed in the previous chapter. In common with the media reportage of Rosie's story, the account of Cherry-Lyn's experiences is at odds with her own interpretation of events. The stories of women like Cherry-Lyn who rail against fines, debts, punishments, missing contracts and denial of salary in their jobs as entertainers in Korea disappear under the gaze of the hapless 'modern day comfort woman'. Missing also are the attempts – sometimes failed and sometimes successful – by the women themselves to manoeuvre these situations by running away to work in a factory or negotiating with their promoter to transfer to a different club or pursuing an array of other tactics.

This chapter explores the migration process to Korea for women like Cherry-Lyn. It examines their deployment and working situations in the *gijich'on* clubs, centring on the labour exploitation and loss of control/freedom inherent in women's migration experiences. Entertainers' sojourns in Korea are riddled with exploitative labour practices and poor work conditions. Exploitation contains multiple layers and expressions relating to women's declining levels of control over their situations induced through debt and contract arrangements that are inherent in the migration process. Further, women are subject to arbitrary penalties and punishments for various infringements of ludicrously strict club rules, which simultaneously inflate their debt and lower their self-esteem. Women in some clubs are pushed to go on bar fines (which may or may not entail sex) or need to perform sexual or intimate labour – pole dancing in Cherry-Lyn's case – under degrading and humiliating conditions for little or no recompense. While it is important to understand these experiences, it is equally as important not to over-generalise them and render other aspects of women's labour migration experiences invisible. By implication this means decentring the 'sex' in trafficking. I approach this task by attempting to answer the question of what exactly trafficking means in the experiences of women like Rosie as well as Cherry-Lyn and her Top Hat co-workers.

Realising the dream: migrating as an entertainer to Korea

The migration process as it is organised and managed in the Philippines is a key site through which women's vulnerability becomes heightened once they arrive in Korea. This is because the process requires a performance of paperwork to legitimise migration which in turn results in the creation of inflated debts for prospective labour migrants. The ultimate consequence of this is low or no salary – often for several months – once an entertainer arrives in Korea. The situation for migrant entertainers is similar to practices affecting other prospective Filipino labour migrants, both to Korea and elsewhere, who must pay often exorbitant agency fees and costs associated with official accreditations and checks in order to migrate abroad for work. Many migrant entertainers face club owners' non-adherence to contracts that the women sign in the Philippines or sometimes upon arrival in Korea, including flouting of stipulations relating to work performed (such as pole dancing) and failure to provide food. Women find it difficult to leave workplaces that do not adhere to contract stipulations because they must pay back the money doled out to various agencies to finance their migration, effectively debt bonding them to errant employers. The conditions attached to working visas in Korea also exacerbate this dilemma since in a case where a migrant worker leaves her initial employer she cannot legally look for a new employer without leaving the country and starting the whole application and placement process over again. I argue that trafficking in this situation relates to declining levels of control and freedom that a woman has over her labour as a result of costs incurred during the migration process and the inability to negotiate changes to exploitative or degrading conditions of employment after arriving in Korea. In these instances, being trafficked therefore relates mainly to debt bondage, removal of freedom and deception about work conditions and duties more generally, rather than to women's exploitation as 'sex slaves', which applies unambiguously to only two women I came to know out of more than 100 who participated in my research.

Stephen Castles (2000) argues that the emergence of contract migration regimes globally in the current period of border tightening measures in developed nations has led to distinct ways of regulating third-world labour and organising and controlling its movement. The specific modes of regulation of migrant labourers from developing countries inflate costs and impose heightened restrictions on them when they reach the migration destination. These contract migration regimes also expand the roles of private sector agencies – commonly referred to as recruitment agencies or labour brokers – in the migration process despite oftentimes a lack of adherence to regulations governing the ways these agencies are supposed to operate. The perception that migrant entertainers are highly susceptible to trafficking has only acted to further heighten the rigmarole of the contract migration apparatus by inserting the need for protection of these female workers into it. In the case of migrant entertainers the paperwork and procedures of verification of qualifications attached to approving visas are subject to increasingly rigorous processes of training and certification. In tracing the recent history of the involvement of both the state and private-sector agencies in contract labour migration in the Philippines, Anna Romina Guevarra (2009) notes that in 1995 the government passed the Migrant Workers Act and Overseas Filipinos Act, which aimed to 'protect' migrant workers but contained an implicit focus on heightening regulations for female entertainers and domestic workers, guided by the rationale that those migrating in these feminised occupational categories were most likely to be subject to violence and abuse abroad. She also suggests that this gendered focus was seen as "a way to correct perceptions of the Philippines as a country of domestic workers and entertainers, which contributes to the marred image of the country and, in particular, of the Filipino women" (Guevarra 2009: 38). Whatever the logic behind the act, the result has been a more elaborate migration infrastructure for those wishing to work abroad as entertainers.

In order to migrate to Korea on an E-6, or entertainer's, visa Filipinas first have to train as either singers or dancers with talent agencies in the Philippines. Some women I knew in Korea paid up to USD 800 'under the table' to receive certification without having ever undergone training, creating yet another debt for these women. On completion of the training, women undergo an Academic and Skills Test (AST) where the routines learned so diligently during training are tested. The talent then receives an Artist's Record Book (ARB), without which she – or more likely her promotion agency – cannot apply for a visa as an entertainer.[2] There are thus two different agencies involved in arranging a woman's migration as an entertainer: the talent agency that trains her and the promotion agency that arranges her deployment into a specific club in Korea. Usually the promotion agency will work in concert with a partner promotion agency in Korea to locate and arrange a woman's deployment to a club at the request of a club.

Thus, once trained, women need to register with a promotion agency, which then handles all aspects of their migration from the Philippines side. Women who buy their ARBs on the black market or acquire them through corrupt state officials would contact the promotion agency first, since agencies often help women secure this document without having to undergo training. What is important to note is that a woman wishing to migrate to Korea to work as an entertainer cannot arrange her migration independently and must utilise the services of one of these promotion agencies, since the Philippines government feels this will ostensibly protect women from trafficking or exploitation in Korea (Guevarra 2009: 38–39). This follows from the model employed for entertainers migrating to Japan (see Parrenas 2006 and 2011).

When women register with a promoter in the Philippines the promoter also arranges an 'audition', and, on this basis, the selection of women to go abroad is made, as in Rosie's description in the introduction. Sometimes the club owners or the counterpart Korean promotion agencies will themselves travel to the Philippines to attend the auditions and meet the women. What the women have to do in an audition varies. Some women perform (sing or dance) while others simply stand on stage. Without exception all women who had an audition stated that they had to wear a 'sexy costume', which revealed parts of their bodies, for the audition. Some women stated that the club owners from Korea or the Korean promoters would touch their body, including their breasts, and check their body for stretch marks. Alma, deployed in Shield Club in TDC, stated that in her case she found out about working in Korea from a friend, who said to her, "I know about entertainers in Korea. You must apply Ashman promotions". Alma applied for Japan, but she said it was difficult and the process took a long time. Her friend said, "To Korea is quick". Alma had an audition in the Philippines before coming to Korea [in June 2003] and then received the visa in August. At the audition they just told her, "You will belong to Shield Club", then took her photograph. Despite Alma's training as a dancer in Manila, there was no testing of her dancing prowess in the audition, presumably because this was not a skill she would require in Shield Club.

The Philippines promoter also pays women's travel costs and handles the minefield of paperwork required to migrate. The latter includes the ARB, a medical check-up, acquiring a passport if a woman does not already hold a passport and obtaining her visa. In order to process a passport application other documents are also required, including a birth certificate and parents' marriage certificate. Some of the women incurred additional costs for false passports. Six of the women I knew entered Korea when they were minors, at either sixteen or seventeen years of age, and they came on false passports because they were underage. Eight others I knew also entered Korea using a passport that was not their own, even though they were of legal age at the time of entry. The reason for using a different or false passport for minors is obvious. For adult women, if they did not have a passport but were to migrate quickly, they were issued with a real passport that belonged to another woman in which the photograph had been changed. Unfortunately buying false passports or real passports that belong to someone else is excessively expensive and entails another substantial additional fee to a woman's migration debt. Entering on a passport that uses someone else's identity or is false also makes it less likely women will run away or make complaints about their situations in Korea lest their identity fraud is discovered.

Promotion agencies also require women to have a pictorial, which is then used by the promotion agency to help place a woman in a club in Korea. The Korean promotion agency arranges for copies of women's pictorials to be sent from the Philippines promoter to club owners in Korea, from which they are able to select particular women. Many of the women put considerable effort into creating these dossiers in order to appear as professional as possible. One of my participants, Honey, had an extensive dossier, which she showed me. It contained photos of herself in professional dance performances back in the Philippines and listings of events in which she had performed during her training with Villa Flor Talent Agency in Manila. Sometimes promoters also lend women money so they can buy costumes, make-up or other items needed for their work in Korea. All these costs are added to women's migration debts and sometimes are greatly inflated by the agencies/lenders. The main effect of the introduction of strict entertainer's certifications for E-6 visa holders in Korea and the involvement of promotion agencies has therefore been to inflate women's debts and consequently reduce their salary. All these logistics and documentation costs, which apply to all labour migrants exiting the Philippines for overseas employment, have deservedly lead Robyn Rodriguez (2010) to label the Philippines a labour "brokerage state".

Given the high costs associated with entertainer contract migration, none of the women I knew paid their costs up front, but instead agreed to repay the costs of their migration to their respective agents and talent managers via an agency fee imposed by their promoter. Women pay this debt out of their salaries once in Korea. Employment contracts normally state that entertainers will receive a salary of approximately USD 400–USD 500 per month, which should commence within two months of a woman starting her work in Korea and after repaying her migration debt.

Honey, Nikki and Penny, who were deployed together in Limbo Club in TDC in early 2003 and whom I met after they ran away from the club a few months later, described the costs and debts incurred in the training and the ways promotion agents can use this to their own advantage to exert control over migrant entertainers. Honey recounted that all women who underwent training in her talent agency had to pay back their talent manager, as well as the Philippines promotion agency, through agreed-to salary deductions once they started working in Korea. Honey was told she had to pay PHP 22,304.50 to her talent manager, Villa Flor, for the cost of the training, for organising her ARB and for living costs associated with staying at Villa Flor's house while completing her training.[3] Just before leaving for Korea, AP Promotions, Honey's and Nikki's promotion agency in the Philippines, asked them to sign a promissory note saying they would accept a USD 50 monthly salary deduction as Villa Flor's talent fee (see copy of Nikki's promissory note, Figure 3.1). The three women were asked to sign these notes in the car when they were already on the way to the airport in Manila, leaving them no real recourse to refuse. As Honey described:

> My talent manager said "You can pay USD 50 every month fee. You can get that back with your drinks". But we didn't know what she meant by this. When we got to Korea Papa Chu [Korean promotion agent] said, "No, that's not correct". Villa Flor was planning to come to Korea in May to get that money for the first four months [USD 50 × 4 months] from each of us three girls and for girls she had in other clubs in Korea.

The agreement that Honey, Nikki and Penny had originally signed was for part of the money owed to Villa Flor to be repaid after the completion of the first twelve-month contract. For Honey, Nikki and Penny, the USD 50 that Villa Flor was demanding led to pressure to make high drink sales in Limbo Club to procure this extra income. Having no idea that drink sales was even part of their work in Korea, Honey, Nikki and Penny experienced a double anxiety related to fulfilling the obligations of their promissory notes – first, paying back the money during the contract and, second, the work they needed perform to pay it back. These types of arbitrary arrangements are difficult for women to contest if they wish to go through with their intended migration, leaving them open to unexpected debt impositions and little real choice in negotiating the work they must perform.

The women I knew rarely received either all or even part of their salaries, making it difficult for them to consider leaving their job. One-quarter of the participants

Date: January 31, 2003

PROMISSORY NOTE

To Whom It May Concern:

I _____, promise to pay the amount of **Pesos Twenty Two Thousand Three Hundred Four & 50/00 (P 22,304.50)** or it's equivalent representing my accountabilities to **VILLAFLOR'S PROMOTION and TALENT SERVICES.**

Moreover, I promise to remit to _____ it's office commission amounting to **US$ 550.00 for eleven (11) months.**

In case I will break my contract for whatever reason I promise to notify the office and will pay the corresponding damages accordingly.

_____   _____
Name of Talent   Manager

Witness:

_____   _____

Figure 3.1 Copy of Nikki's promissory note

in my research, for example, were not paid any salary while working in the clubs for periods up to ten months.

The club owners pay a much higher price to the promoters than the women receive in their salaries, as Alma told me:

> I see that it is USD 900 that the *ajumma* [female Korean club owner, lit. aunty, in Korean] pays to my manager every month. So I wondered where the other USD 500 was going. I knew my manager paid USD 100 to Ashman agency [Alma's Philippines promotion agency], which means Anak Promotions [Alma's Korean promotion agency] get USD 400 for me each month. We never knew USD 900 until I saw it. So why do they pay us below the minimum salary in Korea?

In Alma's case there were eight women working together in Shield Club where she was deployed, which means that Anak Promotions was making a profit of USD 3,200 per month (8 × USD 400) from the club owners' payments to Anak for these women's placement in the club. In addition, Ashman Promotions Agency in the Philippines makes USD 800 (8 × USD 100) from the Korean club owner for these same women each month. Anak Promotions and Ashman Promotions Agency were, from 2002 to 2003 and in 2005 when I conducted the main periods of my fieldwork, two of the biggest promotion agencies operating to deploy Filipinas in Korea. Anak also brings Russian women into Korea, and in 2003 the number of Filipinas and Russians collectively placed by the agency in Korea was around 300. At USD 400 per month from the club owners for each woman deployed in their club, plus the fee (normally around USD 100) the women must pay out of their monthly salaries to repay debts, Korean-based promotion agencies such as Anak Promotions can make up to USD 150,000 per month from the business of placing entertainers in clubs.

With media reports of trafficking becoming more frequent in 2002, and heightened Philippines and Korean government scrutiny of migrant entertainers wishing to work in Korea, petty corruption also started to increase. Cherry told me that whenever the owner of M Club, where she was deployed, travelled to Manila to attend auditions and select entertainers for her club she would take a briefcase full of cash with her to pay off the Korean Embassy and Philippine government officials. She would brag to the Filipinas in M Club that she could buy whoever she wanted with that money. Alma also described that in her visa issuance meeting at the Korean Embassy, the embassy official in Manila did not ask Alma to dance to test her skills (supposedly entertainers were to perform for embassy officials before being granted their visas in order to confirm that they were bona fide entertainers). Instead her promoter passed a bottle of USD 200 whiskey and an envelope across the desk to the official, after which she was granted her visa. The Philippine Overseas Employment Administration, which is charged with controlling and regulating Philippine labour migration, has been criticised for not fulfilling its mandated regulatory role for agencies. For example, a Philippine Migrants Rights Watch (PMRW) study in 2004 found that even though the rule is that the placement fee for an Filipino seeking a job abroad must be equivalent to or less than one month's salary, this was continually thwarted, with many agencies sending women to Korea and charging several times this amount.

Conversely to my argument here that debt increases women's vulnerability in migration to Korea, Cheng (2010) has suggested that debt bondage as an element of trafficking for migrant entertainers in Korea needs to be rethought. She argues that migration debts in the form of promotion and talent agency fees are not sites of financial exploitation or mechanisms to bond women to errant employers but, rather, enabling costs that allow women who otherwise could not afford to migrate the opportunity to go abroad for work. I disagree; if women were able to migrate independently (that is, without the services of agencies) the costs borne would likely be less than a quarter of those they currently pay as there would be no inflation or arbitrary impositions, thus allowing women to earn money more quickly and not remain in employment situations they did not agree to. The agency profits are quite apart from the profits the club owners make from the women's sexual and intimate labour, to which I now turn.

Walang pera [no money]: working for the club

Amongst Filipinas who migrate to Korea to work as entertainers there is considerable variation in their understandings of the type of work they will be performing, making it impossible to locate the Filipina entertainer as a singular subject.[4] First, there are those who have had no previous experience working in clubs as strippers, erotic dancers or sex workers and think they are migrating for other work, such as being a waitress or hostess. Second are those who have previous experience working in the entertainment sector as professional singers and dancers and think they are going abroad for work in this profession. Third are those who have worked in clubs previously as professional strippers and/or sex workers, who may have a good idea that they will be performing sexual or intimate labour but may nonetheless still be deceived about the conditions of work or other aspects of their migration. Finally, there are women who have migrated previously to work as entertainers in other countries, usually Japan, and understand that their work and working conditions will be similar to those of previous migration experiences, including a particular understanding of what it means to be a hostess. None of the women I knew in Korea had engaged in sex work in the Philippines, although Cherry had previously been employed as an erotic dancer in a club in Manila, while Rosa, who was deployed together with Cherry in M Club, had performed strip dancing in Guam, where she was employed as an entertainer. Several women who had worked as entertainers in Japan were skilled hostesses and performed a combination of intimate and sexual labour, what Rhacel Parrenas (2011) calls "illicit flirtation", though rarely prostitution. It is important to note that entertainer's visas are often seen as a rouse by various governments and international organisations for women wishing to migrate for sex work, both in Korea and elsewhere (see Parrenas 2011 on this for Japan). A quarter of my participants told me they were professionally trained singers, and nine said they were professional cabaret dancers, while the remainder were either students, unemployed or unskilled/low-skilled workers in other sectors before receiving training or buying certification to travel to Korea as entertainers.

The women's expectations about the nature of their work duties in Korea varied according to which group they fell into. Professional entertainers (singers or dancers) expected to perform each evening according to the conditions agreed to in their contracts. Angel, for example, was working in a club as a singer in the Philippines when her Filipina boss introduced her to Kim Kyung Soo, an infamous club and promotion agency owner in TDC who makes regular trips to the Philippines to attend auditions to bring women to Korea. Angel said,

> Kim Kyong Soo in Palace Club – my owner – he always goes to the Philippines. I think my work here [in Korea] is a good job. You know, singer – like that. But I get here Monday night and I see Palace and I say, "Where [is] the singer here?" They say, "No singer here, just drinkie girl", like that. And my boss said, "You

practice dance", and I have no choice, because, you know, I'm here already. My boss, Jimmy [Kim Kyung Soo's son], he fight me. I'm shocked because I want a job as singer. I have no choice because the Korean doesn't speak English much and my English is no good. He [Kim Kyong Soo] lied to me.

Angel's reference to 'drinkie girl' invokes the slang name GIs use to describe the foreign women who work in the clubs. The name is a reference to the drink system that operates in all the clubs. Under this system customers buy women's time in the club through the purchase of a drink for her. Another equivalent term is 'juicy girl' since the drink most commonly purchased is a small glass of juice.

Similarly to Angel, Rico was a professional singer in a band and had previously worked in Japan and in the Philippines as an entertainer. She recounted,

> I had a Filipina acquaintance when I was working in Japan. This girl said to me that she'd met a girl who worked in Korea before and so she introduced her to me. This girl from in Korea said "You can earn lots of money there", and she convinced us that we could save money higher than in Japan. She said we would be professional singers. So when I get back to the Philippines after my booking in Japan, I contact Ashman Promotions. They tell us there that we will have 20–30 minutes sets 7 times a night at the club in Korea, and then we just stay backstage between our sets. They said it would be up to us if we decided to sit down with a customer. That was all bullshit what they told us.

Those who are not professional singers or dancers, but instead utilised an entertainer's visa to secure hostessing work abroad, were normally given a job description which included entertaining customers by taking their order for drinks and sitting or dancing with them and chatting to them or serving drinks. Lisa, who had a sister in Japan doing hostessing work on an entertainer's visa, told me,

> The contract said we would be a waitress, entertain and talk and like my sister in Japan. But when we get here [to Korea] we have to sit down on their [customer's] laps, lap dance, VIP and going out on bar fine – only sometimes VIP and bar fine. But we need the money 'coz they don't pay us the salary.

Janice, who was deployed in Shield Club with Alma, echoed Lisa's sentiments:

> We were never told that we going to dance and wear a thong. They [promotion agency in the Philippines] said we're just going to entertain not to dance ... It's my first time to work in a club and dancing wearing a bra and thong. Mr Yoon [Korean manager] is the one who did the audition in Manila. During the audition we just wear sexy dresses. That's why we thought we're just going to hostess in Korea.

Some women know there is a risk attached to being an entertainer that is associated with the possibility of having to perform sexual labouring. But some Philippine promotion agencies pre-empt the concern this can create for women recruited. Cecile said her contract stated she would be an entertainer, which meant selling drinks and talking to customers. Her promoter in the Philippines said something like this to her:

> In other clubs there is dancing all the way [strip shows]. But you don't do like that, just entertain. This is Korea, not the Philippines, so it's okay. Other clubs do bar fine, but not Papaya Club. We don't like that at Papaya Club. But when I got here, papa-san [male club owner in TDC] said, "You need to do bar fine".

This deception created particular anxieties in Cecile's case since she was nearly three months pregnant when she migrated to Korea. She was planning to work for as long as she could waitressing in the club before either having her baby in Korea or returning to Palawan in central Philippines. Once Cecile realised that her papa-san planned to make her abort the baby so she would be able to go for bar fines she ran away and found work in a factory, delivering her baby six months later in the general hospital at Uijongbu, north of Seoul. Cecile had worked right up until she felt her first labour pains, catching the bus from the factory to the hospital, where she delivered her baby an hour after being admitted.

So women have different expectations about the work they need to perform, but the work they *actually* perform once deployed in *gijich'on* clubs always involves pressures to heighten the profits for the club. The two main forms of intimate labour in the clubs are providing customers with companionship through flirting in the context of a ladies drink served in the club and providing customers with intercourse either in a club's VIP room or outside the club on bar fines.

Ladies drinks, VIP rooms and bar fines

All the clubs have a drink system which means the women need to perform hostessing work that may involve anything from just chatting or dancing with a customer to being kissed, fondled and groped. In USA Club where Lisa worked the drink system also entailed lap dancing. Women's gradations of intimate and sexual labour depended on what each club offered and what an individual woman would negotiate with her (different) customers. Parrenas (2006) refers to this negotiation of unwanted advances and physical attention by customers for Filipina hostesses in Tokyo as "boundary work". Zheng (2009) has similarly focused on this boundary work, suggesting that veteran Chinese hostesses in Dailin were more skilled at negotiating advances from customers than newcomers. As well as these negotiations with the customer a woman also has to make sure the club manager does not witness any signs of dissatisfaction from the customer, which could lead to a fine or some kind of punishment for the woman concerned. Manoeuvring intimate labour in hostessing work was a source of incredible anxiety for many of the women in Korea's *gijich'on* clubs, especially those not skilled in the arts of performing boundary work, which applied mainly to those women not expecting to be doing hostessing work in Korea in the first place. Other women experienced some of the greatest anxiety because they did not know how to deflect a customer's advances.

To illustrate this anxiety in performing hostessing duties, I focus on Honey's experience when she worked in Limbo Club. Honey, Nikki and Penny were all expecting to work as professional dancers in Limbo Club. Honey identified having to sit with customers for ladies drinks as her main problem in Limbo Club. Bangladeshi customers caused her the greatest problems. When I first interviewed Honey the day she ran away from Limbo Club she had bruises all over her legs from where she had been pinched and punched by one of her Bangladeshi customers. She recounted,

> He said to me, "You drink Budweiser". Mini [Korean bar manager] said [to him], "Okay, but you pay KRW 30,000 [for Honey's drink]". But I went up to Mini and said, "Mini, it's hard to drink Budweiser". Mini said, "No, no, if a customer goes to the bathroom we replace your drink with an empty bottle. That is how we get him to buy a lot of drinks".

Honey tried to avoid Bangladeshi customers. She said, "They are always horny. Some okay, but most try to touch you. I always hold their hand and I get tired of pushing their hands away. I always get a sore back because I sit like this [curls herself away]". Although she particularly disliked Bangladeshi customers, Honey also felt uncomfortable with some of the GIs. This was because Honey was constantly compared by some GI customers to women in other clubs in relation to the sexual services available. She recounted, "The GI customers will come from the other clubs and say, 'Hey, if I buy you a drink you give me a lap dance'. I say 'No' and I go to the mama-san and tell her. Mama-san says, 'You do that because he buy you a drink', and she gets mad when I won't go to the customer who asks me that. Some customers say, 'This club is boring'. They say, 'We get a fuck at M Club' and one customer just came from Flame Club and said, 'I got a blow job there'". This leads me to a consideration of the role of sex in these women's work in the clubs.

The type of experience illustrated by Honey in relation to performing intimate labour points to the need to complicate discussions of the understanding of sex in women's labouring in the clubs to include an appreciation of the fact that women in some clubs never had sex with a customer. Nonetheless they still felt extreme anxiety in negotiating other forms of intimate labour besides intercourse, as Honey's rendition of relations with customers illustrates. Alma, from Player's Club, stated this most succinctly: "My boss doesn't push me to go on a bar fine. She says, 'It's up to you. If you want to make extra money then go – it's not my decision'. I don't go on bar fines, but I don't have any money because of that".

But bar fines themselves can be interpreted in many ways, and again the type of club in which a woman is deployed is often the key to understanding her experiences with bar fines. Somewhat ironically, it was women in relatively good clubs, like Honey and Alma, who usually avoided bar fines, whilst those in the worst club actively *chose* in many instances to go on bar fines. Although this seems contradictory at first, we must appreciate the fact that bar fines provided women deployed in bad clubs with opportunities to have a break from the club for a while, go on a date or just have a rest. Media reporting often casts bar fines and hostessing duties – including in Cherry-Lyn's case in Top Hat and the other two clubs where she was deployed – exclusively in the realm of forced sex. Cherry-Lyn articulated to me ways that sexual and intimate labour intersect in multiple ways with exploitative situations, only one of which relates to not-agreed-to intercourse with particular customers. Alma from Shield Club; she *wanted* to go on bar fines with her boyfriend so she could take a break and get some rest from the club and to stop the constant nagging of *ajumma* about the lack of money she was generating for the club.

It is important to emphasise therefore that bar fines are not metaphors for forced prostitution. Some women had bad experiences, including being raped, on bar fines, and there is no denying the general lack of redress for women who had these experiences. But women would consent to go on bar fines for a range of reasons, including earning money and tips; avoiding ongoing harassment from the club manager or owner; and in order to further consolidate a relationship with a favoured customer or boyfriend. Cherry-Lyn was not forced to go on bar fines and exerted some choice in matters related to decisions around this, but the need for money was usually the driving factor. Lisa reiterated this point,

> The contract said we would be a waitress, entertain and talk like that. But then when I come here we have to sit down on their [customer's] laps, lap dance, VIP and going out on bar fines; only sometimes VIP and bar fines. They don't push us – it's our choice. But we need the money because they never paid us salary the whole time we were working.

Women's anxieties over bar fines related more specifically to situations where a refusal – usually to go with a Korean or migrant worker customer – would entail a seemingly endless stream of reprimand at the hands of the mama-san or papa-san in the club.

The clubs where sex was sold inside the club itself generally represent the most extreme situation for women as far as commercial sexual exploitation was concerned, but even here this is manifest in ways that resist easy location within the discourse of sexual slavery. In M Club in Toka-ri, where Rosa, Cherry, Jane and Rachel worked, as well as in Y Club where Rosie was deployed, sex was sold in the club in VIP rooms (twenty to thirty minutes per customer), short time (in rooms upstairs for an hour), and long time (in rooms upstairs overnight). But in these venues I found women were often more concerned about the removal of their freedom since these club do not let women out alone at all, the low remuneration for their sexual labour (often further reduced by payment of fines) and the humiliation they experienced at the hands of some customers. Further, some of the women said the single thing they could not endure was performing strip and erotic dancing, *not* intercourse. Rachel, who found dancing the worst of any of her duties in M Club, including over and above performing intercourse with customers, said, "I'm shy to myself. I don't want to see all the guys [look] at my body. It's okay to go to VIP room [for sex], but I don't want to dance. But I have no choice. If you want the money, you have to do like that". Rosa, at thirty-five years old, was a veteran of club work, having been to Japan, Saipan and Korea twice (the first time in Kunsan and the second in Toka-ri). In Japan Rosa never had to perform any kind of 'sexy dancing', but when she reached Saipan she had to strip dance on stage, which she hated. In Kunsan she did not have to perform strip dances, so when a second chance to go to Korea appeared she decided to go, but she was told upon reaching M Club that she needed to do the 'lesbian show' on stage. This meant performing oral sex on another Filipina, whilst another Filipina simultaneously performed it on her. Then they would have to rotate positions. Like Rachel's concerns about strip dancing, Rosa found the show humiliating and embarrassing. Women like Rosa, Rachel and Cherry generally found ways of reclaiming a sense of control over sexual transactions which Rosa astutely described to me as "playing the GIs" (see Zheng 2009 for a similar argument for Chinese internal migrant hostesses).

In sum, then, reflecting on the discrepant narratives of my participants concerning sexual and intimate labour and the conditions under which it was performed and with whom, I am conscious that my participants did not all experience sexual exploitation in the context of trafficking, or indeed in ways that are commonly alluded to in prevailing discourses of sexual exploitation in trafficking. Many of the differences in women's experiences related to differences in their initial expectations about the type of work they were expecting to perform in Korea. Women who were professional singers and dancers usually did not expect hostessing work, and women who were anticipating hostessing work did not usually expect to make decisions about going on bar fines driven by financial constraints and fear of retributions from the club manager or owner. Women in the 'worst' clubs were often prepared to perform sexual labour in the strict sense of a transaction involving intercourse, but these women were often operating under constrained choice, and again, the fact that they were often denied their percentage of the fee for these services was greater a problem than performing the service itself. In these clubs women often found other duties, like erotic and strip dancing, more difficult to perform than intercourse because dancing is performed in a public space (the stage) open to the gaze of all customers while sex is performed in semi-private spaces.

Returning to Cherry-Lyn's experience, the main form of intimate labour for Cherry-Lyn in Yes Club was hostessing which was performed when a customer bought her a lady's drink, allowing him to spend time with her at a table in the club. The lady's drinks in Yes Club were USD 10 (or KRW 10,000) per drink. Cherry-Lyn was supposed to receive KRW 4,000 for each drink sale as her commission but said she did not regularly receive this money. Yes Club, like all the other clubs, has a quota for the number of drink sales each woman must generate in a night. Cherry-Lyn had to sell ten drinks per night at a minimum, and she said the club owner would put pressure on her to generate even higher drink sales. If Cherry-Lyn did not meet the drink quota she needed to go on a bar fine in order to make up for the lack of drink sales. The owner of Yes Club did not physically force Cherry-Lyn to go on a bar fine but exerted pressure for her to do so if she did not meet her drink quota. Sometimes Cherry-Lyn would go if she knew a customer well and trusted him.

Bar fines have come to be viewed by the anti-trafficking sector in Korea as a key mechanism through which women are forced into prostitution. Contrary to this belief, for Cherry-Lyn bar fines were a way of getting out of the club and taking a break with a boyfriend or regular customer, who often gave her extra money when she was outside the club owner's surveillance. Cherry-Lyn was not allowed to receive tips in the club, and if discovered the tip money would be taken by the club owner. Cherry-Lyn related that she only had sex on a bar fine with her boyfriends, and other customers would take her bar hopping or shopping or out to dinner. In other words, it was Cherry-Lyn's *companionship*, not her sexual services, that most customers were buying. She told me, "Some GIs, they help. They say, 'Okay, you need to go out for a break'. They're good. I say to them, 'Just bar hopping and then you can go home for curfew'.[5] They agree and we go out and have fun". Like many other women I came to know, Cherry-Lyn had a few bad experiences with customers who, in Cherry-Lyn's words, thought "being a juicy girl means I am available for sex". She told me that on one occasion a GI tried to have sex with her, so she ran away back to the club. She recounted, "I told the guy, 'No sex', but he's drunk and crazy so I ran away".

Lisa told a similar story about a Bangladeshi migrant worker customer bar fining her and taking her to a hotel for sex. Even though Lisa had decided to 'go all the way' in Korea when she needed extra money to send back to the Philippines, she did not want to go with the Bangladeshi customer whom she found malodorous and unattractive. She said,

> He did it and came, and then after he rested he wanted to do it again. They want to use you as many times as possible when they buy you; like they really want to get their money's worth. So when he took a shower I ran back to the club. Otherwise I have to have sex with him again.

Although the *gijich'on* clubs are generally oriented to American GI customers, Koreans and migrant workers are allowed to patronise some clubs (usually after GI customers return to base to meet their nightly curfew), including in Yes Club where Cherry-Lyn worked and USA Club in TDC where Lisa worked. Like Lisa, Cherry-Lyn was cajoled by the club owner to go on bar fines with Korean customers on several occasions, and in a couple of these cases she said she was forced to have sex with these men. If these Korean customers went back to the club again Cherry-Lyn said she would ignore them and the club owner would get mad at her.

Apart from intimate and sexual labour and the "boundary work" (Parrenas 2006 and 2011) that often accompanies this, migrant entertainers in the clubs also have to clean, cook and sometimes waitress. For all my participants, important conditions set out in their contracts relating to such work were flouted by club owners. Other stipulations relating to days off, working hours, free time and living arrangements were also not adhered to. Depending on the particular club, women's hours of work varied from a minimum of six hours per night during the week and seven to eight hours per night during weekends (Friday, Saturday and Sunday nights) to fifteen hours per night during the week and eighteen hours during the weekend. On week nights women would normally start work between 5 and 6 p.m. and finish at midnight or 1 a.m. During the weekends, however, women normally started work at 1 or 2 p.m. and could finish anywhere between 2 and 7 a.m. the next day. None of my participants ever received any overtime pay for working these longer hours, even though a standard employment contract for entertainers states that "overtime would be paid at the prevailing rate in Korea" (see Figure 3.2).

---

mployment Contract is entered into by and between: _____

The Korean Principal/ Promoter: _____
Address: _____
Telephone No./s: _____ Fax No./s: _____ E-mail Address: _____
Hereinafter referred to as the EMPLOYER represented by its president _____
and by his/her authorized licensed Philippine Private Recruitment Agency or Philippine Agent.

The licensed Philippine Private Recruitment Agency: _____
Address: _____
Telephone No./s: _____ Fax No./s: _____ E-mail Address: _____
Hereinafter referred to as the Philippine Agent.

The Filipino Overseas Performing Artist: _____
Address: _____
Civil Status: SINGLE   Age: 31 yrs. old
Passport No.: _____   Date and Place of Issue: 05 MAY 1998 / MANILA
Artist Record Book No.: _____
Hereinafter referred to as the Talent.

The Filipino Talent Manager: _____
Address: _____
Hereinafter referred to as the Talent Manager: _____

THE ABOVE PARTIES in this contract hereby agree to the following terms and conditions of engagement of the Overseas Performing Artist for the delivery of entertainment services/performances:

DURATION AND PERIOD OF EFFECTIVITY OF THE CONTRACT
1.1 Duration: This contract shall be enforced for a period of six months, extendible by another six months by mutual agreement of the parties.
1.2 Effectivity: The contract shall commence upon the Talent's departure from the Philippines (Date _____) and shall remain in force as stipulated in the duration, unless sooner terminated by the mutual consent of the parties or due to circumstances beyond their control. Booking of the Talent shall be effected within three (3) days upon arrival in Korea, but only after undergoing Mandatory Post-Arrival Briefing at the Philippine Overseas Labor Office (POLO), Philippine Embassy in Seoul.

NAME OF PERFORMANCE VENUE: _____
NAME OF OWNER: _____
ADDRESS: _____
CATEGORY: (As Classified by the Korean Ministry of Culture and Tourism): DANCER
Telephone No./s: _____ Fax No.: _____ E-mail Address: _____
(Subject to ocular inspection, verification, and approval by POLO).

COMPENSATION: The Talent shall receive a monthly compensation of a minimum of U.S.$500 (Ranging from U.S.$ 500 to 800 based on the categories of the ARB, skill and experience of the Talent, and of the Performance Venue) which shall accrue beginning on the day of the Talent's departure from the Philippines and shall be paid every end of the month directly to the Talent by the Employer, minus the authorized fees of the Philippine Agent and the Talent Manager, which shall be deducted at a maximum monthly rates of U.S.$50 and U.S.$ 50 for the Philippine Agent and Talent Manager, respectively.

HOURS OF WORK, RESTDAY AND OVERTIME PAY
4.1 Hours of Work: Maximum of five (5) hours per day.
4.2 Rest day: One (1) day a week
4.3 Overtime Rate: 150 percent of regular rate or the prevailing rate in Korea as required by the Labor Standards Act.

FOOD AND ACCOMMODATION: The Talent shall be entitled to free, suitable, and sanitary living quarters, as well as free, nutritionally adequate and suitable food, or in lieu of the latter the provision of food allowance in the amount of Korean Won 10,000 or $8/ per Talent per day.
5.1 ACCOMMODATION VENUE: NEW YORK
  Address: same as above
  Telephone No./s: _____ Fax No./s: _____ E-mail Address: _____
  (Subject to ocular inspection, verification and approval by POLO).
5.2 Facilities: The Employer shall ensure that the accommodation is safe and secure and has adequate and free provision of electricity, water, heating and ventilation facility.

MEDICAL AND ACCIDENT INSURANCE: Personal Medical and Accident Insurance shall be secured by the Employer in Korea for the Talent in the amount of U.S.$ 10,000 with the Talent's appointed kin as beneficiary. The insurance shall cover work and non-work- related injury, disease, disability or death. The Employer shall likewise enroll the Talent with the Overseas Workers Welfare Fund (OWWA) and its Medicare Program.

VACATION LEAVE: The Talent shall be given no less than fifteen (15) calendar days of paid Leave for every year of service to be availed of by the Talent towards the end of the contract.

TRANSPORTATION: The Talent shall be given free two-way transportation from the Talent's country of origin to the site of employment and back upon the completion of the contract, or when the contract is prematurely terminated through no fault of the Talent or due to force majeure. In case of contract renewal, the Employer shall likewise provide free roundtrip economy class air ticket.

Figure 3.2 Copy of a woman's contract

The services of the Talent as provided [in] this contract shall only be rendered at the Performance venue agreed and mutual agreement of the parties for the Talent to transfer to another Performance venue there shall be executed a new contract. The new contract shall be subject of verification requirement of the Philippine Overseas Labor Office, Philippine Embassy.

10. The Talent shall also be entitled to free emergency medical and dental services, including the attendant fees for medicines and facilities, which shall be for the account of the employer.

11. In case of death of the Talent during the term of this contract, his/her remains and personal belongings shall be repatriated to the Philippines at the expense of the Employer. In case repatriation is not possible, the remains shall be disposed of upon prior approval of the next of kin or of the Philippine Embassy.

12. **TERMINATION:**

   A. Termination by Employer: The Employer may terminate the contract of Employment for any of the following just causes: serious misconduct or willful disobedience of the lawful orders of the employer, gross or habitual neglect of duties, violation of the laws of the host country. When the termination of the contract is due to the foregoing causes, the Talent shall bear the cost of repatriation. In addition, the Talent may be liable to blacklisting and/or other penalties in case of serious offense.
   B. Termination by the Talent: The Talent may terminate the contract for any of the following just causes: when the Talent is maltreated by the employer or any of his/her associates, or when the Employer commits any of the following non-payment of Talent's salary, underpayment of salary in violation of this contract, non-booking of the Talent, physical molestation, assault or subjecting the Talent to inhumane treatment or shame. Inhumane treatment shall be understood to include forcing or letting the Talent to be used in indecent performance or in prostitution. In any of the foregoing cases, the Employer shall pay the cost of repatriation and be liable to garnishment of escrow deposit, aside from other penalties that may arise from a case.
   C. Termination due to illness: Any of the parties may terminate the contract on the ground of illness, disease, or injury suffered by the Talent, where the latter's continuing employment is prohibited by law or is prejudicial to his/her health, or to the health of the employer, or to others. The cost of repatriation of the Talent for any of the foregoing reason shall be for the account of the employer.

13. **SETTLEMENT OF DISPUTES:** In case of dispute between the Talent and the Employer, the matter must be referred by either or both parties to the Philippine Overseas Office, Philippine Embassy, which shall endeavor to settle the issue amicably in the best interest of both parties. If the dispute remains unresolved, the POLO shall refer the matter to the appropriate Labor authorities of the host country for adjudication, without prejudice to whatever legal action the aggrieved party may take.

14. **Ownership of Passport:** A Philippine passport remains at all times the property of the Government, the holder being a mere possessor thereof as long as it is valid and the same may not be surrendered to any person or entity other than the Philippine government or its representative. (Sec. 11, Republic Act No. 8239 of Philippine Passport Act of 1996). The employer thereof is not authorized to hold possession of the Talent's passport at all times. The Talent shall keep his/her passport while the employer may have a photocopy of the passport.

15. **SPECIAL PROVISIONS:**
    15.1 The employer shall treat the Talent in a just and humane manner and in no case shall physical violence be used upon the Talent.
    15.2 The Talent shall work solely for the employer.
    15.3 It shall be unlawful to deduct any amount from the regular salary of the Talent other than compulsory contributions prescribed by law or this contract. Such deductions must be issued a corresponding receipt.
    15.4 The employer shall provide the Talent a copy of this employment contract duly verified and recommended by the Labor Attaché and processed by POEA.
    15.5 The employer shall make sure that the Alien Registration Card is in the safekeeping of the Talent.

16. No provisions of this contract shall be altered amended or substitute without the written approval of the Philippine Embassy or POEA.

17. Other terms and conditions of employment shall be governed by the pertinent laws of the Philippines or the host country. Any applicable provisions on labour and employment of the host country are hereby incorporated as part of this contract.

Figure 3.2 Continued

Rosie had particularly long working hours in Y Club. Friday through Sunday the women in Y Club worked approximately fifteen hours a night (2 p.m.–5 a.m.), and on weeknights 4 p.m.–2 a.m. (ten hours a night). Rosie told me that she and her co-workers in Club Y averaged less than five hours of sleep a night on weekends and were always tired. As a form of punishment, additional work is required of the woman in Y Club who sells the lowest number of drinks each week. As Rosie related,

> The girl who sells the lowest number of drinks each week is punished by having to do all the cooking, cleaning and laundry for all the girls for that whole week. That means getting up 7 a.m., even though on weekends we have to work till 5 a.m. The last week I was there in the club before I ran away I sold the lowest number of drinks and had to do this punishment. If a girl has this punishment it means that on the weekends she cannot go to sleep until after she has cooked breakfast.

Another part of women's contracts normally not upheld relates to time off. Women's contracts normally state they are entitled to either two or, more commonly, four days off per month. Thirty-seven of the women in my research never received a single day off in the entire time they were in their club, and forty-four stated they received less days off than agreed to in their contracts, normally receiving one day per month instead of two or four and sometimes no days in a particular month as a form of punishment (for example, for having low drink sales). Several of my participants also complained that they would not be told they were having a day off until the morning of that day, meaning they would not have time to arrange anything they needed to do for the day. Some women also complained that a day off meant only until 10 p.m. in the evening, at which time they would have to be back at the club and ready to start work. During weekdays around half of my participants said they had some free time in which they could be outside the club. This normally meant they could go out for thirty to sixty minutes, but they were often monitored when they did go out, usually by video cameras which tracked their exit from and entry to their place of residence. The remainder said they were not free to go out of the clubs during the daytime unaccompanied, meaning that someone from the club whom the women referred to as a 'bodyguard' would normally accompany them if they needed to go out. Even women who could go out unaccompanied during their free time often would be subject to a penalty if they returned to the club or their apartment later than the time allowed by the club owner.

As a result of extremely long working hours, few if any days off and limited free time women complained of constant fatigue. Long working hours and limited free time also meant that meal times were disrupted and irregular, with women often eating their evening meal after finishing work (around 1 a.m.) or during work time when the club was quiet (usually early in the evening). Many of my participants said they only ate once a day because they got up too late for breakfast and were not permitted to eat at night because they were working.

In all the clubs the women live either above the club itself in rooms they shared with up to five other women or in a separate apartment, usually within walking distance of the club. The accommodation was provided free of charge by the club owner. In most cases their rooms were crowded and consisted of mattresses on the floor and drawers for clothes. I spent a lot of time in the apartment of Maricel and her co-workers in Songtan. There were two bedrooms with six entertainers in each. There was no real 'living space' in the apartment, and whenever I went to Maricel's room I had to sit on someone's mattress on the floor. Although they did not have to pay rent, most of the women had to cover other costs associated with their accommodation, including oil/heating, even though utilities were supposed to be provided free of charge by the club.

All the women I knew reported restrictions on their freedom of movement, which was mainly expressed by being locked in their rooms overnight. Thus, even though most of the women considered their accommodation to be adequate, they were dismayed by not being able to move around freely. During the day when they wished to go out, some women reported that they had to call the club owner to come to the club and unlock the front door so they could get outside. Some women lived with the club owner or his/her relatives so they could be easily monitored. Some of the clubs, especially those in TDC and Toka-ri, posed extreme fire and safety hazards with barbed wire or bars on the windows, and women living above these clubs would be unable to escape in case of a fire. A lot of these restrictions and surveillance relate to club owners' fears that women will meet boyfriends or regular customers outside the club, thus denying the club owners of their money from the sale of the women's intimate and sexual labour.

The women's food was also supposed to be provided by the club owners free of charge. In most cases the club owner gave the women an allowance of around KRW 10,000 for their weekly food costs. However, my participants maintained that they never received an allowance or that the allowance was not the agreed-upon amount. Cecile told me that in Papaya Club in TDC,

> Eight girls get KRW 50,000 a week for our food. If we have no more food, we must buy ourselves. That week [the week she was in the club] we ran out of food after four days. So I had to pay for my food but I had no money so I had to ask a customer.

All the clubs where my participants had worked imposed a range of punishments and financial penalties if a woman broke club rules. Cherry-Lyn told me she would have to pay the club owner USD 200 if she wanted a day off or if she went out with someone on a date on her own time since this would mean the club would not get their share of the bar fine money. Cherry-Lyn never had a single night off whilst working in Yes Club, and so she paid USD 200 for a night off so she could rest. She recalled that one month she went on a lunch date with one of her regular customers. She explained, "It was 12 o'clock in the afternoon and we only eat in a restaurant. I got USD 200 penalty for that when my owner [club owner] found out". If Cherry-Lyn got drunk at work she also got a USD 200 fine. In May – the month she left the club with Father Glenn – she took a night off work and got the penalty for going on a date which meant that all the money the club owed her for bar fines and ladies drinks that month was deducted and she got nothing. Amelia and Gerry, from a club in America Town in Kunsan, whom I first met when they were bar hopping one night, described another typical scenario. Gerry told me she and Amelia were not working because "the mama-san is sick tonight so she closed the club. She made us each pay KRW 60,000 because we were having the night off – even though it is her fault because she is sick". Clubs in all *gijich'on* regularly make women pay their own bar fine or time off, which further reduces their income and/or increases their debt.

Further to this system of the extraction of excessive profits through migrant entertainers' labour, open pimping of migrant entertainers on the streets of TDC began when anti-trafficking panic took hold in *gijich'on* areas in 2002. This was because it was far more difficult for police to detect prostitution in these hidden spaces and because the practice of street prostitution could not be directly attributable to the club management as it occurred outside the club itself. In these cases women were taken down a *gol mok* (back alley, lit. neck road, in Korean) in TDC and intercourse would be performed there for around USD 10. I knew several women from some of the worst clubs in TDC and Toka-ri, which forced their entertainers to perform intercourse under these circumstances.

I have narrated the club duties and conditions in *gijich'on* clubs in extensive detail here because these aspects of women's experiences are routinely ignored in the discussions of their trafficking experiences by the media in Korea and in the academic and NGO studies cited in chapter 2, despite the fact that they represent key aspects of women's anxieties in their club deployment. Stephen Castles (2000) argues that globalisation has led to a decline in the ability of labour to organise. Part of the reason for this has to do with the increase in migrant labour entering destination countries through contract migration regimes which strictly regulate their conditions and period of sojourn. An Employment Permit System (EPS) was introduced in 2004 to enhance migrant worker's rights in Korea, and the Seoul-Kyunggi-Incheon Migrant Workers Trade Union was formed to monitor the extent to which these newly granted rights were being upheld. Migrant entertainers entering Korea on legitimate work visas nonetheless remain largely outside the purview of these developments, which are oriented almost entirely towards male and female factory and construction workers. The key explanation for this lies in the fact that women's experiences in the clubs were thought of solely in terms of sexual slavery and not labour issues.

Migrant entertainers and the 2010 TIP report

Sex trafficking has been key to the narratives of all Korea's entries in the TIP reports since the country's initial listing in 2001 when Korean women 'trafficked' to the United States were the key object of discussion (as outlined in chapter 2). But the 2010 report included a new problem not hitherto identified; for the first time foreign women working as entertainers on E-6 visas in *gijich'on* clubs received attention as a trafficking concern. The report (US DoS 2010: 176) stated:

> The ROK [Republic of Korea] is a destination country for women trafficked from Russia, Uzbekistan, Kazakhstan, Mongolia, People's Republic of China, the Philippines, Thailand, Cambodia and other Southeast Asian countries, some of whom are recruited to work on entertainers visas and may be vulnerable to trafficking for sexual exploitation or domestic servitude.

In a US military newspaper article that followed, US senator Chris Smith condoned the inclusion of this problem in the TIP report, suggesting it will "prompt the US military and South Korean officials to step up efforts to rid the base-area establishments of prostitution and other problems" (Rabinoff 2010). As mentioned in the previous chapter, the principle reason the *gijich'on* bars were not included in previous reports was because the US DoD developed its own policy to address trafficking for prostitution around the bases, which rested on the key precept of 'zero tolerance' for DoD personnel caught patronising clubs where prostitution and sex trafficking may have been taking place. Arguably the failure of the USFK to be fully committed to implementing this policy resulted in the 2010 TIP report's attempt to highlight the ongoing problems in *gijich'on* and the lack of progress with the DoD's own policy.

The TIP report (US DoS 2010: 177) also stated that one foreign embassy in Korea had "express[ed] concern about entertainment (E-6) visas, arguing that the ROK government should either significantly tighten the visa qualifications or stop issuing the visa altogether". The experiences of many of the Filipinas I knew confirmed they had usually undergone rigorous training as either singers or dancers in the Philippines prior to embarking on their labour migration to Korea. Tightening the visa qualifications would arguably have the effect of further inflating the debts a woman must pay off once in Korea since it would most likely mean she would have to train as an entertainer for longer periods and/or at a higher fee to prove herself a bona fide performing artist. Given that many of the women are fully qualified singers or dancers, this suggestion may induce an unnecessarily inflated financial burden on the women most likely to be paid off during their Korean sojourns. Further, one can only speculate as to the effects of stopping the issuance of E-6 visas altogether, as in the un-named embassy official's suggestion. Anecdotal evidence from other contexts suggests that tightening border controls and restricting the cross-border movements of women from the third world increases the costs and heightens the vulnerability of women who will still attempt to migrate for work. Unless appropriate alternatives for livelihoods are provided in the women's home countries restrictions on their movement are likely to result in unemployment and a lack of other opportunities to engage in transnational projects for upward social and economic mobility. Even then, women often do not want to stay at home, and an appreciation of the gendered nature of motivations to migrate might well bring these desires to leave more clearly to light.

The 2010 TIP report also highlighted, again for the first time since Korea's inclusion, that labour trafficking was "a problem in the country, with some employers allegedly withholding passports and wages of foreign workers, a practice that can be used as a means to subject workers to forced labour". The discussion of labour trafficking in the report continued with the identification of the destruction of contracts signed in the worker's home countries and working conditions which included "excessively long working hours" as a problem. The report therefore recommended that the Korean government "take steps to improve protections for foreign workers by continuing to investigate and prosecute reported cases of forced labour among migrant workers" (US DoS 2010: 178).

As I have outlined here, the Filipinas I came to know over the course of my fieldwork complained most commonly and repeatedly about having their passports withheld by their boss in the club, violations to agreed-to work in their contracts (and indeed, for many women, of not being able to hold a copy of their own contract) such as excessive working hours and inadequate food and accommodation, arbitrarily imposed punishments and penalties and a lack of adherence by their club bosses and promotion agencies to provisions about health. Most of the women also complained about the ways they were treated by mama-sans or papa-sans in the clubs where they were deployed, as well as having to serve Koreans and South Asian migrant workers. Despite this, according to the tone of the 2010 TIP report, these women would not be counted amongst those migrant workers who are trafficked for labour exploitation/forced labour or indeed amongst the many marriage migrants who also experience forced labour in their domestic situations. The overriding perception of migrant entertainers is as sex trafficking victims, presumably because one of a range of possible of violations to their contracts is performing various types of sexual and erotic labour under duress instead of – or in addition to – performing as singers or dancers. This distinction between labour trafficking (applied to other migrant workers) and sex trafficking (applied to camp town entertainers) is even made explicitly in the 2010 TIP report when the (labour) experiences of migrant entertainers are contrasted to marriage trafficking victims: "Most other facilities [shelters] that support foreigners are geared towards women who have married Korean men and subsequently encounter abuse or *conditions of forced labour, rather than sex trafficking victims*" (US DoS 2010: 178, my emphasis). The sex slave discourse that was examined in the previous chapter clearly bolsters this perception of migrant entertainers as *only* victims of commercial sexual exploitation, thus separating and distinguishing them from victims of forced labour in the way that both marriage migrants and factory or constructions workers entering under the EPS may be considered.

Korea's anti-trafficking legislation does not contain provisions for labour trafficking, although other legal provisions such as the migrant worker's code cover abuses experienced by foreign workers in Korea. Since the United States has played a major role in interpreting what counts as human trafficking in Korea I use the United States Trafficking Victims Protection Act of 2000 (TVPA) (US DoS 2000) to define labour trafficking. According to the TVPA labour trafficking is: "The recruitment, harbouring, transportation, provision, or obtaining of a person for labour or services, through the use of force, fraud or coercion for the purpose of subjection to involuntary servitude, peonage, debt bondage or slavery". According to the Labour Trafficking Fact Sheet produced by the Department of Health and Human Services, the TVPA also recognizes sex trafficking, but it is discussed in a *separate* fact sheet.

The failure to recognise entertainers as possible victims of migrant labour exploitation in Korea therefore excludes and disqualifies them from a range of support systems and protections that are being developed to respond to claims put forward by other migrant workers, such as the establishment of twenty-seven support centres by the Labour Ministry to facilitate the recovery of unpaid wages. Responses to entertainers as trafficked persons, however, fall under the purview of a range of support programs to target sex trafficking victims, which include counselling centres, shelters and medical and legal aid. This presumes that the women's overriding need will be support to recover from the trauma and violence of sexual exploitation (for an example of this view see Farley et al. 2003). None of these responses, however, are able to fulfil the most oft-repeated lament of Filipinas I knew – namely to recover lost wages and money for extra work (such as drink/juice money or bar fines) or money they outlaid for medical expenses and food, which was supposed to be covered by the club owner according to their contracts. Returning home to the Philippines without money to display their success as labour migrants is likely to generate only further anxiety for the women and shame related to the inability to meet expectations of family and community about the fruits of their labour migration (see chapter 8). Reflecting on these unmet needs, compensation claims provide an important mechanism of redress for migrant entertainers since such claims work to both demonstrate to club owners and/or promotion agencies the pitfalls of not adhering to women's contracts and fulfil one of the key objectives of women's migration projects – namely, to make money. To illustrate the significance of compensation for *gijich'on* entertainers, I narrate two episodes in TDC – the first in which four women I knew took their manager to task over unpaid salaries and drink monies, the second involving Grace's collection of her unpaid monies from the Centre.

Making claims/claiming respect: subverting the power of bosses

I was heading to the main strip of TDC with Cherry when my phone rang. I hesitated at the unknown number, but Cherry urged me to answer; it could be important. On the other end of the line was Louisa, whom I vaguely recalled meeting briefly in Pop Store Club a few days earlier. I knew from Amy, one of the women who had worked there, that the club owner of Pop Store was not paying women salaries and was denying them food. Louisa asked if I could go around to her place which was hidden in one of the backstreets of American Ally to discuss "something important". When I entered the three-room apartment Louisa was sitting with three other women who were intently discussing some matter which I guessed had a connection to my presence there. I texted Cherry and told her I might not make it to the strip and settled down on the floor to find out what was going on. "We heard you help girls get their money back from the clubs, Sallie. Amy said you could help us", Louisa prompted. I wondered why Amy had said that, since I had only treated her to her lunch one day because her club owner refused to pay for food when there were no customers. She had been far more animated about her three GI boyfriends about whom we joked over our meal since they were all named Chris, providing Amy with an endless stream of funny stories of mixed-up Chrises. In any case, like most of the women in TDC, Amy already knew about Father Glenn and his work in retrieving unpaid salaries of Filipina migrant workers.

Over the course of the next three hours I sat in Louisa's apartment and took detailed notes on their equally detailed descriptions of when they were supposed to have been paid, how much, how much of their salary should have been rightly deducted for migration costs, what deductions were made for fines and so on. Half an hour into our deliberations Julia pulled a carefully folded paper from her handbag and opened it across the table for us all to scrutinise. It was her contract, which the others immediately pointed to with enthusiasm, claiming their contracts – even though they did not hold them personally – contained exactly the same stipulations. We picked over the terms of the contract, focusing on the parts relating to payment of salary (which was KRW 420,000 supposed to be paid monthly) and other benefits of employment (free accommodation, free food, free utilities and so on). We finally all agreed on a figure for each woman and collapsed back into our chairs satisfied with the sum they felt they were owed. I left Louisa and the others with the cautionary note that I really could not guarantee that their promotion agency would agree to pay the sums we devised in the compensation claims. The next day I headed to the Centre and placed the individual and intricately disaggregated claims on Father Glenn's desk. Perusing the pages, he phoned the agency, making the usual threats to contact the police if they refused to pay up. Father Glenn succeeded in arranging a meeting at 11 a.m. the next day at a cafe in Uijongbu, close to the promoter's office. When the manager failed to appear after two hours, Father Glenn was ropable. "Bring the girls to Uijongbu police station, Sallie", be barked down the phone to me. "We need to clear this up through the police. The agency needs to be held accountable for this". I texted Cherry, and together we hurriedly picked up Louisa and the others and piled onto the bus for Uijongbu. An hour later Father Glenn was explaining the situation to the police officer, whose phone call to the agent yielded the desired result. "He will meet you at his office in Uijongbu", the policeman beamed at us. Father Glenn hurried off to collect the money, Cherry and I rode the bus back to TDC, and the Pop Store women decided to stay awhile in Uijongbu and look around, waiting for Father Glenn to come back with their money.

Hutchinson and Brown (2001) write that, in the era of contract labour migration, we must turn our gaze to labour activism that takes place through other organisations and processes that are not strictly "industrial".[6] NGOs and "disorganised responses of workers outside any formally constituted body" (Hutchinson and Brown 2001: 2) must necessarily replace trade unions as loci for achieving workers' rights.[7] In *gijich'on* women who run away from clubs utilise the knowledge circulating within their social networks to seek conduits for making compensation claims, and whilst they rarely seek to transform the system of entertainers' rights in the *gijich'on*, they may nonetheless have more impact on tempering the practices of errant club owners and promotion agencies than they imagine. Through Father Glenn and the *Potdure-jip* NGO in Seoul I assisted fourteen women – from TDC, Songtan and Anjong-ri – to make similar claims Most of the claims related to unpaid salaries and unrightfully deducted fines.[8] Indeed, the very first time I met Lisa and Grace was at the Centre a few days after they ran away from VIP Club. They had come to see Father Glenn to retrieve unpaid salaries to the value of around USD 1,200 each. In her vignette of a similar compensation claim involving *gijich'on* entertainers in Korea, Cheng (2010), in my view, misses the significance of these claims for the women, suggesting as she does that the women involved are far more concerned with love and with their relationships with GIs and that it is intermediaries like Father Glenn who push women to make claims in the name of pursuing NGO advocacy agendas. Yet the initiative to make compensation claims, at least for the women I knew, came entirely from them.

It also struck me that the money itself was not significant to many of the women for its economic value alone, despite their ardent efforts to retrieve it. Why then did the women risk exposing themselves to the possibility of retributions of harassment from errant club owners or promoters if the money itself was not always a key goal of their deliberations? I gleaned the answer through reflections on Grace's and the Pop Store Club women's motivations. After Father Glenn managed to recover Lisa's and Grace's owed salary from their promoter, I went with Grace to Seoul to pick up hers at the Centre. The packet of KRW 10,000 notes was bulging to the tune of KRW 1,800,000. Not bothering to count the money, we left the Centre, and Grace treated me to dinner at a nearly pizza restaurant before deciding she was too tired to catch the train and bus back to TDC. She promptly hailed a taxi. "Grace, do you realise how much the fare will be all the way back to TDC?" I exclaimed (not having ever taken one myself I assumed it must be at least KRW 80,000, or a quarter of Grace's monthly salary in the club). She replied that she didn't care. "I want to feel like I can do what I want to for once. You know what I mean; not think, 'Oh, I have to send money home so I really shouldn't treat myself to anything just like that'". The experience of financial freedom and the taste of economic mobility it conferred was what Grace saw in her money. She desired, in short, to feel mobile.

Whilst the Pop Store women also saw their owed money as enabling particular social relations of mobility, they harboured another equally as significant desire – namely, to exert power over their promoter. Louisa was incensed by the ways the club owner treated them and the constant violations of the stipulations of their contract, as well as the seeming indifference of their promoter to their problems in Pop Store Club. Returning to Hutchinson and Brown's point, then, we might agree on one level that these efforts to recover money from club owners and promoters is a form of "disorganised response" (2001: 2) to exploitative migrant labouring. But it is also more than that. Viviana Zelizer's (1997) exposition on the social value of money enables us to see that, in addition to the utility/exchange value of money, we should also consider money as a social and symbolic resource. If money is a way of expressing and enabling particular social relations, then for Louisa and the Pop Store Club women, it allowed them to achieve the upper hand in their relationship with their promoter and the Pop Store Club owner by targeting the one place where they knew it would hurt the most – their bosses' hip pockets. In the different values these women ascribe to their compensation claims, then, money has a practical (financial) *and* a symbolic (relational) role, with the latter seen in the subversion – at least for a while – of their relationships with their bosses in Korea.

Conclusion

The prevailing global anti-trafficking framework rests on four *P*s – prevention, protection, prosecution and policy – the last of which is cross-cutting for the effective implementation of the other three *P*s. As the United States has adopted and adapted the UN Protocol and begun to rank states accordingly through the TIP reporting process, nations around the globe have become disciplined in their response to 'the problem of human trafficking'. More recently, and once it became clear that sanctioned anti-trafficking responses were not having the desired effects in significantly curtailing the problem, critiques of the impacts of the anti-trafficking framework on trafficked persons and other migrants have been articulated with increasing intensity and vehement. Feminist sex worker rights advocates have consistently and convincingly advanced their critiques of the current anti-trafficking infrastructure. As I suggested in the introduction, academics undertaking in-depth empirical research with trafficked persons also yield divergent views of trafficking and anti-trafficking than those put forward in policy, many of which feed into alterative paradigms of (female) migrant worker subjectivity. Ratna Kapur (2002: 6) has suggested that the current anti-trafficking framework, aimed primarily at trafficking for commercial sexual exploitation, rests on a "victimisation rhetoric" that purports a universalised, hegemonic victim subject which "cannot accommodate a multi-layered experience" of the sort that Cherry-Lyn, Grace and the Pop Store women disclosed. Kapur has articulated the ways liberal feminists have linked campaigns geared towards women's empowerment to a convenient tag line, namely violence against women. Sex trafficking has become the most recent and arguably powerful invocation of this campaign, inducing "state actors, non-state actors, and donors to embrace universalising strategies in responding to human rights violations against women" (Kapur 2002: 11).

Feminist sex worker rights critiques of the "victimising ethos" (Mai and King 2009: 2) of anti-trafficking interventions advance three particularly useful arguments that have some merit in comprehending the ways Filipinas in *gijich'on* clubs *could* be negatively affected by the description of their situations in recent US TIP reporting according to the rhetoric of sexual violence. First, anti-trafficking responses are admonished for their tendency to keep women in their place, restricting their ability to move and possibly heightening their vulnerability in attempts to migrate to advance their economic and social positions; these responses arguably also reflect the moral anxieties of an increasing number of states that make mobile third-world women the object of intervention. In Korea this could mean in the future that a ban is placed on foreign women entering Korea on E-6 visas – as hinted by the unknown foreign embassy representative's comment in the most recent TIP report – since such visas are presumed to be a front for prostitution and other unspecified camp town 'problems'. A large pool of immobile female subjects with limited opportunities in the Philippines – and other countries that utilise Korea as a migrant destination – could emerge in the aftermath of such a restriction. In the prevailing international anti-trafficking framework this nonetheless is referred to by the seemingly innocuous term 'prevention'.

Second, feminist sex worker rights critiques highlight the ways anti-trafficking efforts aimed at protection of victims are also used to justify interventions such as rescues and rehabilitation or repatriation of those rescued, thus involving a range of anti-trafficking stakeholders such as a police, immigration authorities and NGOs. Rescuing victims from their fates as sex slaves arguably leads to a range of actions aimed at further restricting and controlling women's post-exit fates in addition to restricting their mobility, including placement in shelters, being supported with a short-term visa to assist with police investigations or repatriation to the home country for further rehabilitation. Laura Agustin (2007) has coined the term "rescue industry" to describe the pervasive infrastructure of rescue and subsequent interventions on behalf of freed sex slaves. Soderlund (2005: 67) has admonished the rehabilitation process as "a punitive form of imprisonment", which she suggests complicates the binary between captivity and freedom guiding anti-trafficking protection practices.[9] In Korea, these types of actions would mean, as with prevention measures, that migrant entertainers would lose their transnational positions as they are eventually repatriated back home. The ability of these women to work towards overcoming exploitative situations by asserting their own agency in and beyond Korea would simply cease to occur.

Finally, critiques of the emerging anti-trafficking infrastructure that underlie both these prevention and protection responses take issue with the presumed lack of agency of the women/victims who are their object – a presumption bolstered by seeing the 'sex slave' as the embodiment of the trafficked entertainer in Korea. The currently prevailing architecture of anti-trafficking that has been advanced by the United Nations and the United States and that governs responses to trafficking in Korea fails to address their situations, thus requiring that we direct "attention instead to more nuanced anti-trafficking solutions, particularly solutions with a bottom-to-top perspective that would address the self-identified concerns of trafficked persons" (Parrenas 2006). Certainly, self-identified concerns are an almost impossible location from which to speak for women defined – and marginalised – under the current anti-trafficking framework as trafficked sex slaves.

Although these critiques have drawn out the significant practical and ideological limitations of the globally prevailing anti-trafficking framework, there are some shortcomings to them when thinking about appropriate responses to support women like Cherry-Lyn, Grace and the Pop Store Club women in Korea. As the experiences of these women have demonstrated the vast majority of the Filipinas in *gijich'on* clubs are not strictly sex workers, with their understandings of the work they were migrating for ranging across the full spectrum of sex worker–hostess–professional singer or dancer and with the vast majority of women falling clearly into one or both of the latter categories. At best, women like Cherry-Lyn could be said to perform intimate labour as part of their hostessing work with sex often occurring outside the sphere of commodified encounters (see also Boris et al. 2010). Many of the women end up engaging in sex work, especially those deployed in the clubs where customers can purchase sex from the women inside the club itself – most commonly in VIP rooms located at the rear of the club, as in Y Club and M Club in Toka-ri. I found that most of these women were not prepared to engage in sex work when they left the Philippines, and their decision to undertake sex work emerged under conditions of "constrained choice" (Sandy 2007) once in Korea. Notably, the main constraint the women faced was their low or non-existent income and their high migration debt that was also inflated by fines for 'mistakes' such as breaking club rules or not performing work well enough. These concerns ultimately point to a larger problem in which the women lacked control over the conditions of both their migration and labour, including the ability to break their contracts without having a hefty penalty imposed or changing employers.

In sum, where sex worker rights and radical feminist critiques have considerable merit in recognising the multiplicity of processes that fail to understand and then institutionalise women's presumed lack of agency, they are less successful *in this context* in addressing questions of how significant problems related to control over one's labour and immigration status can be addressed in sites like *gijich'on* clubs. Further, the agency that women like Cherry-Lyn express is not limited to the decision to migrate for work (sex or otherwise), but for utilising a variety of strategies to reclaim their lost income and assert some control over their liaisons with customers, co-workers and bosses in the clubs. In this sense the Filipinas I knew often invoked and appropriated the discourse of trafficking to realise private compensation claims – especially from errant managers who ultimately control all aspects of the women's migration and deployment – and to garner sympathy from customers. The latter would usually result in tips or gifts from sympathetic customers, which enabled women to advance, albeit in often limited ways, their poor financial situations. In this sense the women's relationship to trafficking is far more complex than a simple victim discourse can imagine, but one thing is for certain – trafficking as an experience and strategic position is far from irrelevant for migrant entertainers in Korea's *gijich'on*.

Notes

1 Securing an alien registration card from the Seoul Immigration Office is usually the responsibility of a woman's promoter. This should be done within three months of an entertainer's arrival in Korea.
2 James Tyner has provided a detailed description of what goes on during the training process based on his in-depth description of Lisa, who migrated to Okinawa, Japan,

as an entertainer. See James Tyner (2009), chapter 5, "Performing Globalisation". He relates Lisa's description of learning dance or song routines, aerobics sessions, tutoring in correct poses, facial expressions and conversational skills for interactions with clients, application of make-up, personal hygiene and how to dress appropriately, amongst other things. All of this together, Tyner (p. 160) convincingly suggests, "serves to produce a particular feminine body – one that visibly and visually signifies their submissiveness, passivity, and willingness to serve the (usually) man's needs and desires".

3   The costs of doing training will always be much higher for women not from Manila since trainees of provincial origin must reside at the accommodation provided by the talent manager, which adds a significant amount to the fee the talent manager charges a woman.
4   Tyner (2009) and Parrenas (2006) both narrate the story of the migrant entertainer to Japan through the use of a single woman's narrative. Whilst this is useful in gaining deep insights into the lived experiences of women who migrate as entertainers, there is a tendency for such an approach to claim a generalisable Filipina (or other nationality) entertainer subject.
5   US military personnel in Korea have a universal curfew which is normally 1 a.m. on Fridays and Saturdays and 12 midnight other nights of the week. If there is a perceived security threat the curfew is amended, and sometimes GIs are confined to base, something they refer to as a "lockdown". The entire two months following the 9/11 terrorist attacks in the United States constituted a lockdown period. Scores of foreign women working on the *gijich'on* clubs during this time ran away because the managers were not paying them salary and they were not able to earn sufficient commissions from ladies drinks or bar fines. Many women, including some of my participants, ran away to work in factories at this time.
6   I take Hutchison and Brown's (2001: 2) definition of labour organising as "workers responses to class processes and relations that are collective and self-organised (or independent)".
7   Michele Ford (2004) also suggests that there is very little engagement between the organised trade union and labour migration literatures. In her study of Indonesian migrant labour she argues that migrant representatives of labour NGOs and migrant labour associations should be taken more seriously in this scholarship. We might also point out that religious and nationality-based associations representing specific groups of migrant workers should also not sit outside this analytic purview since, as the role of the Centre demonstrates, these organisations can play a vital role in supporting migrant labour rights.
8   Wendy's and Dolores's claims (which I discuss in chapter 5) also related to rape and attempted rape. Wendy was paid USD 5,000 by the club owner who raped her.
9   In a telling critique of the main government-run shelter for sex trafficking victims in Bangkok, Thailand, Pearson and Gallagher (2008) also suggest that conditions in shelters for victims of (sex) trafficking can unwittingly replicate the conditions trafficked persons can experience when in trafficking situations.

4 Health in trafficking

Making my way up the stairs to Cherry's apartment, I notice that the curtains are drawn in her bedroom, which is strange as it is the middle of the day. If she was out I would have to lug my heavy bag back down the stairs and see if I could find her at one of her friend's apartments in TDC's American Alley. I knock on the door just in case and hear movement coming from her bedroom. She feebly calls to say she's coming and emerges to open the front door looking dishevelled and squinting into the pale November sunlight. I go inside to put my things in her spare room where I often stay whilst in TDC and come back out to see if there's anything I can do. "This happens sometimes, Sallie. It's my eyes. Sometimes I can't bear the sunlight and I have to just lie in the dark. It makes my head hurt so much that it feels like it will explode". I ask. How long have you had this? Have you been to see a doctor? Do you have medicine? "It's M Club, Sallie. For a whole year I am in that club and I didn't go out. You've been in the club. You know how dark it is. For a whole year my eyes get accustomed to that darkness. My eyes are very weak now. There's nothing I can really do".

I thought immediately of some of the other women I knew in TDC. After Valerie ran away from USA Club the previous year with Lisa and Grace, she recounted to me that she desperately wanted to go hiking in the mountains because all she could do for a year in the club was look at them from the window of her room upstairs in the club. She went with her boyfriend to a popular hiking spot not far from TDC. Even though she was only sixteen at the time, she told me afterwards that she could not even make it up to the first lookout point. They had to turn back after thirty minutes and make their way back to American Alley so Valerie could rest. One of the other reasons Valerie lamented that she did not want to leave TDC again was that she felt the Korean people she encountered on the train and during hiking looked down at her; "They look at me like they think I'm a cheap Filipina prostitute". It was thus both her level of fitness and her fear of stigma that kept her mobilities circumscribed to TDC. She resigned herself to staying around TDC, declaring that she didn't want to go anywhere in Korea anymore.

I also thought of Alma, with whom I shared a room at the Centre for a few weeks after she ran away from Eagle Club in TDC. I noticed one night just before bed that she had an array of different coloured pills that she was sorting through to take with her glass of water. Responding to my curious glances, she explained that she had a heart problem and had not been allowed treatment while working in Eagle Club. The long hours, poor food and stress she felt in relation to the work and her boss in the club exacerbated her high blood pressure to the point where she was constantly asking her boyfriend to bar fine her so she could take a rest and buy some medicine. Her boss would, she said, occasionally throw some paracetamol in her direction and tell her to stop being so dramatic; she just had a chest pain, after all.

Only a few weeks before I learned of Alma's heart problem, Lisa had confided to me an extreme instance of violence she had experienced in USA Club, which in fact supplied her with the motivation to take the drastic step of running away. I had been thinking about this disclosure a lot because I had been friends with Lisa for more than six months before she had revealed this to me; her difficulty in talking about it suggested how deeply it must have affected her. She had lost her baby through miscarriage resulting from abuse she experienced in the club. She recounted the circumstances surrounding her miscarriage whilst working in USA Club, where Valerie had also been deployed. Lisa told me,

> I got pregnant to David [her GI boyfriend] while I was still working in the club. This should have been our second baby, coz I already have one baby back in the Philippines from another guy. I had a miscarriage because there was a fight between me and the mama-san in the club. Some of the girls – even some of the Filipinas – were holding me down and the mama-san was hitting me and scratching my face. I got a fever and felt sick and needed to go to the hospital after that. Some of the other girls tried to help me and they were punished by mama-san. As punishment she forced those girls who helped me to keep standing up during work time unless with a customer. The daughter of mama-san wasn't there when I got beat up. When the daughter came back I begged her to let me go to hospital and said I would pay all my own costs. After two days they allowed me to go. I had a lot of blood and I knew I had lost the baby by that time. I had the miscarriage two months before I ran away. David was away in the field[1] when this incident happened.

As I sat beside Lisa on the bed in her apartment that day I felt completely disarmed by her disclosure. I thought of the complexities that her narrative held; she wanted to have a baby with her boyfriend, with whom she had sex in the context of her work; she hid her pregnancy from her boss and some of her workmates in the club; she planned to finish her contract and leave the club to have her baby; and it was other Filipina workmates who assisted in the violent episode that eventually led to her miscarriage. I already knew that her first baby, back in the Philippines, had been conceived as a result of rape and in fact had supplied her main motivation for deciding to 'try for Korea' as an entertainer in the first place (see Yea 2004). As these discrepant episodes demonstrate, the story of health in trafficking, including where it is linked to violence and sex, is far from hermeneutically sealed in the rhetoric of sexual slavery and requires that we direct our gaze instead towards nuanced and stark operations of power in and beyond *gijich'on* clubs.

In the previous chapter I suggested that some of the most important aspects of the experience of trafficking for migrant entertainers in *gijich'on* clubs relate to issues of deception and control over their labour and the financial aspects associated with their work, as much as the type of work they are engaged in. In advancing this argument one might come to the conclusion that problems related to sexual exploitation, violence and health that collectively constitute the lynchpin that defines sex trafficking as a 'violence against women' issue are thus not a particularly significant concern for these women. Yet as the everyday fragments of Cherry's, Valerie's, Alma's and Lisa's experiences reveal, problems relating to health and violence are far from absent in their experiences in the clubs or from the ways their post-club trajectories are mapped out within Korea. Yet, simultaneously, their accounts reveal the limits of reductive descriptions of violent clients, abusive pimps, psychological damage and unsafe sex that operate to produce a "damage paradigm" (Frederick 2005) and "tragic victim" (Kapur 2002) of sex trafficking and a range of interventions aimed at her rehabilitation.

Prevailing characterisations of the experience of sex trafficked women put forward by some anti-trafficking organisations and researchers focus on particular readings of the violence and abuse commonly ascribed to these subjects (for example, Farley 2004, Farley et al. 2003, Rafferty 2008, Miller et al. 2007, Raymond et al. 2001). Psychologist Melissa Farley (2004) has been a key figure in advancing this perspective. In particular, her 2003 co-authored study of prostitution in nine countries made some startling statistical claims, including that 71 per cent of participants had been physically assaulted in prostitution, 63 per cent had been raped and 88 per cent wished to leave prostitution but lacked the means to do so.[2] In this study and her other writings Farley argues in line with an abolitionist perspective that there should be no distinction between sex trafficking and prostitution, and she uses the terms interchangeably throughout her work (for example, Farley 2004). She has been rightly criticised on methodological grounds (Weitzer 2005) and for allowing her position on prostitution to bias her research design and findings.

A similar process of bias and elision is evident when health problems in sex trafficking are discussed by those working with trafficked persons from outside an abolitionist stance. Here problems are generally framed within a sexual health discourse and, in particular, anxieties around sexually transmitted infections and, most recently, HIV/AIDS. This, as Lisa Law (1997) reminds us, speaks more generally to the ways the (Asian female) prostitute body is stigmatised and exceptionalised as a vector of disease and, with the onset of anti-trafficking discourses, as victim of unwanted and unprotected sex (for example, IOM 2007).[3] Whilst violence and sexual health are often regarded as separate concerns amongst those working closely with sex trafficked persons, Zimmermann et al. (2003) make a direct connection between violence and health in sex trafficking, suggesting that the sexual violence women experience during trafficking leads to extensive and profound physical and psychological health consequences that extend well beyond health-related discourses of STIs and HIV/AIDS. In both violence-centred and health-centred accounts, as well as those which attempt to connect these two concerns, trafficked women are produced as manageable objects of health interventions in the name of rehabilitation or containment.

This reading of the health issues facing women in situations of commercial sexual exploitation is one that does not go unopposed, and in particular those working closely with migrant sex workers – either as researchers or support workers or both – understand the multiple dimensions of vulnerability to violence and poor health that sex workers experience (for example, Miller 2002). A recent study by Human Rights Watch (2010) on abuses of sex workers in Cambodia has further highlighted that it is often those very authorities charged with upholding the law, such as police, who inflict the worse abuses. Those focusing on migrant sex workers additionally recognise that the migration process, especially where it confers irregular status, can further accentuate violence – for example, by discouraging sex workers from reporting rape – and reduce access to health services (Andrijasevic 2003, Gulcur and Ilkkaracan 2002). Echoing the findings of the Human Rights Watch report on Cambodia, migrant sex workers from the former Soviet Union who took part in these European studies also found that government authorities were directly involved as perpetrators of abuse towards them, demanding free sex and extorting bribes from women in exchange for police 'protection'.

This scholarship provides some extremely valuable insights into the types of problems associated with health and violence that migrant sex workers face, especially in attempts to move beyond the types of reductive discourses that bolster an abolitionist stance towards prostitution as trafficking. In this chapter I wish to extend these discussions of health and violence even further. On the one hand it is important to recognise that abuse, violence and vulnerabilities in health *do* exist for women deployed as entertainers in *gijich'on* clubs, but, on the other hand, it is important to not locate these concerns entirely within the rubric of sex worker education and outreach efforts, which do not always speak in ways central to *gijich'on* entertainer's concerns. Thus, I want to at once re-centre issues of violence, abuse and health but ground this in the multiple and complex experiences of the women in *gijich'on* clubs that are not ascribed a priori from their already imagined vulnerabilities resulting from their positions as providers of sexual and intimate labour under a clearly discernible positioning as either sex worker or sex slave. I wish to argue that these less recognised dimensions of women's experiences in *gijich'on* clubs are significant aspects of their everyday lives, for women like Cherry and Alma conferring longer-term health effects and for women like Valerie and Lisa resulting in shorter-term diminished health, but in ways which remain in their memories as testaments to the enduring everyday violence that marked their sojourns in Korea.

Governance of the prostitute body

STIs and HIV/AIDS

Various scholars focusing on a range of different sites, especially in Asia, have examined the way a particular rendering of the problem of HIV has been utilised by state authorities and international organisations to bring sex workers under the purview of control and management as objects of intervention (Law 1997, Ming 2005, Steinfatt 2002, Sariola 2010). This has led to numerous interventions, including compulsory health checks and attendant registration of sex workers and issuance with health cards, sex worker outreach and education interventions usually aimed at achieving 100 per cent condom use during transacted sex including free distribution of condoms, lessons on how sex workers can eroticise the application of a condom to a client's penis and so on and drop-in centres for clients so they may receive information about HIV/AIDS and STIs and the 'dangers' of unprotected intercourse with sex workers. Some organisations, including various government authorities and abolitionist/faith-based organisations, attempt to insert a moral agenda into these efforts. Nguyen (2008: 107), in his excellent treatment of neo-liberal governance and the sex industry since the mid-1990s in Vietnam, has for example documented the ways expert medical knowledge has been subtly utilised to admonish prostitution as a 'social evil':

> The point . . . is not that the prostitute is simply vilified as the vessel of disease, to be cast out and eradicated. To the contrary, it is the embeddedness of her body in the nation's body that makes her so connected, so visible as an entity. Public health workers draw attention to prostitutes in order to make visible the links that connect individual bodies to the body of the population, said to be threatened with disease and death.

This Foucauldian reading of medical governance through expert knowledge draws attention to the dangers of the prostitute as a vector threatening the body of the nation, often through what Nguyen (2008: 99) labels "the spectacle of consequences", which might include dramatic images of deformed foetuses or emaciated bodies of AIDS patients.

Sex workers rights organisations throughout Asia have also challenged this rendering of sex workers health concerns and its location in unequal power relations of moralising governance and surveillance, arguing that strategies to control HIV and STIs cannot be effectively implemented without recognising the agency of sex workers themselves and the important role they play in protecting their health (cf. Law 1997) and without also understanding the constraining social and economic conditions under which sex workers operate which can reduce their ability to enforce health controls, despite the agency and knowledge they possess (Marten 2005). Whilst these emergent discussions are important in creating discursive space for considerations of sex worker agency, they do not provide a significant departure from the overall view that sex workers need to be regulated and therefore fail to significantly undermine the perception of sex workers as vectors of disease.

The link between trafficking into the sex and nightlife entertainment sector and medical/health interventions over the prostitute body have provided a much less coherent discursive formation than that directed towards voluntary sex workers. What is clear, however, is the dominance of the 'prostitution as violence against women' perspective in trafficking (as in Farley 2004, Farley et al. 2003). Here the concern is not to support sex workers through education and outreach but to remove them from their situations of exploitation, usually through rescue operations, and rehabilitate them from the sexual, physical and psychological health damage that was incurred during their forced prostitution.[4] This rehabilitation-reintegration model has become the lynchpin of post-trafficking interventions to support victims prompted by the inclusion of Article Six of the Trafficking Protocol. Article Six on "Assistance to and protection of victims of trafficking in persons" includes this provision:

> Each State Party shall consider implementing measures to provide for the physical, psychological and social recovery of victims of trafficking in persons, including, in appropriate cases, in cooperation with non-governmental organizations, other relevant organizations and other elements of civil society, and, in particular, the provision of:
> (a) Appropriate housing;
> (b) Counselling and information, in particular as regards their legal rights, in a language that the victims of trafficking in persons can understand;
> (c) Medical, psychological and material assistance; and
> (d) Employment, educational and training opportunities.

Yet, as John Frederick (2005), having worked closely with Nepalese women and girls trafficked to India, rightly points out, this view presumes lack of agency and the presence of severe physical and psychological damage to the victim. Women in my research in Korea move on from their experiences utilising resources available to them largely outside the anti-trafficking framework, thus enabling us to think more broadly about the meanings of agency within the prostitution-trafficking nexus and beyond the sex worker rights paradigm of medicalised agency in the context of remaining in sex work or the victim rehabilitation model central to anti–sex trafficking health interventions.

Sex, empires and tensions of trafficking in women

As seen here, the medicalised discourse of HIV/AIDS dominates understandings, fuels anxieties about and leads to a range of governance mechanisms to regulate migrant sex workers. Since the early 2000s a different narrative of psychological and physical violence inflicted through sexual abuse is inscribed onto the mythical body of the sex trafficking victim, whose health needs must necessarily be distinguished from those of voluntary sex workers and met through her rehabilitation. Whilst rehabilitation of sex workers is admittedly not absent from the HIV/STI discourse, the orientation is less towards restoring the damaged subject's psychological and physical health and more towards rehabilitating her from prostitution itself. In Korea, notably under the anti-trafficking legislation of 2004, this has also been extended to the clients of sex workers who attend 'john's schools' to receive re-education under which heteronormative sexual outlets in the context of state-sanctioned institutions such as marriage are encouraged and the deviant sexual orientation of prostitution explicitly discouraged.

But this is only part of the picture that forms the fraught relationship between sex trafficking, health and violence. We must also consider the role and interests of the (militarised) state and its complex gendered, classed and racialised relationship with sex. Philip Howell (2009) has documented the imbrications of empire and regulation of prostitution focusing on the ways the British Empire differentially utilised the Contagious Diseases Act to regulate sexuality in the interests of empire building. In exploring the early anti-trafficking movement of the twentieth century specifically, Stephanie Limoncelli (2010: 2) has argued that the movement was limited by the central role of women's sexual labour in both nation-state and empire building, as also suggested in Philip Howell's (2009:187) study: "State officials sought to defend and preserve their right to maintain and regulate prostitution in metropolitan and colonial areas in support of militaries and migrant labourers, and as a means of maintaining ethnic hierarchies". State attention to women's bodies and their sexuality, including prostitution, has thus figured in various ways in nation- and empire-building processes (Yuval-Davis 1998, Stoler 1989, Nagel 2003). The important point here is that anti-trafficking initiatives, as well as broader movements centring on women's empowerment or eliminating violence towards women, can often be stymied by these nation-building efforts which, as Ann Stoler (1989) reminds us, can reproduce and perpetuate racialised, classed and gendered hierarchies which often cast different groups of women – prostitutes versus wives/ mothers, for example – as serving different moral roles of the nation.

Chungmoo Choi and Elaine Kim (1998) have explored the ways this nationalist anxiety has been manifest in Korea, including a discussion of the uneasy positioning in the national imaginary of the former comfort women and Korean prostitutes serving the US military. These two groups of women are seen to symbolise the ongoing occupation of the Korean nation by foreign powers expressed through the *sexual* occupation of Korean women's bodies by foreign military forces. In the Korean context the interests of the Korean and United States governments have converged around the need to maintain national security, where the sexualised female body plays an indispensable role. Katharine Moon (1998) has described how the US military in Korea governed the prostitute bodies of the Korean women in *gijich'on* areas through direct regulation and surveillance of their health beginning in the 1970s until recently. With the US government's self-proclaimed global leadership role in the fight against human trafficking since the early 2000s, coupled with attention towards the suspected involvement of US military personnel and peacekeepers in sex trafficking, clearly this formal regulation role is no longer officially tenable. In other words, it is becoming increasingly difficult for the US military to regulate prostitution and attend to the biomedical surveillance of bodies of prostitutes when the US government purports to be a global leader in the fight against human trafficking.

These discussions are significant in understanding health issues in Korea's *gijich'on* in the 2000s. Women that I knew in my field sites could all recount incidents of US military CPs (Courtesy Patrols) entering clubs and 'informally' performing checks on women's health. This entailed CPs asking the club owner or manager to make the women's health check cards (which are part of their contracts to work in Korea) available for the perusal of the CPs. Lisa recounted to me this involvement of the USFK in the monitoring of clubs for STIs:

> One day the CPs were checking the clubs for girls with STDs. They wanted to make them have check-ups. They checked three clubs. In USA Club the mama-san said to five of the girls, "You go upstairs and don't work tonight, and if the CPs come again tomorrow, you have to pay your time off". Because those five girls had some kind of STD, like thrush I think. They had to pay for their own treatment quickly so they could go back to work again, coz none of those girls could afford to keep bar fining herself until she got better.

This demonstrates a manoeuvring of the US military's (specifically, USFK's) sexual health interventions in light of the emergence of anti-trafficking discourses, but in ways that still enable the US military to indirectly regulate and survey entertainers' sexual health in the interests of security at multiple scales from the bodies of US soldiers to the Korean nation and US military empire.

In the remainder of this chapter I focus on sites of violence and health beyond a focus only on HIV/AIDS and STIs or military-inspired regimes of regulation and intervention. Instead I want to turn attention towards the everyday utterances of health, sickness, violence and abuse that render these broader discourses partial at best. In her ethnography of female sex workers in Chennai, India, Salla Sariola (2010: 5) also emphasises the ways the prevailing medical (particularly HIV) discourse of sex workers has rendered "their everyday lives . . . hidden from view". These everyday experiences are further obscured by the spectacle of violence narrative that underwrites much of the abolitionist perspective on prostitution as trafficking. In undertaking a different focus from these narratives I frame my discussion partly in line with recent observations that neo-liberal agendas concerning the creation of compliant bodies for profit are productive of particular negative health consequences (for example, Wallace 2009, Nguyen 2008). In what follows I focus on two sites; first, the inverse relationship between club profits and women's health (the greater the profits the more likely women's health will suffer) and, second, the psychological and physical effects of punishments and power relations in the club.

Inverse relationships: profits versus health in the clubs

Like all legal migrants entering Korea on work visas, every single one of my participants stated that she was supposed to have regular medical check-ups and that these check-ups were agreed to in her contract. These check-ups were supposed to be conducted every four to twelve weeks, and the woman's promoter was responsible for covering the costs of these check-ups and any associated medical expenses. Some of my participants said they did not receive their check-ups on the agreed regular basis, although most said that when they did have check-ups their manager would pay. Fhem, for example, worked in Players Club for just over one year, and in that entire time she was never given a medical check-up.

76 *Health in trafficking*

Whilst the women's regular check-ups are sometimes paid on their behalf, albeit with an expectation of repayment attached, a very different pattern emerges when a woman becomes sick. In these cases a woman must pay her *own* medical expenses. In USA Club in TDC, for example, Lisa told me that the entertainers would have check-ups every two months, and the manager pays these, but "if a girl gets sick, she has to pay her own medical expenses and the cost depends on the kind of sickness she has. When we signed the contracts they said everything would be free. But we have to pay for a lot of things". This happened to Rosie, who said that if she wanted a day off because of illness, she had to pay her penalty (normally the cost of bar fining herself at around USD 200–300) for the day. She recalled one experience when she became injured at work:

> One day I fell down from the VIP room when I was coming out from having sex with the GI because I was so drunk. My leg was swollen, so I went to the doctor and had to pay for that from my own money [KRW 30,000 for injections and more for medicine]. I didn't have any days off after this accident. Only I could sit down in the club and didn't have to dance for three days. But I still had to entertain customers.

Alma recalled a similar accident she had in Shield Club in TDC:

> One time two Bangladeshi customers were fighting over me and they were both pulling me in different directions. I fell over and I broke my ankle. After I got it bandaged I wanted to rest but mama-san said, 'No time off unless you pay. Just wear sandals with no heel'. It was so stupid because, you know, if a customer wants to buy me a drink he has to carry me to the chair and then if another customer buys me a drink he has to carry me to the other chair or the bar; like that, like that.

One afternoon I met up with Cherry and Rosa at Rosa's apartment in American Ally in TDC where she was living with her GI husband. As we sat talking, Jane, who had worked with Cherry and Rosa at M Club, came in, and we invited her to chat with us. The conversation turned to the time when Jane got appendicitis whilst working in M Club. Rosa recounted that Jane was so sick that she was foaming at the mouth. The other girls told the mama-san (the Korean club owner), but mama-san kept saying, "She is just acting". Cherry recalled that none of the other girls could sleep that night because they were afraid Jane's appendix was going to burst and she was going to die in the club. When mama-san finally took Jane to the hospital two days later, she had to have her appendix taken out immediately. After the operation mama-san took Jane straight back to the club and told her to continue working the same day, including going to the VIP rooms with customers for intercourse. Rosa recalled that she was really mad about this, telling Jane and mama-san that Jane would burst her stitches if she had sex on the same day as the operation. Jane said she had no choice but to go to the VIP room because she did not have enough money to pay her day off after the operation and because the operation cost

USD 2,000, which mama-san lent to her. Jane had to pay all the operation money back to mama-san and did not receive four months' salary as a result. When Jane returned to the Philippines Cherry laughed as she recalled saying to Jane, "This scar [from the operation] is so you don't forget your experience in Korea".

When health issues in trafficking involving the commercial sex industry are discussed rarely does money and debt figure as a significant concern. Yet the experiences of Jane, Alma and Rosie suggest that the money – either to pay for time off whilst sick or recuperating from illness or to pay for medicines and treatments – was central to rendering women more vulnerable to health problems and, in particular, making existing health problems worse. Further, paying for expensive operations or treatments – like Jane's appendicitis operation – confronted women with the health/money dilemma of having to return to work straight away *and* to see more customers in order to pay back the cost of treatment to the club owner. In almost every case women related to me that the club owner inflated the cost or charged interest so it took longer for a woman to pay the initial sum back. Health problems were thus used strategically by club owners as a means of extracting higher profits from women through their labour or at the very least of reducing the days a woman could take off through penalising her time off during illness. These penalties are just one type of punitive action taken by club owners. Other penalties, as well as quotas and punishments, were also inflicted on women, often causing women undue stress and humiliation in their club work. It is to the health implications of these that I now turn.

Penalties, punishments and power

In the previous chapter I ended with a discussion of the compensation claims for the women who ran away from Pop Store Club in TDC. In my interpretation of their push for compensation from the owner of Pop Store Club and their promoter I argued that the process of claiming unpaid salaries and other monies owed had as much to do with the women's desire to subvert the power relations between themselves and the club owner as with the money itself, with the compensation claim serving as the key symbolic mode through which to realise this reversal. Here I wish to more fully draw out *why* this is important to many of the women who run away from the clubs by focusing on the ways power relations in the clubs are constructed through punitive actions against the women, including the imposition of monetary fines, physical and verbal abuse and acts of humiliation. In understanding when and how these punitive actions are meted out the distinction between different clubs is important to understand. Cherry explained to me that there are 'good' or 'bad' clubs in the *gijich'on*, and women in 'bad' clubs are subject to a strict system of rules and punishments. Whilst this may appear an overly simplistic distinction, it is one that women in the clubs consistently repeated to me. Laments like, "Oh, such and such a club is a really bad club" or "I hope my promoter doesn't send me to a bad club" were a common refrain amongst the women I knew.

The arbitrarily imposed measures in bad clubs include verbal, physical and emotional/psychological abuse of the women and penalties that include fines, salary deductions and other payments exacted from the women, all of which are also arbitrary. These punishments and penalties are most commonly meted out for breaking club rules or failing to meet drink quotas. In addition, women are often subject to the removal of some of their privileges, such as free time to go outside the club, holding a cell phone or even being able to sit down at work, if they break rules or fail to make weekly and monthly drink quotas. Not all the clubs punish or penalize the women, although these 'good' clubs are a minority. Only two of the twenty-seven clubs where my participants were deployed were completely penalty and punishment free, for example. In some of the good clubs, such as Players Club in TDC, the women are not punished if, for example, they do not meet a weekly or monthly drink quota or are late to work. As Fhem explained to me,

> The mama-san started to introduce a penalty for being late to work, because, Alma, she gets drunk and she sleeps until after eight pm, so the mama-san said, "I will introduce a penalty". The penalty is KRW 20,000 every ten-twenty minutes we are late. We only have that penalty if we miss work time, not if we go out and come back late outside work time. I am always late so I owe mama-san lots of penalty money, but I never paid it yet.

In fact, the Players Club entertainers never paid these fines before they returned to the Philippines when their contracts expired. In other clubs, too, the women were not subject to strict punishments and penalties and instead would receive a reward for high drink sales, as another participant, Julie, explained,

> There aren't really any punishments for drinks. If a girl sells 250 drinks in a month she got USD 50 bonus, and if she sells 300 drinks she receives KRW 100,000. I never got this bonus. Sometimes I would sell just over 200 drinks and that's all.

Nonetheless, in other clubs, like Y Club and M Club in TDC and Toka-ri where Rosie and Cherry were respectively deployed, if a woman does not meet a monthly drink quota she is punished by not being allowed to have a day off in a month. In these clubs, penalties and punishments are taken much more seriously.[5] In NBA Club the women were punished if they stayed outside for more than the time allowed by the club owner. One of my participants who had worked in NBA, Rachel, said this was one manifestation of 'Article 15': "If I go outside for more than thirty minutes I got Article 15. This meant I couldn't go outside at all and I was not allowed to use the cell phone to call my family in the Philippines for six months". 'Article 15' is in fact a US military term that denotes any arbitrary punishment for misconduct inflicted usually by a superior officer over junior ranking personnel. It has been appropriated by some of the camp town clubs and applied by the club owners to their foreign female entertainers.

In Peace Club in TDC the Korean mama-san was, according to Beth, particularly ruthless in her delivery of punishments to the women. Beth told me that "if you are one minute late to work you have to raise your arms to customers for thirty minutes on the stage. So that means if you are two minutes late you have to stand like that for one hour. It's so humiliating". Other punishments in this club were more arbitrarily distributed. Beth recounted another occasion when one of her workmates was kicked outside the club in winter (wearing only her thin costume) for four hours. This punishment was inflicted because a customer paid her workmate's bar fine and the woman thought she would not have to return to work that night after the bar fine. However, upon her return from the bar fine she was told to go back to work, and, when she pleaded that she had earned the required commission for that night, she was kicked outside to stand in the snow in her thin costume.

The conditions of work bear similarities to those of the young female factory workers described in Aiwha Ong's (1987) study in Malaysia. Discipline through bodily practices of surveillance, control of movement and punishment as described by Foucault (1980) has been increasingly wrested from his original site of the prison to the factory, the construction site, the household and, as illustrated here, the club. Yet existing research on such regimes of power within (migrant) workplaces has yet to fully engage with opaque psychological consequences of these everyday encounters. Alma's experiences in Shield Club provide deeper insights into these issues. Alma arrived in Korea on January 31, 2003, and worked in Shield Club for just under four months before running away and seeking refuge at the Centre. Alma's heart problem, which I briefly described at the beginning of this chapter, was, she felt, exacerbated by the situation in the club and, in particular, her relationship with the Korean female club owner whom she referred to as *ajumma* (lit. aunty, in Korean). The following is an unreconstructed account from Alma of her experiences in Shield Club. I wish to present Alma's narrative in this way in order to destabilise the regimes of discursive authority in sex trafficking that would otherwise work to occlude the detailed preoccupation of Alma with the *ajumma* in the club and the constant anxiety she experienced in manoeuvring *ajumma's* changing club rules and penalties.

Alma's narrative

When we arrived in Korea *ajumma* treated us good for a few days till Mr Kim [Alma's Korean promoter] visited the club. We have a license to be a singer; so we thought we are singers to the stage. For two weeks *ajumma* was good – she chose four girls to sing on stage two weeks only. Then she stopped it and we request [singing on stage], but she says, "No more". The owner of Shield Club and Eagle Club, which is upstairs from our club, is also the owner of another club which is a very bad one because there is naked dancing and prostitution in the open part of the club.

Ajumma said that if we go out we have to have a bodyguard. Monday we get the commission from our drinks so we go out and get the groceries. We go out only thirty minutes, from 1 till 1:30 p.m. We understand that we have to follow the rules because we're here in Korea. *Ajumma* said, "You can't go out because you have no alien card yet". But in May we got our alien card and *ajumma* said, "One night you get seven drinks. Then you could go out – only if you got seven drinks". So, even though we have our alien cards she still makes some excuse that we not go out. At the end of May we get our alien card and that's a big bullshit [that we can go out after that]. I say to *ajumma*, "Can I go out alone now?" and she says, "No". I'm shocked. I react; when I react she thinks I'm the fighter woman [the trouble maker] in the club. We go out with a bodyguard again, so we have a meeting again. *Ajumma* says, "If you want to go out alone you get a quota [for drinks]". So, we get that and we follow the rules and we go out alone, but only the girls who get the quota. We follow that for almost three weeks. Then she changes the rule again because we start going out [on dates] with our customers and she doesn't like that because she wants the customer to spend the money inside the club, not outside on a date.

We are also not allowed to hold cell phones. If we hold cell phones we must hide them from *ajumma* and *samchung* [lit. big brother, in Korean; in this case the brother of the club owner]. *Ajumma* also said for the girls never to accept a cell phone from a GI or other customer, but sometimes we would accept the phones and hide them.

From April *ajumma* said, "You have a drink quota now". Ladies drinks in Shield Club are USD 20 for twenty minutes or USD 40 for an hour. One USD 20 drink is two chips, and one USD 40 drink is five chips. The girl gets USD 3 commission per USD 20 drink. On the GIs payday the girls are expected to only spend ten minutes for a USD 20 drink. On payday especially *ajumma* records how many minutes you sit with a customer and, oh my God, she writes it down in her book behind the counter and times us with the customer.

When she started with the quota it was really difficult for us because often the GIs did not have money. I have to tell the customers, "If not payday you must be understand [that I cannot sit with you]". Not always the GI has a lot of money. Payday is okay, but how about next week? The commission for the drinks is paid to us every Monday, when we also have a weekly meeting. There are two Korean women working in the club, and if those girls get drinks they perform lap dances for their customers. So because the Korean girls do the lap dances, at one of the meetings *ajumma* says to us Filipinas, "Why you six girls don't do that position?" *Ajumma* says, "I know you're new and never did this work, so I give you a chance. We give you time so starting to April you have a quota". But we know that the labour attaché at the Philippines Embassy in Seoul says there should be no quota and no lap dances.

So sometimes we sit on the lap after that. We have a meeting – just the girls – and we all say that we must follow [the new rule]. The style of *ajumma* is that if she sees you are a good worker she treats you good. I'm a sales cashier in a gas station in the Philippines. This is my first time to work in a club. So I don't know how to do like that. Me and *ajumma* argue because she thinks I stop all the girls to do the lap dancing.

In May a new group of eight girls arrived and were put in Eagle Club upstairs on the third floor. The new girls have no idea how to work and get drinks. So we work Eagle Club for a while, but that's no good because our booking is Shield Club. Mr Kim said, "Keep quiet about that [changing clubs]". When Eagle Club is open we work there and Eagle Club girls work in Shield. But we already have regular customers in Shield. After two weeks in Shield Club those new girls have our regular customers there. And for those two weeks our drinks are less. Eventually *ajumma* decided to close Eagle Club unless it was payday, so all thirteen girls began to work in Shield together. Now it's even harder for us to make any money from the drinks, so no getting the quota and no time to go out of the club.

Starting June *ajumma* never follows the rules she made anymore. We work 6 p.m. till midnight, but she opens the club 5 p.m. till 2 a.m. We still have a drink quota. We're always confused because she always changes the rules. I feel she gives me embarrassment. Twelve midnight when it's the GIs curfew we sit down. If she knows I get six chips she yells and asks who gets eight chips, just so I look like the bad one who never works hard. When me and *ajumma* were fighting *ajumma* punished me – no day off in May. One month four days off in the contract, but we only get two days off in other months. In May, no day off at all. *Ajumma* changes the rules again; Friday to Sunday 3 p.m. till 4 a.m. and twenty chips per night. I ask, "Where can we get [twenty chips] if not GI payday?" If we get high drinks we can finish work early but some girls never get that so from midnight to 4 a.m. they stand up in the door, like standing the whole time".

The contract says no bar fine, but when the new girls for Eagle Club arrive here in May after one week *ajumma* says they have bar fine – USD 500 for the customer – the girl gets only USD 50. Some customers say they want to bar fine us too so we can have a day off, but *ajumma* says no. She never agreed to let us Shield Club girls go out. If I get a day off I go out with my boyfriend. *Ajumma* never knows. We never tell about our boyfriends because we get in trouble. But when the new girls come they get a bar fine; Friday 11 a.m. till 9 a.m. the next day. *Ajumma* says to the new girls, "You come to Korea to make money so we help you". She gives the girl the bar fine money – USD 50 – in front of our group. Then she says [to us in our weekly meeting], "It's up to you if you want bar fine. Why don't you just try?" We don't say anything. Two weeks later one of our group needs money and asks her boyfriend about a bar fine. *Ajumma* agrees and we think it's unfair. I don't want my boyfriend to do like that and spend money for *ajumma*. My boyfriend says, "I'm very serious to you. I love you. I don't want to treat you like a prostitute". *Ajumma* is scared of our group if we make trouble, like tell the police or something. That's why she doesn't let us go on a bar fine, so our group no bar fine.

We are punished if we don't achieve high drinks in a night. If we get a certain number of chips then we can sit down, but *ajumma* always changes the quota for the drinks and the chips. *Ajumma*, she's never contented. If you do not get six or seven chips you are standing in the door for like five hours. In May a lot of customers went back to the USA because they finished their tour, but she doesn't understand why our drinks are low. It's hard to get new customers because you must begin new conversations again and see if you are compatible, like that.

February and March I'm a good employee and I have a lot of customers. I have top drink sales two months in a row. Then I have a serious boyfriend. *Ajumma* knows and she is mad because that's not the rule. Starting to April I lost all my drinks because of my boyfriend and I have pity for the GIs because they give all their money but it only goes to *ajumma's* pockets, not to us. Some GIs tell us, "You know what? You make money for them [the owners]". Sometimes we lie to the GIs. Sometimes the GIs say, "Okay, if I give USD 20 how much do you get out of that USD 20? I say, "USD 10". I lie. I say, "If you want to help [me] you buy [a drink]. Some GIs are good and help the situation, but some if they know I just get USD 3 they say, "I give you the money, not drinks". If *ajumma* knew that she gives us big trouble.

You know, some GIs are jealous. They say, "I treat you a lot of drinks. Why don't you want to have lunch with me, but you have lunch with the other guy?" So, *ajumma* changes the rules again: ten chips [five drinks] because she's afraid we are going to lose the customer. That's the big problem with *ajumma*: she doesn't care that the GI doesn't have any money. You know, another thing, the bodyguard said, "We don't care what the GI does to you at the table. We just want the drinks. So *you* have to know how to handle the customer, not us".

I have a new customer. He's only staying in Korea two weeks. He's a little drunk and he buys my drinks. When I sit down, my customer goes to the bathroom and stays there fourteen minutes, so when the guy gets out he goes to his friend's table. So when he comes back over to me *ajumma* signalled for me to stand up. My customer said, "What's going on? Why did you drink your juice quickly?" He's starting to get mad. He said, "You stand up – you only entertain me for five minutes". I'm confused because *ajumma* gets mad. Then he says, "I want to buy you another drink", and he starts counting his money. *Ajumma* is mad because I'm wasting time. He only has USD 15 so he said, "I can't buy you a drink anymore". I say, "Come back tomorrow and we'll talk". When I return my glass to the counter *ajumma* is mad at me.

I have a KATUSA customer and *ajumma* knows he really likes me and he gives a lot of juice. He says, "Alma, I want to know you outside the club". He asked to bar fine me a day off. He asked *ajumma* and he said to me, "I want to take you to Seoul". He said he would pay. But he wanted to go for three days. I never went because *ajumma* doesn't let me go and I don't want because I have a boyfriend and I'm loyal to my boyfriend. Every night he buys a lot of drinks – USD 100 or USD 200. *Ajumma* knows the guy is Korean. Then, because I can't go on the bar fine [with him] he says, "It's just business for me. You just entertain me".

One day my boyfriend says to me, "When is your second day off [for May]?" I'm waiting in May and I'm waiting, but no day off. One day I get twenty chips with the Korean guy so I'm hoping *ajumma* says that I get a day off the next day. But in May the only day off is 9 May and the day off is only 10 a.m. till 10 p.m. The day after my day off in April – I was with my boyfriend on Thursday – *ajumma* says, "Alma, who were you with yesterday?" I told to *ajumma* that I called the Korean guy first but he said he had no time, so then I called the fat guy – actually that's my boyfriend. *Ajumma* says, "You know, I know the fat guy he spend you a lot in February and March. Why the last two months he only gives you a small juice and not spend money? Why?" I say it's because he's divorced and he have a daughter and he's only an E-5 [low rank]. *Ajumma* says, "That's bullshit. You [should] only care about the juice. You don't care about the problems of the GI. You care only about yourself and the money and the juice".

Reflecting on Alma's narrative

To subject Alma's narrative to my own interpretation would be to defeat the purpose of its inclusion as a self-articulation of the main preoccupations Alma, and many other women I knew, faced in *gijich'on* clubs – namely their bosses in the clubs. Yet some comments are warranted about her situation in relation to discussions about health and well-being in this chapter. Foremost, Alma's fractured relationship with the *ajumma*, the constant pressure and confusion she felt in relation to *ajumma's* changing rules in the club, the arbitrary nature of penalties and punitive actions and the humiliation they caused were the focal points of Alma's anxiety in the club. Notably, her narrative did not ever touch on sexual exploitation by clients, and iterations of verbal, physical and sexual abuse were limited to those imposed by *ajumma* and *samchung* ('older brother'), rather than customers. In Alma's case her pre-existing health problem of high blood pressure was exacerbated by the particular anxieties she felt in her relationship with *ajumma*, and *this* was her main health concern. Because most of the *ajummas* and mama-sans in the *gijich'on* clubs were themselves once in similar positions to the Filipinas they employed in the clubs (bar women serving the US military in the post–Korean War period) the exercise of power over Alma by *ajumma*, at least in my reading of Alma's narrative, is as much about the renegotiation of the Korean *ajumma's* position and status within the club regime as it is about her preoccupation with extracting profit from migrant women's labour per se.

Pregnancy, abortions and babies

Pregnancies – both unwanted and planned – were a major preoccupation amongst women in the clubs, especially those that offered intercourse as a service to customers either in the club or in the context of a bar fine. Even with high levels of condom use some women would not use condoms when going with a favoured or regular customer or boyfriend. This practice is guided by women's belief that a boyfriend would not 'go' with another woman since, as his girlfriend, she had exclusive claim over his sexual release. In fact, of the ten entertainers in my research who admitted to having abortions, three, including Lisa, revealed that they were pregnant to their GI boyfriends. The other two aborted because of the negative repercussions they would face while working in the club if pregnant and because of supposed problems with the foetus respectively. The other seven women became pregnant to customers who refused to use condoms or deliberately broke or pricked condoms. Where women became pregnant to their boyfriends or favoured customers the customer normally bore responsibility for the cost of the abortion. Rhea became pregnant to her GI boyfriend when she was in Songtan in 2003. She explained,

> Last June I had an abortion because I got pregnant to my boyfriend here. I was one month already and he asked me what I'm going to do about it. I said I have to have an abortion because I don't have enough money [to stop working and look after a baby]. He gave me USD 350 to pay for the abortion. We still

have a relationship after that, but then his tour in Korea finished at the end of June and he went back to the United States. I told my mum about the abortion and she was mad. She asked, 'Why did you abort your baby?' I said that I didn't want to go back to the Philippines with no money. I feel guilty and sad about it and sometime I have a regret about doing the abortion. I want to tell my mum before I go to the hospital but I tell her after. I went straight back to work the next day. I got two brothers and two sisters and my mum and dad. I'm the only one to work abroad. I'm the only one who is single and can earn money for my family. I try to send USD 100 home every month. If I have the baby I can't do this anymore.

In cases where women became pregnant through their work in the clubs and may not have known who the father was, they normally had to pay the cost of their own abortion. In nearly all these cases the manager or club owner would lend the woman the money or pay for the abortion and the abortion cost would then continue to be deducted from her salary until it was completely repaid. Some women who became pregnant through work opted to take powerful, unsafe abortion-inducing drugs, such as overdoses of strong painkillers that would abort the foetus straight away, instead of paying for the high cost of an abortion at the hospital or medical clinic. Cherry once told me,

I don't use the girl's toilet at Club M anymore because a lot of the girls lose their babies in those toilets. They take a lot of aspirin or other medicine and then they abort the baby. The baby comes out in the toilet. There are a lot of the baby's souls in that toilet. That's why it's haunted.

Because nearly all the Filipinas I knew were highly religious, abortions were also emotionally distressing for many women and induced a range of religious and symbolic practices aimed at reconciling their decisions within their own minds. None of my participants who had an abortion ever received any counselling prior to or after the abortion, and every woman stated that she had to return to work the day after the abortion. Rhea even asked me one day if I could bring some Holy Water to her from Father Glenn in Seoul on my next trip to Songtan. At first I failed to connect this request to her abortion, but after asking her why she wanted water blessed by Father Glenn she replied that she could not get the guilt she felt in aborting her baby out of her mind, even when she was asleep. She planned to put the vial of Holy Water above her bed in the hope that it might help her overcome her distress and restless sleeping patterns.

The case of Cecile was a little different to other women who became pregnant. Cecile was pregnant to her Filipino partner prior to leaving the Philippines. When she was recruited by a promotion agency in Santa Cruz, Manila, she was told that she could have an abortion in Korea if she wanted to, and that it would cost her about KRW 100,000, or that she could keep her baby if she wanted. Cecile wanted to keep her baby and never planned to have an abortion. She was told by her promotion agency that she would be a waitress in Korea, so it was okay if she decided to continue her pregnancy. However, when she arrived in Korea the papa-san in the club where she was deployed insisted that she have an abortion. She told me,

> I went to the clinic to have an ultrasound and check up on April 20, the day after I arrived in Korea. I had to pay KRW70,000. Then I was told by the papa-san that I would have an abortion the next day [April 21]. I said, "I don't like abortion". He said, "Okay, if you don't like, you go back to the Philippines". That was when I decided to run away from the club. If I have an abortion I have to pay. It costs W870,000 in total. That money would come from my salary – like W100,000 every month until it is paid. That means out of W450,000 salary each month, W100,000 goes for the abortion and USD 100 also goes to my manager for his agency fee. What do I have left? So I ran away three days after arriving in Korea. Also, there was another girl in our club who was also pregnant – she was five months. I don't know what happened to that girl because I run away, but I overheard the owner saying to our manager that they had a plan to send her back to the Philippines before it was too late.

Women who are discovered to be pregnant by the club owner or promoter are routinely sent back to the Philippines or forced to have an abortion. As Cecile's narrative suggests, some women also exercise a degree of capacity to control decisions around terminating pregnancies; in her case this meant running away from the club and working in a factory until her baby was due in order to continue her pregnancy. This is contra Lisa's case, where physical abuses in the club led her to miscarry and where control over any decision about her pregnancy was wrested from her hands.

Conclusion

The stories explored in this chapter disrupt the certainties of the sex slave discourse regarding health and violence as they related to trafficked entertainers in *gijich'on* clubs. This is because issues of violence, sexual health problems, and psychological and emotional difficulties were experienced in ways that are markedly different from those put forward in accounts such as Melissa Farley's (2004) discussed at the beginning of the chapter. As Alma's narrative attests, the *ajumma* was the figure mainly responsible for Alma's stress and health problems in the club, but even for her the problems she experienced were expressed in ways that find very little resonance in existing discourses of the relationship between violence, health and sex trafficking.

The stories about health, pregnancy and abortion that I have narrated in this chapter are suggestive of the ways money and pregnancy/abortion intersect. Although Cecile wanted to continue her pregnancy because the father was her Filipino partner, her narrative also indicates the significance of money in making this decision. This was because she calculated that she could not afford to repay the excessive cost of an abortion. Cherry's rendition of M Club's female toilet being 'haunted' by the ghosts of babies also speaks to the importance of money in women's decision-making about different procedures to terminate an unwanted pregnancy. In these cases lack of money to repay the cost of an abortion leads to unsafe termination practices involving ingestion of abortion-inducing drugs. Women like Rhea who ostensibly knew the paternity of the baby was their boyfriend were lucky to escape these self-induced abortion techniques since a boyfriend would almost always shoulder the financial burden of an abortion.

Many Filipinas run away from their club to marry or live in a de facto relationship with a GI boyfriend and become pregnant either before or after running away in the hope of securing a long-term future with their boyfriend. Lisa became pregnant to her boyfriend a second time a few months after running away from VIP Club. As we were walking down a backstreet of American Alley one afternoon she whispered as we passed another heavily pregnant Filipina, "That's Janice. She is almost the same as me; six months and due in April". Pointing to a closed door to our right she continued, "Over there in that apartment is Dana, who is five months, and then there is Lorna who is seven months who is in the next street". Pregnancies are so common amongst the women who run away that any time of the day walking through American Alley, or the backstreets of Songtan, one can see Filipinas pushing strollers or clearly in advanced stages of pregnancy. Pregnancies to customers-cum-boyfriends are one element of a broader range of health issues that women negotiate in their relationships with their boyfriends. The ways romantic relationship both enable women to regain some degree of control over their situations and compromise these very processes are taken up in the next chapter.

Notes

1 Meaning away from the base, usually in remote areas for the purpose of conducting military exercises.
2 The nine countries included in the study were Canada, Colombia, Germany, Mexico, South Africa, Thailand, Turkey, United States and Zambia). Farley and her co-authors interviewed 854 people (782 women and girls, 44 transgendered individuals and 28 men) currently active in prostitution or having recently exited. The sample included street prostitutes, brothel-based workers and strip club workers.
3 IOM's (2007) handbook devotes an entire chapter (chapter 5) to health and trafficking. Included in the chapter are comprehensive, but generalised, health problems affecting trafficked persons, especially women and children. Prominent amongst these are STIs and HIV/AIDS, trauma and psychological problems.
4 In practice, however, these polarised strategies often break down. During fieldwork for a separate study of trafficking for commercial sexual exploitation in the Philippines I witnessed Catholic priests distributing condoms to trafficked women and girls in lower class red-light districts of Cebu City. The Catholic-run rehabilitation centre in Cebu City also worked closely with a sex worker rights organisation that conducted outreach in Cebu's red-light districts, despite their differing stances towards sex work.
5 Recall, for example, Rosie's description in the introduction of her experience of being locked in the closet in Y Club for up to half a day with the used condoms and tissues.

5 Romancing (in) the club

There is now a burgeoning literature on the interrelated subjects of sex tourism, militarised prostitution and trafficking in Asia. Despite the central importance many women who are the subjects of this literature place on relationships, romance and sometimes love in narrating their migration experiences and discussing their lives at work in the clubs and bars around military bases or tourist areas, very little of their concerns have figured in this literature until quite recently. Relationships that circumvent or contradict client-entertainer norms are producing some interest in a growing multidisciplinary body of recent work (for example, Brennan 2004, Cheng 2010). This work allows us to better understand and frame experiences of many women in *gijich'on* clubs, who are often preoccupied with the tensions between work and relationships, by the way relationships are both expressed and constrained by their status as 'trafficked entertainers' and by negotiations over their financial and emotional security.

The previous chapter contested some of the ways in which the perpetrators and sites of violence, abuse and health problems within trafficking have been (mis)characterised, especially by those who sustain an abolitionist stance towards prostitution. This chapter focuses on women's resistance in the club aimed at minimising harms and maximising their economic and personal welfare and simultaneously changing their overall situation by leaving the club. The significance of romance as an exit strategy lies in large part in women's imaginings of their transnational trajectories. To elaborate, most of the women I came to know did not wish to return to the Philippines. Forming romantic associations with customers is the key strategy by which women attempt to maintain their transnational positions in Korea by becoming the legal spouse of a boyfriend from the club. In this sense, and in the context of unfulfilled labour migration goals in the *gijich'on* clubs, Korea becomes a transnational platform for further socio-economic mobility. However, romance as a strategy to redress an oppressive work situation holds complex and sometimes contradictory outcomes for the women concerned. The anxieties of romance are central to women's experiences in the clubs and – like women's anxieties around relations with their bosses – form a central place in their narratives of working in the clubs.

In the chapter I draw on Cornwall, Correa, and Jolly's (2008: 38) recent observation that "development has generally seen sexuality as a problem needing to be controlled – related to population control, disease or violence – rather than as a source of affirmation, pleasure, intimacy and love". I explore two key sites through which situations of *gijich'on* entertainers speak to issues of intimacy, romance and love – first, anxieties by women in performing gradations of intimate and sexual labour; and second, the romantic scars women bear as a result of their hostessing work. Correa and Jolly are concerned both with centring sexuality, love and intimacy in positive ways within development discourses and with elucidating the manifold links between sex and poverty. Taking this observation further, I am interested in the ways sex, love and intimacy can be productive of particular operations of power that produce significant anxieties for migrant women like those in Korea's *gijich'on*. Foremost, the Filipinas I knew in *gijich'on* used strategic intimacy to negotiate their situations in the clubs in ways that provided important guards against their oppressive working situations. Nonetheless, women's strategies are enmeshed with romance in complicated ways that often contain multiple and amorphous meanings as strategies slip into the realm of real emotional attachments.

Strategic intimacy

Intimacy, emotion and affect have generated a crescendo of interest in the social sciences of late, including in geography where they have nonetheless rarely led to a focus on commercial sexual labour or, indeed, human trafficking. This may be, as Viviana Zelizer (2005) explains, because the transacted nature of commercial sexual services tends to preclude its location within intimate and affective relations. Despite this, several recent anthropological accounts of sex tourism in the Caribbean and Southeast Asia have disrupted this view. Brennan's (2004) account of the tourist town of Sousa in the Dominican Republic illustrates the significant role that open-ended prostitution plays in enabling women to attempt to achieve immediate goals of financial stability but also long-term ones associated with their movement beyond the site in which their sexual labouring takes place. Her analysis nonetheless highlights the precarity of such strategies, which for many women did not ultimately improve their situations either in Sousa or abroad.

Kempadoo's (1999) analysis of sex workers in the Caribbean also explores the ways sex workers utilise strategies for social and economic advancement that hinge on sexual labour beyond the client-prostitute transaction. Re-working subjectivity through the expression of agency is a key theme in studies of migrant and tourist-oriented sex work. In tracing the historical situatedness of contemporary forms of sex work in the Caribbean Kempadoo (1999: 8) suggests that historically under slavery sex was a strategy by women to acquire freedom from oppression: "Exoticism, while constituting a form of control and domination over women of colour, was thus also strategically transformed through sex work to economically and socially empower women, men and children", leading to the subversion and reconstitution of power relations since it "disrupts notions of prostitution as simply a relationship based on an exchange of sex for money or as a source of oppression for women". Discussing Filipinas specifically, Hildson and Giridharan

(2008: 612) also note the ability of those working in Sabah's nightlife industries to "resist, negotiate and participate in forging their subjectivities", rendering domination incomplete (cf. Scott 1985).

This work indicates that money is tied to intimate relationships with customers-cum-boyfriends, but not in ways that suggest sex is only a transaction or encounters are primarily about transacted sex. Visas as an emblem of onward and outward mobility, and sincere romance with a customer, further complicate these encounters as women attempt to enmesh their own transnational mobility and romantic aspirations within them. The concept of 'strategic intimacy' illuminates the ways in which women attempt to negotiate and resist their marginal circumstances in *gijich'on* clubs by strategically cultivating intimate relationships with selective customers. Cabezas (2009:23) applies the similar concept of 'tactical sex' to the sex tourism sectors in Cuba and the Dominican Republic in order to "capture the diverse, amorphous ways in which sex is deployed in tourist economies". I found that most Filipina entertainers in *gijich'on* do not position themselves as sex workers, with intimacy being a more readily acceptable resource for their encounters with customers than sex. Moreover, while a tactic can be understood as a focused manoeuvre in response to a specific situation, a strategy implies an overall plan realised through a range of possible manoeuvres. Filipinas in *gijich'on* clubs became extremely competent strategists whose manoeuvres were ultimately directed at leaving the club in a way that would enable them to realise either socio-economic or geographical mobility or both.

Ladies drinks and bar fines as sites of possibility

I begin my exploration of these strategies by arguing that ladies drinks and bar fines comprise important sites of possibility in which Filipina entertainers and American GIs can come together in relationships that transcend the positions of hostess and customer. The drink system described in chapter 3 emerges because the women normally receive less salary than has been agreed to in their contracts (or salary is withheld completely). In order to have a constant source of cash income, they must generate money through the drink sales system and, for some women, by engaging in the provision of sexual services at the clubs. If we recall from chapter 3, the drink system entails having customers buy them drinks for which they receive a percentage from the club. A drink for a woman normally costs between USD 10 or USD 20, and, as an unwritten rule, each drink allows the customer to spend between fifteen to twenty-five minutes with the woman, after which the customer must buy her another drink. From the purchase of drinks the women get between KRW 1,000 and KRW 2,000, or between 10–20 per cent of the money, the rest going to the club owner. A book is usually kept behind the bar in which a record of how many drinks each woman sells in a week or a month (depending on the club) is kept.

It is the drink system that supplies the nickname GIs give to the women who work in the clubs; they are dubbed 'juicy girls', 'juices' or 'drinkie girls'. The name 'juicy girl' denotes the fact that the usual drink for the women is a tiny glass of juice. So buying a 'ladies drink' is a symbolic act in that the drink represents a period of time for which a customer buys a woman's company. What the woman is expected to do in the fifteen to twenty-five minutes of time she will spend with her customer for each drink will usually depend on the price of the drink, whether the woman works in a good or bad club and what the GI expects. Usually, the higher the price of the drink, the greater the services to be rendered by the woman. I asked Fhem from Player's Club what happened when a GI bought her a ladies drink. She said,

> If a customer is drunk he tries to touch you. I say, 'No touch me'. He says something like, 'Why? You're working in a club, right? I can do whatever I like with you'. I don't like that because I have no self-respect. I want respect.

Charie had similar experiences with customers when they bought her drinks in Papaya Club. She stated,

> I never wear a short skirt like that [shows a photograph of herself in the club] in the Philippines. I have to pull my skirt down all the time. And I have to hold some customers' hands so that their hands don't go over my body.

There is often an expectation by GIs that buying a drink for a woman allows him to fondle and touch her on any part of her body and kiss her. Thus, although the drink system does not entail penetrative sex, it allows GIs to do anything short of that with a woman while they sit together in a booth or at a table within the club.

Some customer's expectations surrounding buying ladies drinks fall more closely into line with those of the women themselves. Here, the purchase of a ladies drink entails conversation and dancing with the possibility of some minimal physical contact. It is *these* encounters that normally provide the space in which romantic relationships develop since the interactions between the customer and the woman are based around conversation and forms of entertainment that do not compromise the women's self-respect. Customers who show respect for the women – as well as customers who are willing to spend a lot of money on the women – are held in higher esteem, and the women draw a strong distinction between good and bad GI customers on this basis, as Charie explained:

> I have met some GIs who understand our job. They know already what our job is. If a girl sits down they will buy [a drink] or they will tell us if they don't have money and they will say, "Another time, because it's not payday". Sometimes they tell us if they are already married. But sometimes they say, "What do I get if I buy you a drink?" Some guys are for fun, other guys are disgusting. They look like this [Charie gestures up and down with her eyes] and I get embarrassed. I like the guys who are just [there] for fun. They spend money. Their parents have good jobs back in America, so they can spend their salaries – not like me [Charie remits most of her salary to her family in the Philippines]. So they can have fun. Like two guys who come to Papaya Club

a lot and they are fun. They play cards and dance with us. They have fun and we give them fun too.

The women view customers who wish only to purchase their time for physical pleasure as disgusting, while GIs who go the clubs for socialising are fun.

Other women had similar things to say about "the dialogue of GIs," as Alma put it to me. Some GIs would go to the clubs and compare the availability and cost of sexual services available to them. For the women in the clubs these GI customers were a source of tension, and this reinforced the women's views of them as disgusting. The women also distinguish between GIs who are honest – in stating whether they have money to buy a woman a drink or revealing if they are married, for example – while deceitful GIs will lie about their marital and financial circumstances.

As discussed briefly in chapter 3, a bar fine can be described as the purchase of a women's time to take her outside the club. The length of time varies, and there is usually a set price for different periods of time. Again, as with the drink system, what a woman is expected to do with the customer on a bar fine depends on the club, the customer himself and his negotiations with both the bar manager and the entertainer concerned. If the woman has already established a relationship with a customer – through, for example, repeated encounters in the context of the drink system – a bar fine is viewed in far more benign terms than if a customer purchases the woman's time without establishing some preceding relationship with her. Some customers – especially those who already 'know' the women – view bar fines more like dates on which they take the woman bar hopping, to a restaurant or shopping. In these cases, even if the woman spends the night with the customer there is not necessarily any expectation on his or her part that they will have sex. Many of the women rail against customers who objectify them for sex and who eschew the discourse of romance. Given the restrictions on women's freedom of movement and free time in many of the clubs, the drink and bar fine systems offer the only real space for romantic relationships to develop between the entertainers and their customers.

The distinction between good and bad GI customers provides a basis by which women can select potential boyfriends, but it is not the only distinction women make concerning customers who may eventually become boyfriends. Although the clubs in *gijich'on* areas are established primarily for the entertainment needs of the GIs, Koreans and migrant factory workers also patronize the clubs. Players Club, where Alma and Fhem worked, is similar to many of the others in that it generally only receives GI customers unless there is a lockdown (meaning the GIs are restricted to base) or if there are no GI customers. Migrant workers and Koreans are normally not allowed in the clubs until the GIs have returned to base to meet their nightly curfew, in part to avoid fights between the Koreans and GIs from breaking out in the clubs.

Most of the women I knew, apart from Charie, who developed a serious relationship with a Filipino man, said they preferred American GI customers to customers of other nationalities. This preference was constructed as a result of a number of factors including: linguistic affinity, as English was the medium for conversation between the Filipinas and GIs; the benevolence expressed by some of the GIs towards the women; and the regularity with which GIs were able to visit the clubs because of the proximity of the bases to the clubs as opposed to migrant workers, who, because of constraints of time, money and proximity, could often only visit the clubs on the weekends. Favoured GI customers would give women money or buy women food and personal items – even if the GI was not the boyfriend of one of the entertainers. In addition, when Koreans or migrant workers (although normally not Filipino migrant workers) went to the clubs they would usually do so only for the purpose of sexual gratification whereas, as Charie suggested earlier, many GIs would go to the clubs simply to socialize and have fun.

Most of the women did not like South Asian, especially Bangladeshi and Pakistani, customers because they do not have much money and are less physically attractive to the women. A combination of their perceived exaggerated sexual drive, their lack of physical appeal to the women, the limited amounts of money they have to spend in the clubs and their sometimes violent tendencies situated factory workers, especially from South Asia, as undesirable, both as customers and as boyfriends.

In an interview at the Philippines Embassy shelter in June 2001, one of the eleven women who ran away from Stars Club in TDC, Ronnie, recounted how different nationalities of customers are marked differently as potential boyfriends:

> We only go out with our GI boyfriends on bar fines. They [GIs] always asked us first before they would go to the boss and to request to take us out. If we agreed then they would take us out but if we refused they respected our wishes. Though the GI's intention of taking us out would be only to take us out to do some shopping and so on it was really up to the woman if she agreed to have sex with him. In our case we only went out if he was our boyfriend. The GI's reason for wanting to take us out was to give us some free time to go out from the club because they knew that we were locked up once the club closed and to have our company. The GIs knew that we didn't get anything from the bar fines so they wouldn't really spend that often on bar fines.

Filipinas are sometimes said to desire relationships with foreigners and, more specifically, Americans. As Santos (2002: 10) notes, for example, a "colonial mentality" acts to construct Americans as desirable partners (see also Rafael 2000). While many of the women I knew did not necessarily aim to marry a GI most viewed a GI boyfriend as a positive investment in their immediate futures within the context of the work in the clubs and life in *gijich'on*. Whether or not a customer is considered a potential boyfriend is based on a coalescence of factors including a distinction between good and bad GI customers and customers of other nationalities. This distinction relates largely to customers' attitudes towards sex and objectification of the women. Men who exhibit kind, benevolent and sympathetic attitudes towards women are viewed by the women as possible romantic partners or friends. These relationships lie outside the bounds of commodified sexual encounters in the context of women's roles as the providers of sexual and intimate labour in the clubs.

Practical love

The women I knew became involved in romantic relationships for a number of reasons. Their boyfriends provide emotional and financial support particularly through repatriating money to the women's family in the Philippines; they assist with meeting day-to-day material needs by buying them food, clothes and sundry items; they provide their girlfriends with limited freedoms by buying their time and/or taking them on a bar fine; and they buy their girlfriends' time in the club whilst they are at work so they do not have to go with other, less desirable customers.

Buying time and earning respect

The most common form of support, discussed by virtually all the women in my research, was their boyfriend buying their time through buying them ladies drinks. Buying drinks or sex meant the woman did not have to entertain or service other customers. Rosie, introduced at the outset of the book, told me about the three different boyfriends she had in the three months she worked in Y Club. Her first boyfriend was a Korean GI[1]:

> He would buy me lots of drinks so that I didn't have to go with other customers who wanted to go to the VIP room. He went to the USA last year, and he sent me USD 300. If he took me to the VIP room, he would leave the door open and we would just talk. We had sex once, just before he went away, as boyfriend and girlfriend.

Lisa had two GI boyfriends when she was in USA Club, both of whom were initially her regular customers before they became romantically involved. She became engaged to her second boyfriend, David, shortly after he assisted her to run away from the club. In a situation common in the clubs, both Rosie's and Lisa's boyfriends would buy them drinks so that they did not have to serve other customers. While she was still working in the club David bought Lisa out on bar fines three times at a cost of between USD 200 and USD 500 each time. She said they did not have sex until their third date, and even then he did not want to push her. He bought her out so she could have some free time. Lisa recalled,

> The first time he took me out on a bar fine was overnight – after I finished work at midnight. We went to a hotel but he told me to just sleep because I am so tired. The next day we went to Second Market [the local town market] and we had lunch. I felt like I had a day off.

94 *Romancing (in) the club*

Cherry's thirty-five-year-old GI boyfriend, Bill, would often spend the night with her by buying her time for a night (long-time sex). As with Lisa's case, he would do this so Cherry did not have to go with other customers. Each time he bought her overnight it cost him between USD 250–300. When we discussed this one day in Cherry and Bill's apartment in TDC, Bill emphasised,

> When I stayed the night with Cherry and we had sex I was sure to make it good for her. These women are taught how to give pleasure but they never get it. They stop enjoying sex and see it as a job. I wanted to make sure Cherry had a good time when we were together.

In the case of both Bill and David, being concerned with what their girlfriends wanted was important in distinguishing themselves from other customers. Being concerned was almost always expressed through considerations based around sex and intimacy, either showing women they cared by not pushing them to have sex or by wanting women to experience sex as pleasure, rather than work.

In contrast to Cherry and Lisa, Cherry-Lyn did not have a serious boyfriend. However, that did not stop some of her regular customers from taking her out for a break. They also "respected her", as she related to me, by not wanting to have sex with her. She produced an excerpt of the diary record entry for her bar fines, which she had kept to document her situation (see Figure 5.1).

Table 5.1 Excerpt from bar fine and ladies drink record for May 31–August 31, 2002, for Cherry-Lyn

Night off		
June 22		Sup $90
July 3		Cezar $200
July 12	1 juice	Mr. Kim $100
July 16		Sup $120
July 19		Cezar $200
July 26		Jessie $40
August 2		Cezar $200
August 3	2 juice	Danny $100
August 6	2 juice	Andy $120 – Mama $100
August 7	1 juice	Steve Y10,000
August 13		Steve $100
August 15		Dave $60
August 16	1 juice	Cezar $200
August 17	1.juice	Cezar $200
August 30		Andy $200

```
                    nite off  No.
                              Date.

June 22              Sup    $90.
July  3              Cezar  $200.
                     Mr. Kim
July 12   1 juice            $100.
July 16              Sup    $120
July 19              Cezar  $200.
July 26              Jessie $40.  — Taxes
Aug  2               Cezar  ~~XXXX~~ $200.
Aug  3   2nd juice   Donny  $100 — Daniel
Aug  6   2 juice     Andy   $120 → Mama $100  3.00 Tip
                                                knot miss
Aug  7   1 juice     Steve  ¥10,000 yen — simon
Aug 13               Steve  $100.
Aug 15               Dave   $60.  Hunter
Aug 16   1 juice     Cezar  $200.
Aug 17   1 juice     Cezar  $120.
Aug 30               Andy   $200
Aug 31               Bryan  $150
*Sept 1  1 juice     Cezar  $180.
*Sept 12             Gabe   $110. ¥10 won  ⎫
Sept 13              Gabe   $120.           ⎬ 6 9 B E
Sept 14              Gabe   $                ⎭
Sept 15  1 juice     Gabe   $80.
                                    ¥10
```

Figure 5.1 Excerpt from bar fine and ladies drink record for May 31–August 31, 2002, for Cherry-Lyn

When perusing her records we discussed the men whose names appeared frequently:

C: Look, you see that Sup and Cezar and Gabe keep buying my time so they can help me out.
S: What do you mean by 'helping you out'?
C: They take me out so I can have a rest or shopping and enjoy myself. So I can forget the club.
S: So these three guys didn't expect anything from you for buying your time?
C No. That was only the customer I didn't know who expected that.
S: So, what would you say your relationship was with these guys?
C: They are my friends. That's why they help me out. But we have fun too and I help them out by giving them some companionship.
S: What about Cezar?
C: Yeah, he bought my contract out, but we are only good friends.

Cezar eventually paid USD 1,000 for Cherry-Lyn's contract, although by mutual agreement he did not expect that he would have a relationship with Cherry-Lyn beyond friendship after buying her contract.

Money for love

Apart from providing opportunities for time off and to avoid having to serve other customers, boyfriends are also a source of financial support. They provide their girlfriends with money and goods, including food, sundry items, phone cards and clothes. In addition, by buying drinks or time, they assist the women in earning commission. Some also repatriate money to the women's families in the Philippines. Boyfriends become financial providers in the context of poor work conditions in the clubs, under which the women are often denied all or part of their salaries. If women were paid the salaries they were promised, and not debt bonded to the clubs, the financial support from boyfriends may well have been far less relevant for the women. Rosie's first boyfriend (the Korean GI) put USD 1,000 in her bank account in the Philippines for her use. Rosie's mother withdrew all the money, telling Rosie she needed it for operations and medical expenses for the family.

Lisa's boyfriend David sent money back to her family in the Philippines three times, totalling USD 500. She told me, "My brother's wife will have a baby soon. They didn't have enough money for an ultrasound, so David sent them USD 200 for that. I didn't know he sent money like that to my family. I never asked him to". In fact, several weeks later Lisa explained that her brother was involved in a car accident in which the person he hit was hospitalized with serious injuries. The victim was willing not to press charges but wanted a payment of USD 500, which Lisa's brother asked her to pay. She said, "I will not tell David about this because I don't want him to feel like he has to pay". I asked Lisa how she planned to raise the money, to which she replied, "I will sell some of my gold jewellery. See, I have three gold necklaces and these two bracelets. Maybe I can get USD 200".

The anxieties of romance

Women's anxieties about negotiating club work and romances emerged in two intersecting ways. First were the tensions involved in juggling relationships between different customers-cum-boyfriends, and second were the tensions between performing sexual labour/club work and maintaining a serious relationship with one particular boyfriend. As the aforementioned discussion has suggested, women often distinguish between fun and serious boyfriends as well as good and bad customers, with the former being defined by women as customers who also take them on dates and, perhaps, assist them financially or in other ways. As such, there appears to be a great deal of fluidity between fun boyfriends and good customers, and often women use these terms interchangeably when describing the same guy. Because women need to maintain a host of regular customers they act to instil in each customer a belief that he is somehow in a 'special relationship' with her. Wendy Chapkis (1997) calls this management of emotions in the context of erotic work "emotional labour", which can be expressed through lying, performing different personas to different clients and so on. The failure of some women to manage their performances of intimacy with customers through these tactics can produce emotional ruptures.

For the Filipinas working in the clubs, it can be particularly challenging to juggle relationships with various good customers and boyfriends. The experiences of Amy from Pop Store Club (introduced in chapter 3) exemplify the tensions of many women in this respect. Amy was separated from her Filipino husband but did not discount the possibility of reconciliation with him when she finished her contract and returned home. Meanwhile, in Korea she has managed to develop romantic relationships with three of her customers, all of whom she refers to as her boyfriends, and also suggested that some other customers, also in her words, "act like boyfriends" because they want to go on dates with her outside work time. She laughs about her situation because all three customers have the name Chris. She said she hopes to marry the "oldest Chris" because he is thirty-seven years old and more mature and stable as a long-term partner than the other two, who are both only twenty-one years old. In non-working hours Amy cleverly uses her cell phone to juggle the demands of these three boyfriends and other good customers. On one occasion, for example, she lied to one of the younger Chrises about having a day off since she already had a plan to travel to Seoul for a date with the older Chris. She does not discount the possibility of forming a more serious relationship with one of these three men and half-jokingly said to me, "I will marry the one who comes to the Philippines to be with me. But what will I do if all three come?" Despite the stress that being involved with different men can create for her in Korea and the effort she devotes to maintaining the illusion for each that he is the only special one, she nonetheless views her situation in pragmatic terms:

> I have to rely on my customers and boyfriends because the club doesn't give the girls food. We all wake up in the morning and think, 'Where will we get our food today? How will we eat today?' If we don't have boyfriends then maybe we can't eat.

Women who only have one serious boyfriend face different kinds of tensions. When a woman enters a serious boyfriend-girlfriend relationship with a GI whilst working in the club she is caught in a complex catch-22 situation with her bosses. On the one hand she receives support through the various financial and emotional mechanisms discussed earlier. On the other hand, such relationships are incompatible with her duties within the club, particularly generating drinks sales, going on bar fines and undertaking intimate and sexual labour. When an entertainer begins to neglect these duties she becomes subject to verbal abuse and unceasing pressure from the club owner or bar manager to improve her work, as Alma related in her narrative in chapter 4. At the same time her boyfriend will exert reverse pressure on her to stop these duties and live entirely on her salary and financial contributions from him. Some clubs prohibit the women working from having serious boyfriends or discourage them by making negative remarks about the boyfriend since these relationships can compromise the profits the owners can make from the women's sexual and intimate labour.

Cherry's experience of the incompatibility between club work and a romantic relationship was telling with regard to these tensions. Cherry moved back to TDC to live with Bill after returning from the Philippines, where the pair had married upon her running away from M Club. She told me in several lengthy accounts about the stress her relationship generated when she was still working in M Club. On one such occasion she said:

> Mama-san kept saying to me, "You'd better work harder because your drinks are so low compared with the other girls". I didn't want to do that [work harder by going with other guys] because I have my boyfriend. I only want to go with him. When I met him I started to wear a long costume in the club [she shows me a photograph of her and her boyfriend sitting in the club; she wears long pants as part of her costume], so that the GIs wouldn't want to go with me. The month before I ran away [July 2002] my drink money was so low. It was only KRW 200,000 [100 drinks].

The mama-san did not know Cherry had a boyfriend, or she would have been punished. The Korean bar manager in M Club would, however, let Cherry spend time with her boyfriend in the club when the mama-san was not there, raising interesting questions about the relationship between the bar managers and club owners in some clubs.[2] The club owners normally policed women's relationships with customers vigilantly because of their concerns about loss of profits should a woman be supported by a boyfriend(s). Women often recount stories of punishments associated with having a serious GI boyfriend. Ronnie, from the group of eleven rescued women I met when I first arrived in Korea to commence my fieldwork, stated, for example:

> There was another incident where one of us got a mobile phone as a gift [owning a mobile phone was strictly prohibited] and the boss heard about

it. He went to our room and reprimanded us to surrender the mobile phone. But no one said a word and he went on a rampage and searched through our closets and he eventually found the mobile phone. Also he went through our wallets/purses and found some dollars and he said that we were not supposed to have any money and inquired how come we got some dollars. In his anger he destroyed the mobile phone and tore the dollars in front of us. Then one of us had about USD 65 dollars in her purse. She pleaded to him not to do anything with the money because it was gift from her boyfriend and she intended to send it back home to her son but to no avail the boss burned the money.

Lisa was also under pressure from her boyfriend David to stop some of her duties in USA Club. She explained,

> When I went with other customers it caused big problems in our relationship. One time David saw me go into the VIP room with a customer. I had to do that because I needed the money. My brother got in trouble with the police for assault. After that David gave me a letter, which said that he could not accept the work I was doing in the club if we were to be boyfriend and girlfriend. In the letter there was USD 1,000. In the letter David asked me to accept the money and not to sell myself for money anymore. After that I stopped going to the VIP room.

Nonetheless, the consequences of Lisa's decision were difficult for her to tolerate since her manager was constantly telling her to stop spending time with her boyfriend in the club and pushed her to serve other customers. She made the decision to run away after one particularly distressing episode in which David bought her food because she was hungry. She sat with him for ten minutes longer than was allowed under the club rules. She recounted:

> I was with David one day in the club. He had bought me a drink, so I was sitting with him. I was very hungry, so he had bought me something to eat. I was just finishing to eat and was walking to the toilet. The mama-san threw ice at me and it hit my back. Mama-san yelled at me, "Why you stay with him so long? You spend too much time with him for that drink". I went to the toilet and started crying. My manager came in and I started yelling at her. I said, "I was hungry and I was only eating". I went back out to the club and I was so mad. I sat at the bar and I refused to work. I just sat at the bar. That was basically when I decided to run away.

Lisa's disclosure speaks to the ways poor working conditions mesh with romance in practical ways, such as the provision of food or taking a short rest, and the ways surveillance censures women's attempts to ameliorate these same conditions. In this episode Lisa openly defied the mama-san by refusing to work, thus demonstrating how anxieties around romance cannot always be separated easily from expressions of defiance.

Charie faced similar conflicting pressures to Lisa whilst working in Papaya Club. She was constantly berated by the papa-san for having a serious boyfriend. These criticisms led to conflicts and tensions between her and her boyfriend and led her to engage in a series of lies to the papa-san, to her boyfriend and to other customers. After she ran away with the help of her boyfriend Charie and I discussed the dilemmas caused by relationships with GIs:

C: Papa-san says all GIs are liars. They discourage us in the club to fall in love with guys. Like Tim – papa-san says he's a bad guy because he's divorced three times and he's only thirty-four. If you fall in love with a guy you won't get drinks. A guy will give money to a girl instead of buying her drinks – some money for her future. If you have a boyfriend and he buys you a drink, instead of fifteen minutes maybe you spend twenty to twenty-five minutes. They allow boyfriend, but not serious boyfriend. All our customers are our boyfriends [laughs]. Some customers introduce like, "This is my girlfriend". Like that. I feel bad when they say that. I think, "Oh, if only Tim know that".
S: What do you think about the GIs? The ones who are not your serious boyfriend, I mean?
C: Some GIs say to me, "You just tell us you love us. But we heard about you. You don't love, you just want us to buy a drink". Customers get jealous of each other. Even Tim gets jealous. He thinks he's just my boyfriend because I want him to buy me drinks. I have to lie to other customers and say Tim is not my boyfriend, just a sweet guy. Sometimes customers insult me and call [me] liar. Tim and I had fights [about that] and he wanted me to leave the club.

In addition to the conflicting pressures exerted on the women by their boyfriends and the club owners, some of the women also experience extreme insecurity over the fidelity and sincerity of their boyfriends. Grace's romantic relationships with GIs formed a very big part of her experiences in Korea (see chapter 6). Grace was deployed on two occasions. During her first contract period (2000–2001) she became engaged to a GI, whom she said she really loved, but he broke her heart. She recounted the moment when she discovered his infidelity:

One night my brother [another GI, friend] took me out to drink [on a bar fine]. We went to his friend's house and when I went inside I saw my fiancé. He was with another girl. All I did [after that] for a long time was drink and have fun and get fucked up. I didn't care about anything or anyone.

Alma from Players Club made a similar discovery. When I interviewed Alma her contract was almost finished and she was due to return to the Philippines. I asked her what would happen to her relationship with her boyfriend, and she said,

In November my boyfriend said he will visit me in the Philippines. I wish he would marry me so much. I love him very much. I accept him for everything, even though I know he has other women. I knocked on his door one day like twenty times, because I knew he was in there and he didn't answer. Finally another Filipina answered and my boyfriend told me to go away. I walked back to the club crying and then I drank. I talked to my mama-san about it because, you know, I have no one else here. My mama-san, she talked to my boyfriend for me.

Often the conflicting pressures exerted by the boyfriends and club owners or managers, as well as the women's own insecurities about their boyfriends and their desire to pursue relationships with their boyfriends outside of the restrictive context of surveillance and control in the club, become too great for the women to bear. Boyfriends often help the women negotiate their departure from the club, especially since they sometimes put pressure on the women to cease club work. Women either run away from the club with their boyfriend's assistance or the men will help their girlfriends seek assistance from the police or other authorities. Sometimes a boyfriend will buy the woman's 'penalty', which is the cost of buying her contract so she becomes 'free'. Often the woman will be granted her freedom to leave the club when her boyfriend pays her penalty – which can be as high as USD 5,000. However, the manager or club owner will sometimes retain the woman's salary and documents, such as her passport and alien card, in an attempt to extract further payments from the woman's boyfriend. Despite its widespread practice, the 'penalty' system is illegal in Korea. Over half the participants in my research relied on the assistance of their boyfriends to help them leave the club. Some ran away, one sought assistance from the police and some had their boyfriends pay their penalty.

Media and NGO accounts of foreign entertainers in Korea's *gijich'on* explain women's decisions to run away from the clubs in terms of the human rights abuses they experience in the context of their work. A newspaper report by the *Air Force Times* (2002), for example, cites one story of a Filipina, Jennifer, who ran away from the club where she was working in TDC with the assistance of her GI boyfriend. The media account stated,

Army Pfc [private first class] Brian met Jennifer in a bar in South Korea where she was being held against her will and forced to work as a prostitute. With the help of a Catholic priest, he helped her escape the bar. Here [in a photograph of the couple riding in a taxi that accompanies the article] they ride through the streets of Seoul on her first day of freedom.

Contra the aforementioned interpretation, in one early NGO report on the situations of women in *gijich'on* clubs, running away is explained as a response to "the poor working conditions, unfair contracts, and other arbitrary practices in the business" (KCWU 1999: 87). Whilst women's decisions to run away can certainly be in part explained in this way, there is no doubt that women run away because of the anxieties generated by their romances and also the personal conflicts they often feel about lying to different customers-cum-boyfriends and concealing relationships from customers and bosses. However, the anxieties and tensions around boyfriends and romances also go beyond the clubs to when women run away. The romantic scars incurred after running away are also important to consider.

Romantic scars

I had just returned from my Christmas vacation in Australia and was sitting in my bedroom unpacking my clothes when my cell phone rang. Josie's name flashed on the screen, and I answered the phone eager to find out how everything was going in her new factory job near Songtan, where she went together with Honey after they both ran away from clubs in TDC. But my questions were quickly thwarted by the incessant sobbing that came down the other end of the line, "Sallie, please come to meet me in Songtan right now. I have a knife. I want to cut my wrists. Please come".

I hastily arranged a place to meet Josie and got straight on the train and bus that took me to Songtan. When I arrived an hour and a half later Josie was already sitting in the cafe with puffy red eyes, and I could see her face was swollen from crying. Her misadventures over the past month came spluttering forth as we sat in a quiet corner booth of the cafe. As I had half suspected, the problem was her ex-boyfriend, who was still based at Camp Casey in TDC. When Josie ran away she had done so with the expectation that she and her boyfriend would get married – a common enough occurrence for women who run away from *gijich'on* clubs (and discussed at length in chapter 6). But when she left TDC, her boyfriend began calling her less frequently. The week before I came back from Australia he did not call her at all and told her he was too busy to meet up with her on Sunday, her only day off from the factory. Josie suspected he was seeing other women in the clubs and called one of her Filipina friends in TDC, who confirmed her worst fears. When Josie called her boyfriend and confronted him about his liaisons with other entertainers he told her she should focus on her new job and forget about him; their relationship was apparently getting 'too difficult' and she was making too many demands on him. Josie was devastated and fell into a state of depression; she had no-one to talk to at the factory apart from Honey, and her fatigue from the twelve- to fourteen-hour shifts at the factory was making her even more mentally exhausted. The dormitory was located on the premises of the factory, rendering it difficult for women to go out during the week, and so Josie was resigned to staying in her room and mulling over her life whilst lying on her bed during her time off. It was at this point that I received her phone call.

That day I convinced Josie to go back to work at the factory and to think about other outlets for her social life. The Filipino Church service in Hyehwa-dong every Sunday had become a popular outlet for Filipino migrant workers to gather. Filipino food stalls set up outside the gates of the church, and the Centre organised various sports competitions. I knew I did not sound convincing when I made these suggestions, but Josie did not want counselling; she just wanted to talk to someone who understood her situation. There was nothing else to suggest. Ironically, moving away from TDC left her without the opportunity to consolidate her relationship with her GI boyfriend. For this reason, many other women chose to forego factory work away from where their boyfriends are based in order to continue 'working' on their relationship and, importantly, monitoring their boyfriends' off-base activities in the clubs (as we shall see in chapter 6).

Josie's experience illustrates one of the key dangers for migrant entertainers in forming romantic relationships with customers in the context of their club work. Failed relationships can affect the emotional and, sometimes, physical health of women like Josie who run away in the hope contained in insincere promises of love and marriage. In all, five women I knew through my research in Korea either threatened or attempted to commit suicide after running away from their club work. In all cases these dramatic actions were related to failed relationships with GI boyfriends, rather than conditions in the clubs themselves.

The position of the women as irregular migrants also has considerable bearing on the dynamics of these physical expressions of depression. Women become irregular migrants once they run away from their workplaces in Korea as they are not allowed to change employers without their promoter's permission, and many promoters refuse to give this to women. Thus, as irregular migrants upon running away, the women come to live clandestine lives, whether working in factories or staying in *gijich'on* areas as girlfriends in rented apartments. This presents enormous difficulties in cases where women require formal medical assistance. Anna, whom I knew through Amy and the other Pop Store Club women, exemplified this dilemma of illegality. One of the Pop Store Club women, Louisa, called me and urged me to come to her apartment because one of her friends, Anna, had overdosed, and they did not know what to do. Because I was only five minutes' walk away I rushed around to the apartment to find Anna lying on the bed. "She's swallowed sleeping tablets, Sallie. We don't know how many, but she won't wake up". Having no training in basic first aid I was at a complete loss as to the appropriate medical treatment and also started to panic. I decided to call Father Glenn; he would know what to do. Father Glenn told me over the phone to take Anna to the local hospital in TDC, which was about a ten-minute taxi ride away. I related this suggestion to Louisa. "No. Absolutely not. We can't take Anna there. She's illegal; she will be deported". Of all the possible responses Louisa could have made, this was the one I had least expected. But she was right; if we took Anna to the hospital she would eventually be deported. I had seen this happen a few weeks earlier with another woman, Jane, who had called the police to complain about her Ecuadorian migrant worker boyfriend beating her up. Both she and her boyfriend were detained and subsequently deported for overstaying their visas. Jane had been held in the Mok-dong Immigration Detention Centre in Seoul for two weeks before she was eventually deported. The only reason Jane was eventually able to leave Korea was because I gathered the necessary sum of KRW 260,000 and bought her one-way air ticket from Seoul to Manila, which was passed to her via an immigration officer at the Mok-dong centre (discussed further in chapter 7). I knew the same fate would await Anna. Finally we called one of Louisa's GI friends, who was a trained medic. He assisted us, and Anna survived. It turned out that the whole debacle created by swallowing sleeping tables was the result of Anna's break-up with her GI boyfriend the previous day. Anna's situation also illustrates the importance these women attached to retaining their transnational positionings in Korea, especially where their attempts to re-work their situations were not (yet) successfully assured.

The danger for women like Anna and Josie is that the fine line they walk between romantic love and the heuristic and rational pursuit of relationships embedded in the desire to pursue upward transnational mobility can, and often does, break down. Zheng (2009: 231), in her ethnography of internal migrant Chinese hostesses, also found that many of the hostesses in her study who succumbed to men's romance "get lost in the game and are left broken-hearted", often self-inflicting cigarette burns or knife cuts on their bodies to remind them of their failures, both to control their emotional desires and their abandonment by the men upon whom these are centred. So it was with women in Korea's *gijich'on* who run away from the clubs having truly fallen for their boyfriend and pinning all their aspirational hopes of mobility on him. If the relationship fails, love *and* mobility, which are interminably mixed together, both are lost.

In their respective discussions of migrant sex workers in Europe, Andrijasevic (2003) and Gulcur and Ilkkaracan (2002) suggest that irregular status induces additional forms of violence in negotiating the already uneven terrain of performing sex work. These relate to police harassment and bribes, inability to report rape, physical abuse or theft of money by clients and an array of other experiences of violence and injustice at the hands of both clients and authorities. Although their findings are underscored by the experiences of my participants in Korea, what I found quite specific to Korea's *gijich'on* was the extent to which negotiations of physical and emotional violence *after* exiting the clubs were also dramatically affected by the relationship women had to Korea's migration regime. Specifically, their irregular status as runaways impinged negatively on their ability to negotiate harm. Interventions, medical and therapeutic, fell back on friends and social networks of 'trusted others' (like myself and Louisa's GI friend) who would ensure that women's position in Korea were not compromised by an unnecessary collision with the state. In this sense the networks that helped women make informal compensation claims that were discussed in chapter 3 also provided other forms of support for women in ways that were often serendipitous and unanticipated, even on occasion by the women themselves.

It is also fair to say that in Korea's *gijich'on* by far the most common cause of women's anxieties concerned ruptures within their romantic liaisons with customers-cum-boyfriends, especially post-exit from the club. Running away from a *gijich'on* club entails considerable deliberation by women, and writ large into many women's decisions is the prospect of a long-term relationship with a boyfriend. Because women rarely receive all, or even any, money from their sexual and intimate labour in the clubs, they often have literally nothing when they run away. The failure of these relationships to *materialise* as women had hoped leads to various attempts at self-harm, including attempted suicide.

Conclusion

A singular sexual slavery discourse of trafficked women does not capture the agency of *gijich'on* entertainers as they negotiate work, relationships and their financial and emotional security. Nor does it fully capture the roles of many of the

GIs who frequent the camp town clubs, who are often a priori viewed as customers or clients complicit in the sexual and financial exploitation of the women by the media and NGOs. Often this is true, but, just as the women cannot be easily located as sex slaves, neither can these men be understood only as customers under the auspices of exploitative masculine/militaristic desires. This understanding of customers in prevailing discourses on sex trafficking pits encounters between customers and entertainers/sex workers as always exploitative. Liz Kelly (2002: 25), for example, has described situations where "the despair that some women feel can be seen in the fact that some risk (and sustain) physical injury through jumping out windows (they are locked in rooms), rather than continue their current existence. Others 'escape' through establishing relationships with customers". Relationships with customers thus tend to be dismissed as a strategy to facilitate women's escape from their places of work, even though ethnographic work across diverse contexts has revealed the prominence of romance and its anxieties in women's narratives about their experiences (Cheng 2010, Parrenas 2011, Zheng 2009, Brennan 2004).

The women I knew in Korea certainly exerted considerable agency in strategising about their choices while labouring in the clubs, and the particular conditions of their work often have an important bearing on whether or not they enter a romantic relationship with a customer. But failing to then unpack the experiences of the women and men who enter these relationships, the often confused meanings they attach to them and the longer-term consequences of these romances is to perpetuate an instrumentalist view of such relationships and reinforce a reductionist understanding of the women's participation in them as located only through a singular 'victim' status. Romance and human rights abuses are interconnected sites through which agency is asserted and (dis)empowerment experienced. This chapter has attempted to demonstrate that many of the women and men who are subjects of these sexual economies do not necessarily construe their encounters entirely – or even predominantly – through commodified or exploitative lenses. *Gijich'on* entertainers are not simply victims, nor are clients always exploiters of women's sexuality. Recognising this can help us move beyond essentialist descriptions that tie these subjects exclusively to sexual exploitation and commodification. The women in my study privileged the subjects of relationships, love, marriage, work and their futures. Neglecting these women's relationships with GIs in the context of discussions about how best to assist trafficked entertainers only acts to reinforce circumscribed understandings of these women's lives and everyday preoccupations (see also Cheng 2010). Whilst, for example, these relationships initially allow women to assert a degree of agency and control over their situations, these power reversals are often incomplete, fractured and short-lived. Although some women are considered by their peers to be success stories, having left the club and married their GI boyfriend, other women attempt suicide or experience emotional breakdowns, abandonment, lower self-esteem and heightened, rather than reduced, emotional and financial vulnerability through these relationships. Finally, focusing on the emotional and relational lives of these women and the conflicts and challenges that their work and positions as trafficked women creates helps establish their identities in terms that recognise the considerable agency they attempt to assert in their lives abroad. Further, relationships with GI customers often come to play a pivotal role in these women's imaginings about their futures once they are in Korea and, sometimes, prior to their migration from the Philippines as well as after they return. Thus, what often starts as a one-year stint in Korea as an entertainer often becomes a much longer-term transnational movement in which their futures become intimately intertwined with those of their boyfriends. In this sense Korea comes to figure as a transnational platform, rather than a destination in and of itself. Seeing Filipina entertainers as transnational subjects who resist exploitative aspects of their deployment and who negotiate and strategise in/from their locations in *gijich'on* clubs enables a focus on what registers and frames these women use to resist their marginality and re-craft their mobility projects

Existing work on both Filipina entertainers in Korea (Cheng 2010) and hostesses performing sexual and intimate labour in other contexts (Brennan 2004, Kempadoo 1999) highlights the meanings and implications of romances with customers, including the ways these strategies can sometimes break down after exit. Like these works, this chapter attempts to unsettle normative renderings of sex trafficked women as always and necessarily sexually exploited by customers by focusing on various ways the discourse of 'love' is strategically deployed by the women. In focusing on narratives of love and romantic relationships with boyfriends amongst Filipinas working in Korea's *gijich'on* I demonstrate that romance as a strategy for reducing vulnerabilities and maximising opportunities in transnational migration can be never singularly celebrated or admonished. Many of the women who participated in my research experienced highly exploitative situations while working in Korea. It is simply that such abuses do not capture the complexity of these women's experiences (as also suggested in chapter 4), or the strategic use of romance and love that the women attempt to employ in negotiating their everyday lives, relationships and status in Korea or the self-understanding and imaginings about their futures the women are constantly attempting to shape whilst in *gijich'on*.

Notes

1 In South Korea there is a period of three years' compulsory military service for all adult males. Some of these Korean soldiers are conscripted to the USFK (United States Forces Korea) for the period of their military service and become based at US military installations in South Korea. They are known by the acronym KATUSA (Korean Augmentee to the United States Army).
2 I knew from Sunny, the Korean manager in Harley's Club with whom I was on friendly terms, that some bar managers viewed the Filipinas and Russian entertainers as 'younger sisters' to be looked after in the club. Sunny herself referred to the Filipinas working in Harley's Club as "my girls". Perhaps this relationship is explained by the fact that many of the Korean bar managers were former entertainers and had to endure the stricture of the club owners themselves previously.

6 Running to the future

My phone buzzed in the pocket of my jeans. It was a text message from Maricel: "Can u meet us for lunch in Songtan today, Sallie? It's important that we meet asap". I texted back "ok" and made the one-and-a-half-hour bus trek down to Songtan from Seoul. I met them at their apartment, still having no clues as to why they were keen to meet up with me so urgently. We decided on a popular sushi place in one of the back lanes of Songtan, where we sat in a quiet corner booth. We'd missed the lunch rush and so had virtually the whole restaurant to ourselves. After eating and chatting about the latest happenings in the club, Maricel finally spoke up. "Sallie, our contracts all expire in a week, and we will be sent back to the Philippines. We want to talk to you about our options". I asked her and the others what they would like to do. Three clearly well-thought answers were immediately disclosed, "We could work in a factory, or we could go back to the Philippines or we could try with our boyfriends". Notably, taking a new contract in a different club was not presented as an option. Running away to work in a factory would automatically confer irregular status, but certainly far higher salaries than they ever received working in the club. Going with their GI boyfriends would mean entrusting their entire futures to the success of the relationship. Very few women worked *and* stayed with their GI boyfriends after exiting the clubs as their boyfriends would not allow it. Anna's dramatic step of overdosing, as described in the previous chapter, although extreme, clearly exemplifies what can happen if these relationships go awry.

We spent three hours mulling over the different options that day, and still no decision was conclusively reached. One thing was clear, though; the women wanted to make sure they remained closely connected to each other, whatever option they chose. When I came to visit them at work three nights later, the women had made a collective decision; they would all go back to the Philippines. Eva and Jules had boyfriends who were supposedly willing to continue supporting them from there, Maricel was tired and just wanted to go home to her family, AJ and Sandra also wanted to spend some time at home before looking for another contract as an entertainer in a different country where they thought conditions might be better. Two days later Maricel texted to say they were at the airport. The next time I saw Maricel and Eva was six months later in Bulacan in central Luzon, where they were both living. AJ was preparing to fly to Hong Kong, Sandra was pregnant to her Filipino boyfriend and was not going anywhere and Jules was anxiously waiting for her boyfriend to fulfil his remittance and marriage promises to her.

108 *Running to the future*

For all but a tiny handful of women, exiting the club is a long-drawn-out process in which options are carefully weighed and choices thought through to the fullest extent possible. Advice is sought and given by compatriots or knowledgeable individuals such as Father Glenn, inquiries about factories made, intentions of boyfriends confirmed and the risks of running away continually weighed against these options. Whilst much of the literature on trafficking suggests that exit is a dramatic event and an immediate, desperate response to heightened abuse and exploitation, this was not the case for women I came to know in Korea's *gijich'on*. The *gijich'on* are what we might refer to as 'rescue absent' contexts, meaning that rescue as the prevailing and normative model for exiting trafficking situations was not a significantly invoked mode of departure from the clubs. Only two groups of women who participated in my research were 'rescued' by police, and in their cases links to trafficking were not the major reasons for their removal from the clubs.[1] Often the impetus to run came from a singular incident, as in Lisa's disclosure in chapter 4 of her beating at the hands of others working in the club and her consequent miscarriage, but in these cases the intent to leave the club was usually already well established, even if the immediate plans for the future were not yet clearly put in place.

Nina Glick-Schieller et al. (1992) suggest that the positions and identities of transnational migrants are inherently unstable as they negotiate (changing) aspirations, expectations and stereotypes placed on them by other migrants and groups within the host society, as well as disappointing economic and social circumstances in the destination. As migrants respond to the multiple possibilities that transnational positions can offer, these negotiations become more intense and, often, complicated (Smith and Guarnizo 1998). This chapter draws on the proposition that migrants' agency should neither be overstated nor overly sentimentalized, thus pointing to "a more complicated view of agency and selfhood" which would be capable of recognizing contradictions, uncertainties and anxieties as migrants attempt to "construct new arrangements of meaning and power as they craft their lives" (Kondo 1990: 225). The challenges required in negotiations of mobility are as such not just one-off matters that occur at a single point in a migrant's trajectory; they are ever present, even within a single destination, and thus reflect these inherent instabilities. With this in mind, running away from a workplace in a migrant destination is a means by which migrants aim to recover mobility aspirations lost in the mismatch between their expectations about work, salary and social life and a reality of exploitation and marginalisation. In discussing the practice of former Filipina entertainers running away from their Japanese husbands in rural Japan, Lieba Faier (2008: 634) calls this "runaway agency", by which she means "underground micromovements: disjointed and frantic patterns of small-scale movements made by individual migrants in an effort to manoeuvre around dominant social relations and legal structures they find abroad". Whilst Filipina entertainers' movements in Korea are not necessarily frantic or impulsive (as suggested in the vignette at the outset of this chapter) the significance of Faier's characterisation resides in her suggestion that runaway discourses are *shared* and so social and friendship networks and *gijich'on*-based communities comprise an important element in their realisation. Thus, in Korea's *gijich'on* runaway discourses circulate through such networks and become emplaced, crystallising into various options like factory work or marriage to an ex-customer.

In the chapter I explore the principal and secondary subject positions in which "runaway agency" crystallises in Korea – namely, the bride and the factory worker respectively. Through each I wish to suggest, in line with Glick-Schiller et al. (1992), that new negotiations and uncertainties emerge as these transnational trajectories are played out, many of which are tied in formative ways to women's prior positionings as migrant entertainers. By exploring the negotiations that accompany the subject positions of bride and factory worker we can also recognise how the realities of these transnational negotiations "blur the artificial and still dominant analytical division between marriage migrants and labour migrants" (Lauser 2008: 85) to an approach that instead embraces an emphasis on how women "negotiate their options within a transnational migratory space" (Lauser 2008: 88)

The aim of this chapter is to explore migrant entertainers' post-exit trajectories in Korea and the ways they attempt to craft futures beyond the clubs, but almost always in ways intimately tied to their sojourns in the clubs. I argue in this and the following two chapters for the need to unfix the 'sex trafficking scenario' from one in which exit necessarily entails intervention in the form of rescue, rehabilitation, repatriation and reintegration to a prior living situation, usually in the 'home country', and in ways which usually mark an end to transnational mobilities. I suggest instead that futures are crafted in the main by staying put in Korea, at least in the short term, but with longer-term strategies for upward and outward mobility from/through Korea in mind. These strategies form the crux of women's efforts to move beyond the club, both literally and figuratively, in ways that are not tied to clichéd scenarios of removal and intervention. However, as with the previous chapters, I refrain from overly sentimentalising such projects; running does not mean that these aspirations become within easy reach, even where they are carefully planned and crafted. In fact the artificial binary between 'bad' space in the club and 'good' space beyond it constructs a misleading interpretation of the continual negotiations and their micro-geographies that characterise women's trajectories upon running away.

Runaway brides

As we saw in the previous chapter, prominent in women's decisions to run away was their unwillingness to continue to endure the tensions between their work in the clubs and their romantic relationships. Thus, although their decisions to run away were informed by a coalescence of factors, their relationships nonetheless assumed paramount importance amongst these. Once they ran away both Anna and Josie became illegal migrants in Korea, and their relationships with their boyfriends took on a formative role in shaping their migration trajectories, though in disparate and sometimes unexpected ways.

When Filipina entertainers run away from clubs in Korea's *gijich'on* areas to marry or cohabit with their GI boyfriend or to find a GI with whom to build a romantic relationship, they are attempting to sculpt their identities and futures in

110 *Running to the future*

more positive and self-fulfilling terms. Here I explore exactly how these women negotiate the shift from being migrant entertainers to 'runaway brides' or 'GI wives' – both terms used by these Filipinas in describing themselves. The label of entertainer continues to influence women's attempts to move beyond the club, and women must continually negotiate – both individually and in their relationships – as a result of their shifting labour and migration status while abroad.

In this part of the chapter I discuss the experiences of some of the many Filipinas who ran away from the clubs where they worked but remain in Korea and continue to live in *gijich'on* areas with their husbands or boyfriends. In these locations the women are intensely subject to the stigma of the 'entertainer-prostitute' label because they continue to reside near their former workplaces and interact with ex-customers. Their anxieties around shifting status and identity take on a particularly exaggerated significance in their everyday lives and relationships in this context. Their marriages to GIs consequently suffer numerous conflicts resulting from tensions around issues of fidelity, money and independence. The label and experiences of Filipinas as 'entertainers' – or as GIs like to call the women, 'juicy girls' – can thus profoundly affect the dynamics of their marriages and relationships and the ability of these Filipina migrants to craft transnational futures beyond the club. This stigma, which Kelly (2008) discusses at length in her ethnography of Mexico's largest regulated brothel, not only plagues women in their workplaces, but also makes strategies for upward and outward mobility difficult to realise as women are hampered by identities and roles located within their club origin. In this sense the discussion in this part of the chapter takes issue with the view purported by some that sex work should be treated like any other work and should not be regarded as a significant part of one's identity (Kempadoo 1998). Whilst "this attitude removes stigmas associated with victimization" (Tyner 2002: 110), the experiences of women in this study point to the inadequacy of such a view in understanding the concrete challenges women face in re-sculpting their identities beyond the prostitute-entertainer label.

I draw on the stories of four of the women I knew well in TDC – Valerie, Grace, Lisa and Mary – to illustrate the tensions in negotiating post-club futures in Korea through romance and marriage. I was able to gain insights into the 'everyday' in these negotiations because over a six-month period I stayed in Lisa and her boyfriend's apartment whenever I was in TDC. Occasionally I stayed in Grace's apartment once she had moved in with her GI husband. These four women ran away from USA Club together in September 2002. Both Lisa and Mary had serious boyfriends at the time and ran away with the intention of marrying their boyfriends. It was their boyfriends who found apartments for the women to rent in American Alley after they fled and who took care of rent and other expenses. Valerie and Grace also had boyfriends but did not leave the clubs with the sole intention of marrying them. Valerie shared Mary's apartment and Grace shared Lisa's apartment in the few weeks after running away. Lisa and Grace hardly left their apartment for over two months after running away because of the initial danger of being caught – either by their manager, their boss in the club or the immigration authorities.

Valerie and Chris

Valerie came to Korea in August 2001 at age sixteen (her false passport stated she was twenty-two) and worked in USA Club for just over eleven months before running away. She has four younger brothers and two small children of her own back in the Philippines. She had her first child when she was thirteen and split with her boyfriend after her second child was born a few years later. Valerie's father abandoned the family, so her mother takes care of Valerie's brothers and her own two children. As both the oldest child and a mother, Valerie was expected to support all these dependents as best she could, which prompted her to come to Korea to work.

After running away Valerie faced a highly uncertain future in Korea. Although she had an exclusive boyfriend, Chris, she reflected, "I love him, but I think he is too young for me [he was nineteen at the time]. I'm young, but my mind is older than him because I have experienced a lot". After six weeks of hiding in Mary's apartment Valerie went with Grace to work in a factory in the nearby town to Uijongbu, but she left the factory after hired thugs from TDC who were working for the club apparently contacted the factory manager looking for Valerie and Grace. Grace recounted the incident to me: The manager called Valerie and Grace into his office and told them he had just received a phone call from a man (who the manager presumed was mafia) asking if two new girls had started working at that factory. The manager said that he did have some new girls working there. The caller then said to the manager that if he held the girls there until he arrived he would pay the manager off. Grace said, "We were so lucky that the manager is a nice guy and he told us about that. Valerie and I discussed what to do and we decided to pack our things and run away back here [to the apartment in TDC]". So they both returned to American Alley and continued to lead an existence based on eluding the police, Immigration officials, the club owner and these thugs. In the interim, Mary had managed to successfully marry her GI fiancée.

Having to act like a fugitive and unable to work in a factory without fear of getting caught, the possibility of marriage became more and more appealing to Valerie, so she broke up with Chris briefly and began contacting some of her previous customers in the club. She hoped to find someone to support her and provide her with a fiancée or marriage visa that would restore her legal status in Korea. However, as Valerie recounted, none of the other GIs wanted to be 'serious' with her, and in late October she decided to change her original decision and marry Chris. They were married on November 4, 2002, and soon thereafter moved into their own apartment in American Alley.

Grace and Stuart

Grace's parents abandoned her when she was a child. Her father physically abused her mother, so Grace was forced to live with her grandfather in Manila. She said, "As far as I'm concerned I don't have any parents. My grandfather is my family. He is the only one I care about". Grace was only halfway through her second contract when she ran away from the club. Although she had never worked in the sex or nightlife entertainment industry before coming to Korea in mid-2001, Grace became extremely competent at her work and continuously earned the second highest sum of money of all the USA Club entertainers. Nonetheless, she had not always been so enthusiastic about her work. She revealed the heartbreak she experienced over a failed romance with a GI, whom she caught cheating on her, during her first contract period in Korea. She said that from then on, "All I did for a long time was drink and have fun and get fucked up. I didn't care about anything or anyone".

Since running away Grace had several boyfriends before she finally became engaged to Stuart (twenty-one years old) in January 2003. When she ran away she had an exclusive boyfriend, Craig (nineteen years old), who had promised to support her financially if she decided to leave the club. In reflecting on her relationship with Craig she told me,

> I ran away because I wanted to change my life. The club was like hell and I didn't want to do like that anymore. Craig said he would pay for everything if I ran away, so I decided to leave the club with Lisa. But Craig hasn't paid anything yet. I paid [rent for her share of Lisa's apartment] out of my own money to Lisa because I am so embarrassed. That's okay, I don't need money from him.

Because of Craig's lack of support, Grace eventually decided to leave him. She called her regular customers from USA Club in the hope that one would agree to be her boyfriend. After several weeks of long phone conversations – many of which Lisa and I had to endure when I stayed in Lisa's apartment – and dates with numerous GIs, she became involved with Andrew (twenty-three years old), who wanted to marry Grace and support her in an apartment of her own in American Alley. However, although Andrew was separated from his wife back in the United States, they were not yet divorced, and this proved a financial burden on Andrew, since he also had a one-year-old son to support back in the United States. Grace was concerned that Andrew's continuing connection with his ex-wife could compromise his potential as a marriage partner. She said,

> I think he is the one. I haven't felt like this about anyone since my ex-fiancée [her first boyfriend when she came to Korea in 2001]. But there is a problem. You know, he still has a wife back in America. They aren't together but he still has to pay for her. That uses up all his salary. He only has about USD 20 for spending over here out of each salary. So he doesn't have any money. He said to me he will go back to America in January for leave and he is going to fix the divorce then. I said I would wait for him to do that . . . so I'll just see what happens. I don't want another guy with no money. I have to think about my future.

Grace had begun to think of her future as exclusively bound to a financially stable husband, and even though she left USA Club for other reasons – because she was "sick of the work" and wanted to "change her life" – she soon became preoccupied with marrying a GI. She began to feel inadequate in comparison to Mary, Valerie and Lisa. Phone calls and dates became an important investment in her future.

While Andrew was in the United States, Grace returned to Uijongbu from Lisa's apartment in TDC and began working in another factory, even though she complained that the work was extremely difficult in the frigid below-twenty-degree temperatures of winter in the north of South Korea. She began drifting between the house of one of her Filipina friends who ran away from USA Club several months prior to Grace and the house of a Filipino male co-worker at the factory who was providing Grace with a place to eat and sleep in return for sexual favours.

In Andrew's absence Grace was becoming increasingly agitated and obsessed with the idea of finding a GI to marry. Both Mary and Valerie were already married by this stage, and Lisa, who was engaged to David, was only awaiting the arrival of documents from the Philippines before she too would marry. Grace wanted her own marriage to be based on genuine love but recognized that this was unlikely given her work history in the club and the type of men she formed relationships within that context:

> I will wish for myself to find a good guy and fall in love. I want to find the right guy and get married. I want that so badly . . . I want a guy who is quiet and doesn't just say "I love you, I love you", like that. Most of the guys I know say "I love you" so easily and I don't even know them very well. I don't want a guy like that. I'm sick of being with guys like that.

The discourse of love which was central to Grace's – and indeed Lisa's and Valerie's – marriage aspirations were noted in Lieba Faier's (2008) study of Filipina entertainers and their Japanese husbands. She notes, "Love is a powerful condition of these women's transnational lives, a term for global self-making that is made meaningful through and that enables their transnational everyday practices" (Faier 2008: 157–8). Whilst Andrew was away on leave in the United States, Grace visited a friend's apartment in American Alley for a New Year's party and met another GI, Stuart. Stuart had recently divorced his American wife of two months. Within six weeks of their meeting Stuart and Grace became engaged, and he rented the apartment next to Lisa's where they lived briefly and where I sometimes stayed whilst in TDC. Andrew returned from the United States to find that he was too late. Grace confided in me a few months later that she still loved Andrew and was sorry she had chosen a quick compromise with Stuart, whom she married in March 2003. She was resigned to her marriage with Stuart, despite her continued love for Andrew.

Lisa and David

Lisa arrived in Korea in June 2001 and worked in USA Club for just under twelve months before running away. Lisa had two serious boyfriends when she was working in VIP Club, including David, whom she married in February 2003. David spends as much time with Lisa as possible and, since they married, has been allowed to live off-post with her in their apartment. When men marry in-country they are provided with different accommodation from those personnel who live in the communal barracks and are also eligible for a financial subsidy to cover the cost of renting a house or apartment. Unlike Valerie and Grace, Lisa never had any doubts about the direction in which her future would unfold when she fled from the club. Not long after she ran away, David destroyed the cell phone she possessed where the phone numbers of her ex-customers were stored. She and David were very much in love when I knew her in 2002 and 2003, and their first apartment together was adorned with photographs of them together and presents they have given each other. Lisa communicates regularly with David's family back in the United States, and his family, in turn, often sent them small gifts.

"You can take the woman out of the club, but . . . "

The saying "You can take the woman out of the club, but you can't take the club out of the woman" was one that was repeated to me many times by GIs who were in a relationship with a runaway entertainer. Although it jarred to hear this, and I would often argue with GIs when they verbalised this platitude, I nonetheless knew it was not something to be ignored or dismissed since the saying undoubtedly encapsulated the ways runaway entertainers were positioned in *gijich'on* and in the post-club relationships they formed. Indeed, while women ran away so they could take back some of the control over the crafting of their lives and futures, the sentiments behind this platitude often left women reeling in the wake of a continued tide of stigma that embedded them further in the entertainer subject.

For Lisa, Grace, Mary and Valerie, marriage was supposed to fulfil some of the same objectives as migration for work, including financial security, restored legal status and continued residence in a transnational space where they perceived their life chances to be enhanced. In addition, for Lisa and Grace at least the aspiration to marry carried with it the hope of fulfilling a personal desire for romantic love and a stable family life, things that eluded both women in their pre-migration lives and, for Grace, was bitterly denied during her first contract period in Korea. Yet despite their 'success' in exercising considerable agency to craft post-club, transnational futures by marrying GIs, all four women experienced heightened anxiety in their marital relationships. It is bitterly ironic that the cause of this anxiety was their previous work as entertainers: while this status allowed them to get to Korea and meet GIs in the first place, it also stigmatized them in the eyes of their husbands and boyfriends, as well as in interactions with others in and beyond *gijich'on*, and influenced, to various degrees, their own manoeuvrings and relationships. The result was conflicts and anxiety expressed predominantly around three, constantly intersecting issues: money, financial and personal independence and fidelity.

Conflicts over money

After Valerie married Chris she was forced to return to factory work to support herself. Chris was not willing to provide her with money or pay the rent on their apartment. This is despite the fact that the USFK provides an additional allowance of approximately USD 500 per month for military personnel supporting a spouse in Korea. Chris had also told Lisa he was not going to repay a considerable loan Lisa had extended to Valerie, nor was he prepared to assist Valerie in repatriating money to the Philippines to continue supporting her family. In early December 2002 Valerie quit working in the factory because the factory was bitterly cold and she could not perform the dexterous manual work. Back in American Alley she proceeded to establish pen pal relationships via email with three other men (two in the United States and another GI stationed in Korea), despite her marriage to Chris. When I asked Valerie about these pen pal relationships with other men she told me she felt financially insecure in her relationship with Chris and was hoping to divorce him if she could craft a 'serious' relationship with one of these other three men. For Valerie the "work for a marriage", as she put it to me, continued even after she had succeeded in marrying a GI precisely because of the mismatch between financial expectations and reality in her marriage to Chris.

Lisa also encountered substantial problems in her marriage relating to money and family obligations back in the Philippines. I was surprised at this because I knew David adored Lisa and loved her deeply; he would do anything to make her happy, and this made her the envy of all her friends. On one occasion Lisa's brother had been involved in a car accident in Manila, where the car he was driving had seriously injured a pedestrian. The family of the injured man demanded USD 500 in compensation to avoid formal charges. Because Lisa had no money of her own and did not want to ask David for help she was unsure how she was expected to raise such a substantial sum. We discussed this one day when she was trying to work out how to raise the money:

L: I don't want that kind of relationship with him.
S: What relationship?
L: Where he thinks I'm just using him for money.
S: But aren't financial issues and problems part of a marriage?
L: That may be the case for you, because you weren't working in a club before, but for me there is an idea that the GIs have that you are just using them for money when you marry them.
S: So it's because you worked in the club before that they have this idea?
L: Of course. We have to do like that in the club. I told you that before. The GIs think we are still like that now [after running away]. And in some cases it is true. But it's not true for me – you know that. So I must make sure David doesn't come to think I'm like some gold digger. So I can't discuss this problem about my brother with him.

As my conversation with Lisa reveals, runaway entertainers are acutely conscious of the stereotype of Filipina entertainers as 'gold diggers'. Reflecting on the potentially negative role this stereotype could play in her own marriage, Lisa decided to conceal her family problems from David. She eventually decided to solve this dilemma by selling three of her pieces of gold jewellery that she had bought herself whilst working in the club. She still had only raised USD 200 to send her brother and did not know what to do. She sent the USD 200 back to the Philippines and was still trying to save the additional money needed by taking money out of the food allowance David gave her each week, amongst other strategies.

For both Valerie and Lisa these conflicts with their partners occurred because Chris and David both saw their wives as largely liberated from the constraints of family obligations, since they had gone abroad to work, presumably, for themselves. For Valerie this manifested itself in Chris's refusal to assist with her family obligations in the Philippines, and for Lisa it meant concealing such obligations so they did not produce conflict in the first place. In addition, because Chris met Valerie at a time when she demonstrated considerable independence and self-reliance, and where her natal family was absent, it was difficult for him to perceive of her requiring his continual financial support after marriage.

Financial (in)dependence and bored brides

When women leave the clubs and pursue relationships with their GI boyfriends some inequalities expressed within the context of their work are perpetuated, rather than ameliorated, because the women's dependence on their boyfriends and husbands generally increases. They may become pregnant, for example, or their partners may not allow them to work and so they lose whatever limited financial independence they might have had as entertainers. Lisa experienced problems as a result of this dependence. She would often say that she had to ask permission from David before she could go out of the house. Lisa also discovered she was pregnant about six weeks after she ran away from the club, and her baby was born in June 2003. Until she discovered she was pregnant she was intending to work part-time in a factory or to secure a job on nearby Camp Casey in one of the restaurants or the commissary. However, once her pregnancy was confirmed David would not allow her to work, so she spent her days cleaning their two-room apartment, preparing meals for David and walking down to the local market with me to go shopping or eat a meal. The dilemma Lisa experienced with regard to her brother's problem, discussed earlier, was undoubtedly compounded by Lisa's further financial dependence on David after she ran away. Asking for money from David would always require an explanation and rebuke from David about having her own family (with David and their unborn child) to think about now.

Similarly, when Grace became engaged to Stuart and moved into his apartment he made it clear he did not want her to go back to work in a factory. She recounted, "He wants me to be at home when he finished work each day. That was a condition of him getting me the place [apartment]". Whilst Lisa would keep herself extremely busy in her apartment by taking up embroidery and going shopping in the market, Grace became bored with the idea of being a full-time housewife. Although she had considerable freedom to move around American Alley without Stuart's permission – even going with me back into clubs on several occasions – on every single occasion I visited her the apartment was spotless and she would flop on the sofa, light a cigarette and launch into a series of complaints about married life that invariably began with, "I'm so bored". My presence offered Grace an outlet to get dressed up, put on make-up and go downrange. She knew she would not get in trouble for going out with me since, as an Australian woman perceived to be associated with the Filipino Catholic Church in Seoul, Grace could, in Stuart's words, "not be led astray when with me". Grace's attempts to overcome boredom were not only aimed at finding something to do, but also at reclaiming her sense of self as a young, attractive woman. Getting dressed up and going downrange provided an opportunity to be 'admired' by GIs and, on several occasions, be flattered by offers of being bought a drink.

Apart from going downrange, Grace's attempts to overcome the boredom of married life were manifest in her gambling habit. After a few weeks of married life she began to visit the apartment of another Filipina, where lengthy card games would be held each day involving substantial sums of money. When I asked about why she wanted to get involved in this, Grace replied,

> It's fun because, like, what else am I going to do. Plus I can use the money, coz I don't have any money that's mine. Stuart gives me an allowance and if I double it with money from cards he doesn't know.

In fact, Grace accrued a gambling debt of over US$2,000, which included money she had withdrawn from Stuart's bank account without his knowledge. Grace justified her gambling habit as a means to simultaneously overcome her boredom and restore her financial independence. Each justification can be read as a reflection of Grace's emerging views about her experiences in her married life (tedious and generally unfulfilling) and the importance she continued to attach to having her own money. Because Grace earned a great deal of money through her work in the club, it was difficult to accept reliance on only the small allowance Stuart gave her each pay.

Infidelity and trust

Whilst Valerie compromised her marital relationship with Chris by engaging in pen pal exchanges with other men, she was not the only one to experience conflicts over infidelity. Just before Christmas 2003, an argument almost led to David and Lisa's breakup. When I arrived to stay with Lisa in her TDC apartment one day on I found her extremely upset, and she recounted to me what had happened:

> I'm fine now. But I have a big problem last week and I get sick and stress. [What happened?] I don't know why, but one day David came to the apartment and he say to me, "Are you still keeping touch with some of your customers from the club?" I [was] shocked. I thought he knows my mind and my attitude is not like that. Remember I told you before that he broke my old cell phone with the phone numbers of my customers. Then he said to me, "How do I know the baby is really mine?" I felt sick. I couldn't believe he say like that. I told him, "You know I'm not like Valerie and Mary. Why do you say this?" You know the problem is that he thinks the other girls influence me because, like I told you, they still keep touch with some of their old customers. He

told me before not to let Mary or Valerie into his apartment. So we split and I asked him if he want me to move from the apartment because, you know, he's the one to pay [the rent]. He says it's okay for me to stay there. I cried and didn't sleep. Then, a couple of days later he came back. We sat outside on the step and talked and he started crying. He said he was sorry and we are together again now.

The anxiety Lisa experienced over David's suspicions arose because some of Lisa closest friends – including Grace and Mary – still kept in contact with customers from the club, even though they had both already married their GI boyfriends. In addition, the Internet liaisons Valerie had established with the three American men took place on David's computer, so David was aware of her indiscretions after marrying Chris. Had David decided not to return to Lisa she would have been left to find money for the following month's rent on the apartment and unable to undertake the difficult work required by factory jobs because of her pregnancy. In addition, Lisa was receiving regular medical check-ups during her pregnancy from the clinic on Camp Casey, so she would have had to find money for these medical expenses elsewhere and transfer to a Korean-run clinic, where English would not be spoken. Her living costs would have had to be covered somehow. Lisa's reflections on these potential problems were the obvious cause of the stress and sickness she felt the week before, while the thought of losing David left her emotionally distraught. Because she rarely engaged in sex work when she worked in the club (at David's request) and repatriated most of the money she did earn to the Philippines, she had very limited savings on which she could draw and had sold most of her jewellery.

Infidelity, financial conflict and independence formed the collective locus for the anxieties experienced by many women who ran away from the clubs. These anxieties in turn were tied to their continued positioning according to an entertainer identity, despite their exit from the clubs. Much of the recent literature on Filipina transnational migrants has focused on questions of identity in the context of migration, suggesting that – as for other migrants performing low-skilled work – negative host society attitudes and stereotypes are frequently encountered in transnational sites (for example, Chang and McAllister Groves 2000, Hildson and Giridharan 2008, Yeoh and Huang 1998 and 1999, Suzuki 2000a). The occupation of entertainer tends to be the most stigmatized category of overseas employment for Filipinas due to its apparent associations with prostitution. Suzuki (2000a), for example, discusses how in Japan groups of Filipinas married to Japanese men carefully distinguish themselves from the image of entertainer, exerting considerable agency in their own self-representation. Similarly, Chang and McAllister Groves (2000) identify various ways Filipina domestics in Hong Kong attempt to distance themselves from popular associations with the sex industry by actively contesting the 'prostitute label'. In both cases these women attempt to project themselves variously as good wives, filial daughters, responsible citizens and sexually moral women. A common theme running through such studies is the assertion of considerable agency by these women in shaping not only their experiences whilst abroad, but, more importantly, in contesting negative stereotypes through affirmative projects that lead to positive self-constructions. Amongst migrant entertainers, these negotiations are emotionally and relationally intense because running away produces new anxieties that are tied to both their previous work and their unstable legal and migration status in Korea and sense of selfhood after exiting the clubs.

Femmes fabrica (factory women)

As the experiences of Valerie and Grace reveal, the trajectories of women who run away from *gijich'on* clubs not only involve developing romantic relationships with GIs, but also taking factory work. The women I knew who went to work in factories either saw this as an opportunity to support themselves whilst also working towards developing a romance or as a livelihood option in its own right. Whilst far more women remain in *gijich'on* areas, such as American Alley in TDC or the backstreets of Songtan, after running away, factory work was clearly the second most common option for women who were not ready or willing to return to the Philippines. It is important to also consider the trajectories of these women in order to understand the complexities of the crafting of post-club futures for runaway entertainers. This is not only because the factories attracted many women – Russians as well as Filipinas – but because, like the status of GI bride, factory work/life was also fraught with anxieties, uncertainties and desires for a better life in ways that often underscored the concerns of women who remained to marry boyfriends. A brief narration of the post-club trajectories of Jane, Cecile and Charie illustrate the fluidity and contingency of projects that emerge from running away to factories and the ways they are multiply tied to desires for, and anxieties around, love, money and community. Some women, like Honey, had extremely positive experiences working in factories after running away from the clubs. Honey found a well-paying job on the periphery of Songtan and was able to remit almost USD 1,000 per month to her impoverished family in the Philippines. She enjoyed the independence the factory gave her as opposed to working in Papaya Club in TDC. She would take the bus to Hyehwa-dong in Seoul every Sunday to go to the Filipino mass and see her friends. Although ex-customers from Papaya Club and Filipino workers she met vied for her attentions, Honey remain single and returned to the Philippines at the next amnesty for illegal migrant workers, having earned enough money to support her family for the following year. But not all women were able to achieve this break from their previous stints in the clubs.

Jane

It was already 4 p.m. when I arrived with a Filipina NGO worker, Marissa, at a small freestanding dwelling in north Kyunggi province. We stepped off the bus in a predominantly semi-rural locale about forty-five-minute bus ride from Uijongbu. I remember thinking at the time that it was a far cry from the bustle and activity of TDC. Jane was waiting for us, and we stepped inside the house to a large room which contained a bed, couch, enormous television, small dining table and kitchen in the corner. Through another door was the bathroom, the only other room in the house. Jane was residing here with her Korean boyfriend, which surprised me as very few women developed romances with Korean men during or after working in the clubs.

This was the first time I had met Jane, who ran away from a TDC club several months prior to my arrival in Korea. Jane had migrated to Korea to work in a club as a singer and had trained professionally for this job in the Philippines. She was separated from her partner back in the Philippines and had two small children there who were being cared for by her sister. Like Grace and Valerie, Jane found work in a factory not far from TDC. She had been working there for two months when her Korean boss began making advances towards her. He had started offering her money for sexual favours, and she accepted because of the ill-treatment she began to receive when she refused. When she began going to his house for sex after her shifts ended, she became the main subject of gossip in the factory. She recalled that the other Filipinos in the factory associated her relationship with the manager as a result of her previous club work. She laughed when she recalled,

> They never asked me why I ran away. It was because of that work, so why do they say that I am just continuing like in the club. Stupid. If I wanted that work would I take the chance to run to the factory? Wouldn't I just stay in TDC?

Gossip can fulfil many functions for marginally situated migrant workers, including as a form of resistance to oppressive work regimes. But it can also be a means of social disciplining of other migrant workers:

> Migrants use gossip to enhance discipline and adhere to cultural and moral virtues embedded in their home society, to protect *amor propio* (self-respect), enhance *pakikisama* (belongingness) and support within the migrant community, and to avoid *hiya* or shame; most of all to keep their jobs.
> (Guy 2004)

Jane keenly felt the injustice in the comments of her fellow workers. It mirrored, in my view, the ways GIs often explained certain 'behaviours' of the women who ran away from the clubs and remained in TDC and spoke more broadly to the ways the job of entertainer is seen as an identity in ways that factory work is clearly not. Jane quit working at the factory because, as she said, she did not "have the energy" to defend herself against this gossip. She moved in to the Korean manager-cum-boyfriend's house and stopped working altogether, relying on his support for her daily needs.

One night not long after I met Jane she called me to say that she was back in TDC staying at the apartment of another Filipina with whom she had previously worked in the club. The previous night her Korean boyfriend had beat her violently and accused her of meeting other men in TDC whilst he was at work. In fact, Jane was spending time in TDC and other *gijich'on* areas, but this was tied to her volunteer work with the Filipina migrants' advocacy organisation, KASAMAKO, itself linked to the Centre in Hyehwa-dong. Jane would sometimes go to the clubs and talk to the women, asking if there was anything she could do for them. She spent a lot of time at one particular club in TDC where there was karaoke and would usually end up singing there.

Jane's Korean boyfriend had a history of being abusive towards her. The first day I met her we saw bruises on her legs and arms as she walked around the house in her shorts and T-shirt. So it was not surprising that Jane had left him. But when I met Jane later in TDC she told me:

> I didn't leave him just because he hit me sometimes. Of course I was scared about that and I knew I would not stay with that guy for a long time because of that attitude. But I left him because of his words. I already got accusations from my friends at the factory, and now my boyfriend was laying his suspicion on me. I'm not with other guys, even though I keep touch with some of my ex-customers. There is no reason to accuse me like that.

Whilst Jane was back in TDC with no job and little money and mulling over her options, she met one of her ex-customers from the club, a Peruvian man named Luis. Luis was a factory worker and told her he could get her another job in the factory where he was employed. Jane went with him, and they soon started a live-in relationship, working and living together in the factory. Momentarily, Jane was satisfied with her life in Korea, and for the first time she made enough money to send back to her kids in the Philippines. But this situation did not last long. Six weeks after Jane began cohabiting with Luis she called the police in a state of panic to come and arrest Luis because "he was drunk and hurting me". She recalled how, in hindsight, this was a rash action. When the police arrived at their quarters in the factory they arrested both Luis and Jane and took them to Mok-dong Immigration Detention Centre's detention facility in southern Seoul for being illegal overstayers.

Cecile

Cecile migrated to Korea as an entertainer in April 2002 but ran away from Papaya Club a few days later. As discussed in chapter 4, she had been two months pregnant to her Filipino boyfriend when she decided to accept a contract as a waitress in a bar in Korea. Her promoter in the Philippines, as well as her boss in Papaya Club, had assured her that she could proceed with her pregnancy in Korea and terminate her contract to return to the Philippines when she was ready to have her baby. But the day after she arrived at Papaya Club her boss told her to have a medical check-up, after which he disclosed that she was scheduled to have an abortion two days hence. She explained to me that her boss had told her that she could not possibly entertain customers in her condition and that if she came to Korea to earn money then she had better get rid of her unborn baby before it was too late. Cecile was distraught and saw her only option as running away. Through another entertainer in Papaya Club, Cecile was put in contact with Beth, a former entertainer who had run away from Peace Club in TDC eighteen months previously. Beth was now living in an apartment in TDC with her GI husband and six-month-old daughter and was widely known in TDC as a woman who helped entertainers leave clubs (see chapter 7).

Cecile packed a small bag of possessions on her third night in Korea and told her boss that she felt sick and was going out to get some paracetamol from the nearby store. Beth was waiting for her and took Cecile to her apartment, where Cecile stayed until Beth found her work in a factory. Cecile worked in that factory, living in a two- by four-metre shipping container on the premises for the next six months. She maintained twelve-hour shifts for six days a week and sometimes was obliged to work on Sundays. As irregular workers, many migrant factory workers who failed to comply with their bosses' demands for overtime were often reported to the immigration authorities. Factory employers would often call immigration authorities saying that some of their workers were illegal and requesting a check to be conducted on a certain day. The boss would then ensure all the compliant workers would be away from the premises when the check took place. The threat of deportation that came with illegality was an effective way for factory bosses to ensure that their employees were malleable to excessive working demands.

Cecile began experiencing contractions one day during work and told her boss she had to leave straight away for the hospital. She caught the next bus back to TDC and collected her belongings from Beth's house. She then caught another bus to a public hospital in Uijongbu and delivered her baby boy an hour after arriving at the hospital. After spending two nights in the hospital she made her way to the Centre and stayed there with her baby for six weeks. In that time she had to go back to the hospital in Uijongbu for check-ups and to the Philippines Embassy to register the birth of her baby. After six weeks of staying in the Centre she completely ran out of money, and Father Glenn advised her to return with her baby to the Philippines. But Cecile refused because she was sure her ex-boyfriend in Palawan who was "from a rich family" would take her baby from her. She went back to the factory where she had been working and tried to claim her unpaid salary for the two weeks of her final month of work. Accompanying her and her baby that day to a remotely located tin building north of Uijongbu, I witnessed her boss's refusal to pay her the KRW 280,000 she claimed he owed her. Her boss took us to one of the shipping containers located at the periphery of the factory complex, opened the door and told me to translate to Cecile. He said, "You have ruined this room now; the furniture is wrecked. I can't put another worker here. I will pay you KRW 100,000 and I am keeping the rest for the cost of fixing another room for my new worker". We did not know when or how the room had become "wrecked", but, loathe to accept this sum, Cecile pleaded with me to phone Father Glenn, who advised us to accept the money and leave before the owner of the factory called the police. Cecile was even more distraught as we made our way back to the Centre. She knew she would have to hurry to find another job with only KRW 100,000 in hand and a baby to support.

Soon thereafter Cecile began working at a different factory. But the difficulty of having a small baby made it extremely challenging for her to keep to her assigned work hours. The costs of clothing, feeding and looking after her baby depleted her earnings. Diapers were a major cost for Cecile, amounting to around a quarter of her monthly income. She began going back to TDC to ask some of her GI friends, including Beth's husband, to buy her diapers from the Commissary on Camp Casey, where they were about half the price of a Korean store. Sometimes she would leave her baby with Beth or other Filipinas in TDC whilst she worked, and at other times she would ask her factory co-workers to mind the baby. But her friends soon tired of this, and Cecile was forced to find an *ajumma* (lit. aunty, in Korean) who babysat whilst the mothers worked. When Cecile began doing this, the money she was able to save from her salary evaporated; she was working just to maintain her and her baby's transnational positions.

Unlike most of the women who ran away from *gijich'on* clubs, Cecile did not remove herself completely from the realm of commercial sexual labour. Even though this work was new to Cecile when she entered Papaya Club, and even though her stay in the club was so brief that she was not compelled to go on bar fines with customers, she began returning to TDC and working on the street to solicit customers for sex after she was dismissed from the second factory job. Motherhood as a source of anxiety and simultaneously an act of love were intimately intertwined in the lives of many of the women who ran away. I encountered many other runaways who were either pregnant or had babies to former customers when I visited other factories. Cecile's was an unusual case because her pregnancy was not conceived in Korea, but in other respects her post-club micro-movements resonated with many of these other women. Whilst Cecile had a particular preoccupation with staying in Korea with her baby due to concerns about sending her baby back to the Philippines, many other women who had babies after running away had to send the babies back to the Philippines whilst they themselves remained in Korea to work and support the child. Indeed a veritable 'baby transportation industry' emerged in *gijich'on* areas during the course of my fieldwork, with women who had regained legal status in Korea (usually through marriage to a GI) accompanying babies of other women back to the Philippines for a fee, which sometimes reached USD 500 per baby. Whilst Rhacel Parrenas (2001, 2005) has discussed the emotional work involved in "mothering from a distance" for Filipina migrant workers and their children back home in the Philippines, what I found in Korea was that this simple transnational divide between the migrant worker abroad and the child at home was not the most common dialectic of transnational mothering and care work for runaway entertainers in Korea. As Cecile's situation demonstrates, the specific contexts, trajectories and materialities of post-club manoeuvring with a baby depart significantly from those described by Parrenas and lead to disparate expressions and anxieties of transnational mothering.

Charie

Charie had run away from Papaya Club with the assistance of her GI boyfriend, Tim, and he had provided an apartment for her in TDC with the expectation that they would be married soon after her exit from the club. Two weeks after she ran away I received a distressed call from Tim saying that he came home to the apartment one day after work to find Charie and most of her clothes and her passport gone. Although I tried to call Charie many times over the following weeks there was no sign of her and no answer to my calls.

I had almost given up on contacting Charie again when she unexpectedly called me. She explained that she had decided she could not marry Tim, a man she respected but did not truly love. She had left Tim's apartment to be with another man, a Filipino customer, Ronny, whom she had also met whilst working in Papaya Club. Ronny worked at a plastics factory in the peri-urban area of Anyang, south of Seoul. In the interceding four weeks Charie and Ronny had rented a three-room basement apartment in a neighbourhood where most of the residents were also irregular migrant workers. Ronny's boss had given Charie a job at the same factory as Ronny, and the two of them rode on Ronny's pushbike to and from work six days a week. I visited Charie a week later in her apartment, and we sat on their bed whilst Ronny cooked us *pancit* (Filipino noodle dish) and chatted about the interceding series of events that had taken place since our last meeting.

Charie was earning a considerable sum at the factory, and she and Ronny hoped to save around USD 800 a month between them before returning to the Philippines in a few years to marry and start a family. Charie mused over the difficulty of the work in the factory, where she was packing plastic injections, which was much more physically tiring than work in Papaya Club. But the money she made and the freedom to be with her boyfriend without having to lie about it to the mama-san or play off her real affections against customers like Tim was more than enough compensation. Although Charie had crafted an immediate post-club future through her relationship with Ronny and job in the factory, the decision to go to a factory was tied to – and indeed facilitated precisely by – her romance with Ronny. She was fully cognizant of the fact that one dependence (Tim) had more or less been replaced with another (Ronny). In other words, Charie's position was to a significant extent contingent on Ronny's continued affections for her.

Anxieties of aspirational mobilities

The experiences of Valerie, Grace and Lisa are indicative of those faced by many of the former Filipina entertainers continuing to live in American Alley and other *gijich'on* areas in Korea after running away. Charie's, Jane's and Cecile's experiences illuminate the trajectories of women who live and work in Korea's peri-urban factories but with aspirations that are also tied to transnational desires for a better life through love, work and community. The experiences of all these six women and many others who run away from *gijich'on* clubs demonstrate that life out of the clubs is not easy, thus exposing the inadequacy of discussions of trafficked entertainers that focus largely on women's problems at work in the clubs. Valerie's, Grace's and Lisa's post-club experiences also reveal the partiality of the common perceptions that women who marry American customers are clearly and unequivocally 'successful' as migrants. The ability of Filipinas to successfully make the transition from entertainer to bride is profoundly influenced by the way they continue to be positioned as migrant entertainers/former prostitutes by their GI partners and husbands and their own sense of independence and life experience gained as a result of working in the clubs. Sexual labour clearly had enormous ramifications in the lives of runaway entertainers in Korea. Living in the same community where they had worked previously, or in factories where there were other Filipino migrants, only acted to magnify these anxieties.

Their status as entertainers affected the way Lisa, Grace, Valerie and Jane were perceived by their GI partners. GIs like David and Chris met their future wives initially through the purchase of their intimate and sexual labour – a relationship that is only transcended after considerable time has passed. GIs also invariably see their girlfriend going with other customers, concealing the fact that she has a boyfriend, and know that their girlfriend's explicit objective is to make as much money from a GI as she can. Given these circumstances GIs often doubt the sincerity and fidelity of their fiancées and wives. The boyfriend of my Korean entertainer friend from Harley's Club, Sunny, summed this attitude up well when he confided to me one day in Harley's Club, "Sometimes I don't know if she's my girlfriend. Sometimes I just think it [our relationship] is a higher form of her work". Sustaining longer-term relationships while having to negate the stigma of being a former entertainer was enormously challenging for many of the women in the clubs. Lisa had to endure David's unfounded suspicions about her fidelity even though, unlike some of her friends, she did not keep in touch with her ex-customers. Valerie's husband, Chris, refused to give her money to send to her family or pay back the money she borrowed from Lisa because he thought it would indeed confirm that she was only using him for money, thus forcing Valerie to go back to work in a factory to meet these obligations. Ironically, this led Valerie to initiate pen pal relationships with other men and thus employ a survival strategy she had commonly utilized in the club.

Grace and Lisa both attempted to actively negotiate and counter this common perception of marriage for money or 'marriage for visas' (see also Brennan 2004). In Grace's case this meant holding out for a marriage that was based on love – "I want for myself to find a good guy" – even though she admits she was not patient enough to realize this desire in the end. In Lisa's case negotiating this perception meant concealing her family's financial burdens from David. For Lisa the importance she attached to love in her marriage also meant that any accusations about infidelity or money hurt Lisa on an emotional, as well as pragmatic, level.

With all the media and military attention to trafficking in the early to mid-2000s, many GIs in Korea's *gijich'on* began to view women in the clubs as 'sex trafficked' and therefore vulnerable and exploited. In both sexual and financial terms this also led to marital tensions for many women. Their financial and emotional dependence on their boyfriends also affected their married lives. Neither Grace nor Lisa was 'allowed' to work after marrying, thus perpetuating their dependence on their husbands and resulting in Grace's gambling habit. Lisa did not go out of her apartment for two months after running away because David considered it too dangerous for her. Thus, many of these couple's marital conflicts emerge because relationships with GIs are established in circumstances of women's vulnerability and insecurity and become subject to andocentric power dynamics that were established previously in the clubs. For Charie, working with Ronny in the same factory and far away from TDC meant that conflicts were minimised, although Charie nonetheless remained highly dependent on Ronny to sustain her post-club factory and social life in Korea.

Just as Filipinas' former work as entertainers can influence GIs' attitudes towards their wives, the reverse is also true. Although Cherry was the only one of my participants who had previously worked as an erotic dancer in the Philippines, many of the women were, in the words of one GI informant, 'influenced by the job' once in Korea. For some women the bar system that marks their interactions with customers is extended outside the clubs, particularly if they do not have a serious boyfriend when they run away. Valerie and Grace both attempted to engage in liaisons with ex-customers that closely approximated arrangements they had with customers while still in the club. The view that GI customers represent money and a visa certainly caused problems in Valerie's relationship with Chris as he began to distrust her motives for marriage. Valerie only married Chris when all other options were closed to her and her situation was deteriorating. During this period of about seven weeks she faced physical confinement in her apartment or, if she did venture out, wore disguises to conceal her identity, and after that she made an unsuccessful attempt to regain her financial independence by taking a factory job. Had Valerie been able to continue working in the factory she probably would not have married Chris, and she saw her eventual marriage as a strategy to restore personal security. In her case security meant legality – with her legal status now restored with the conferral of a spouse/Status of Forces Agreement visa – and freedom; as a legal resident in Korea she can move around TDC without fear of repercussions from the police, Immigration or the owner of USA Club.

Valerie's relationship with Chris was greatly affected by the circumstances precipitating her marriage to him. Chris came to realize that Valerie's motivations were based around the restoration of her personal and financial security. In fact, Chris also began to cheat openly on Valerie – a situation she accepted with little difficulty. Grace and Lisa keenly discussed Valerie and Chris's indiscretions with me, frustrated at having to repeatedly explain to me the apparently obvious reason why they were still in the marriage. Grace nodded in agreement as Lisa tried to explain for the umpteenth time, "It's convenient, you know. She gets what she wants and so does he. [What's that? I ask.] She gets to stay here and he gets regular sex for nothing and his meals cooked for him". The marriages I encountered in *gijich'on* were undoubtedly heterogeneous, and I could not read Valerie's marriage in terms I had established to understand Lisa's or Grace's. This difference in large part explained the rift that began to develop between these three women. Valerie's marriage was like many of those between Thai sex workers and foreign sex tourists described by Cohen (2003: 66) as ambiguous, in which "there is no sharp division between the two (prostitution and marriage), but rather a degree of continuity; indeed, marriage . . . is in a sense the ultimate consequence of open-ended prostitution".

Such circumstances are particularly important in Korea because Filipinas who run away have already positioned themselves as illegal migrants, and this fact can form an important part in many women's decisions to marry their GI boyfriends.

This can lead to problems and conflicts in marriage, especially if a husband begins to feel his wife is just looking for a means to restore her legal immigration status in Korea. Failure to secure a spouse visa can certainly deny further mobility in the same way that an entertainer's visa to Korea can initially facilitate it.

For Jane, Cecile and Charie, as well as other women such as Honey, moving on from trafficking experiences after running away from *gijich'on* clubs was tied to monetary and personal goals in which factory work was seen as a key medium for the crystallisation of these aspirations. Unlike Valerie and Grace, who viewed factory work as a temporary interlocutor to fulfil immediate survival needs whilst they worked towards other romance-related projects, Jane, Cecile and Charie all saw factory work as a 'legitimate' form of work and one that pronounced them as clearly *not* entertainers. Ironically, many of the women I came to know through my research in Korea had left factory work in the Philippines to migrate to Korea precisely because of the poor remuneration and advancement opportunities the factory represented. In global Korea factory work was interpreted in quite different financial terms and was additionally bound up with notions of respectability ascribed by gendered and racial positioning as Filipinas in Korea. However, in ways that played out differentially for each of them, their experiences revealed their continued positioning as 'women who behave like entertainers' in this new space of the factory and in the wider Filipino migrant worker community. For Jane this was most directly experienced: the factory community's suspicions about the ways her relationship with her Korean boss/boyfriend was tied to money and (sexual) favours and the ways this same boyfriend saw her visits to the clubs as evidence of her sexual transgressions against him. Cecile's experience of pregnancy and childbirth in Korea as a runaway entertainer and irregular migrant portended other types of suspicions. In addition Cecile had to face the myriad practical challenges created by single motherhood in Korea which themselves were made more complicated and finical by her inability to recover salary from her former boss.

Often ethnographic studies of third-world women working in factories, either as internal or transnational migrants, discuss at length the ways the factory is a gendered and racialised space and the women's own negotiations of these structures and practices of inequality (for example, Ong 1987, Derks 2008, Mack 2004, Hewamanne 2009). None of this scholarship connects these concerns with the prior experience of exploitative work in other fields, but in Korea a large number of migrant women workers in the factories had run away from clubs. For former *gijich'on* entertainers who attempt to craft their futures through the factories of global Korea, romance, sex, pregnancy, departures from the workplace and return to *gijich'on* portend intense anxieties of their aspirational mobilities that are tied, like runaway brides, to their previous work as migrant entertainers.

Conclusion

The numbers of Filipinas who come to Korea on entertainer's visas, develop relationships with GIs in the context of their work in *gijich'on* clubs and run away from the clubs to pursue these relationships is substantial. Similarly, a large number of migrant entertainers run away and end up working in factories as irregular migrants. In this chapter I have explored the geographies of transnational mobility projects of Filipina entertainers after they run away from clubs. I attempted to highlight some of the anxieties faced by trafficked Filipina entertainers in Korea as they attempt to move between different roles, personas and identifications offered by their positioning as clandestine transnational migrants. The idea of Korea as a transnational platform speaks to such movements and the in-betweenness of identity and identification that often accompanies the experience of migration. Indeed, only by embracing the perspective that Korea is a formidable transnational platform can we begin to untangle the neat conflation of migration per se with a singular migrant position (such as 'migrant entertainer'). From the vantage point offered by the concept of a transnational platform one can engage in a much wider exploration of these women's lives and experiences in the context of transnational migration. It is thus not surprising that so many women run away from their places of employment in the clubs to pursue the other opportunities offered in Korea. Indeed, the wish to remain abroad should not be underestimated as, contrary to the official discourse on sex trafficking that presumes women will want to return home, the vast majority of women I knew did not wish to return home and will pursue various means to ensure they remain abroad, where their dreams for a better life are seen to hold a greater promise of realisation. A GI spouse visa, like an entertainer's visa, enables Filipinas in Korea to do this, thus to some extent allowing them to "capitalize on the very global linkages that exploit them" (Brennan 2002: 155).

Finally, focusing on processes that mark actual movements, such as running away, going to work, staying at home, networking in *gijich'on* and leaving Korea, and symbolic movements of transition and transformation that suggest fluidity and in-betweenness can help temper discussions that perhaps overly sentimentalise migrant agency. The women whose stories figure in this chapter certainly exercise considerable agency in various aspects of their post-club lives, including work and relationships, but the overriding theme of their experiences of negotiating transitions between is nonetheless anxiety. For Filipinas who decide to chart their post-club futures through their boyfriends/husbands, the intimate space of the household and the local community of American Alley or Songtan – and their relationships with their husbands, boyfriends, ex-customers and other Filipinas who make up this community – provided a challenging environment for these women. While American Alley in TDC and Songtan provide opportunities to develop relationships, these *gijich'on* areas simultaneously mark those relationships with the often contradictory meanings and expectations attached to 'entertainer' and 'bride' as both the women themselves and their partners often differentially understand these terms. For Valerie, Grace, Mary and Lisa there was no discrete post-entertainer persona that was not affected by their previous status as entertainers and the reasons they originally migrated to Korea. Insecurity expressed around fidelity, conflicts over money and frustrations over financial and personal independence, as well as practical questions concerning legal status, visas and financial security, all pervade these women's lives beyond the club in Korea.

This chapter extends discussions of migrant Filipinas by focusing on "anxieties of mobility" (cf. Lindquist 2005) involved in attempting to fulfil the expectations attached to the roles of 'GI bride' or 'factory worker' and shirk the stigma attached to the 'Filipina entertainer' label. This anxiety draws momentum from conflicts with husbands/boyfriends, other women, *kabayan*, Korean society and women's own internal struggles with their new roles as wives and/or undocumented factory workers. As the stories of Valerie, Grace and Lisa illustrate, these women's lives as transnational migrants involve more than just the recognition that migrant women "plan and take responsibility for their own life trajectories" (Suzuki 2000b: 115). Extending understandings of these migrant women's experiences requires attention to *how exactly* they negotiate changing circumstances and persistent aspirations and the expectations and stereotypes which are part and parcel of the process of mobility in which they find themselves. To neglect these other dimensions of women's experiences is to ignore the significant effort they invest in renegotiating their positions and status whilst abroad and the difficult and complicated nature of these negotiations aimed at enhancing their mobility and transnational positionings. It also has the effect of silencing the communities forming in destination countries and the challenges the women who live in these communities must face in their new positions as, in this case, runaway brides and femme fabricas.

Note

1 These groups of women were removed from their respective clubs because infighting between club owners and managers resulted in one of the club owners tipping off the police that the clubs had women employed there who had not been paid for several months and that some were underage. Although in both cases the allegations were true, the women were not rescued because they were trafficked.

7 Anti-trafficking by NGOs and entertainers

The first thing I discover when I return to Seoul after a month away from Korea in December 2002 is that the E-6 (entertainer's) visa to Korea has temporarily been suspended for Russian and Filipino nationals. The combined effects of bad press (including the *Time Magazine* story that featured Rosie), pressure from the Philippines and Russian Embassies and several meetings between Father Glenn and the chief of the Seoul Police, amongst other efforts, finally produce this dramatic measure.

The club owners in TDC and Songtan panicked. According to Cherry, the president of the Korean Special Tourism Association (the organisation representing the interests of club owners in *gijich'on* areas) had called a meeting of bar owners and promoters in TDC and Toka-ri to discuss how to deal with the situation. Their response was revealed a few days later when I arrived at the Catholic church in TDC to attend the once-a-week mass Father Glenn held for the Filipinas in TDC. That day there was an unusually large contingent of vans in the parking lot and a large group of Korean men and Filipinas milling around outside the church. Cherry looked at me with raised eyebrows as we walked past the crowd and into the church. Father Dong, another priest from the Centre, was giving the service that day and seemed oblivious to the goings-on outside. None of the regular attendees, including several women who ran away from the clubs and were residing in TDC or Toka-ri, as well as women from Silver Star and Harley's Club, were present. A loud Korean male voice suddenly echoed from the back of the church: "We have women here to attend your service, Father". Father Dong replied that the women were of course welcome to join mass if they wished but that this was a Filipino service and Koreans were to wait outside. Many of the women who were quickly shepherded into the pews by their bosses looked utterly confused and entirely uncomfortable. I had seen many of them before and knew their faces from fleeting encounters when I visited the clubs. The women filled the church to capacity, something that rarely happened at the Tagalog mass in TDC. All the women were heavily made up and wore tight-fitting costumes. I knew they would start to get ready for work as soon as mass finished at around 3:30 p.m.

In the church, and beyond the scrutiny of their bosses, most of the women took communion, and some apologised to Father Dong as the service ended. "Why are you sorry?" Father Dong asked. "Because", answered a woman I had seen several times in Black Jack Club in Toka-ri, "we don't come here by ourselves because they don't allow us. I'm embarrassed that you see me, Father, and I'm sorry that our bosses ruin your mass". Before Father Dong could reply the rear door opened and the voice of one of the club owners came bellowing up the aisle, "We must take the women back now, Father. I hope that you can see that we are making effort to allow these women to go out and to attend your mass. We are not stopping their human rights". Two weeks later the E-6 visa was reinstated, and I never saw any of those women at mass again.

One of the main effects of the global anti-trafficking effort has been the tightening of border controls in both migrant sending and receiving states and the attendant heightening of restrictions on the transnational mobility of 'third-world women'. The temporary suspension of the E-6 visa described earlier was one such reactive policy to keep these undesirable migrant women in their place, figuratively and literally. Trafficking as a discourse and anti-trafficking as a practice had begun to produce "truth effects" (cf. Foucault 1990) in Korea which had important consequences for the entertainers in *gijich'on*. The particular significance of the incident I described above is that it reveals how the efforts of external actors and organisations – meaning those located outside the subjects of trafficking themselves – to 'do good' through advocacy, support and policy interventions in anti-trafficking work are far too often discordant with migrant entertainers' own efforts to this end, with the everyday impulse of the latter remaining largely invisible within the anti-trafficking work of governments and NGOs alike. In TDC on the day of the mass the discourse of human rights invoked by anti-trafficking advocates in Korea and the United States was appropriated by club bosses in ways that compromised the very same rights of the women when they had *no choice* but to attend mass. Their presence that day was certainly not an expression of their freedom of movement or association, but only of its very denial. The actions of the club bosses reverberated beyond their employees. Vivian, a runaway entertainer whom I met the day before the mass, had planned to attend mass in order to discuss her situation with Father Dong. When she neared the church and saw club bosses milling outside she quickly left, advice unsought. Other women who considered the mass a safe space in TDC also turned away before reaching the church that day, and it took Cherry and Lisa considerable effort to explain to the usual attendees what had happened and to convince many of them to return in the following weeks.

Local NGOs and support workers' constructions of trafficking as a problem, and their subsequent interventions in the name of anti-trafficking, are important to consider in order to understand the impact of anti-trafficking efforts on migrant entertainers in Korea. Understanding the practices of religious organisations such as the Centre and Korean women's NGOs (such as Turebang in Uijongbu and Saewoomt'uh in TDC) helps explain why few women avail themselves of these resources or do so in minimal ways. Drawing on her ethnographic observations with international NGO CATW and local NGO Saewoomt'uh, Sealing Cheng (2010) has concluded that the NGO and the entertainer are on 'disparate paths'. But the path Cheng describes for entertainers is one in which 'love' is the principal preoccupation of the women, leaving the efforts of entertainers to respond to exploitative situations in and beyond the clubs in Korea through the transnational communities and networks they develop largely undocumented. Many of the entertainers I knew in TDC and Songtan were equally as interested in anti-trafficking as the organisations and individuals that purported to represent their interests, but in ways that were almost entirely at odds with these. The decision of runaway Filipinas in *gijich'on* to distance themselves from formal anti-trafficking supports is partly explained by the mismatch between these women's needs and desires and the work of third-sector organisations in Korea. In this chapter I turn from the personal projects of women upon running away to those situated within social and community networks and spatially within the *gijich'on* locale. Although many women living in *gijich'on* provide a range of supports to other entertainers that work towards ameliorating the experience of trafficking, these are rarely named as anti-trafficking interventions, and even more rarely do they invoke the emerging global architecture of anti-trafficking as a movement or industry.

Third-sector organisations and anti-trafficking

Before examining runaway entertainers' own support networks and projects, it is important to outline the ways these women are simultaneously excluded from consideration in discourses of both migrant worker rights and women's rights in Korea. The discursive rendering of entertainers' problems by these third-sector stakeholder and the exclusion of their concerns that follows this helps explain the intensity of *gijich'on* communities' own efforts to support each other. In this part of the chapter I look first at the Filipino migrant worker community's advocacy work and second at Korean women's NGOs and religious associations' support work.

The Filipino migrant community and the Centre

The spiritual and social locus for the Filipino community in Korea is the Centre in Hyehwa-dong in Seoul and the nearby Catholic church where Sunday mass and community events are staged every Sunday, organised under the direction of Father Glenn. The Centre has played a pivotal role in providing a range of services to Filipino migrants in Korea, including health support, consular assistance, filing unpaid wage claims and sheltering migrants who run away from or fall out of work. Filipino migrant worker volunteers for the Centre also provide support under its auspices, mainly through advocacy activities intended to highlight the plight of foreign workers in Korea and by organising social activities, such as a basketball competition after Sunday mass. These activities are predominantly oriented to the majority of the Filipino community in Korea, which are the male and female factory workers who number in the tens of thousands and most of whom contribute to the ranks of Korea's irregular migrant workers. It was only in the late 1990s that the population of Filipino workers began to swelled with the arrival of Filipina entertainer and foreign bride migrants.

Outside the church in Hyehwa-dong, Filipino street traders have begun to open stalls and sell Filipino goods and food to the workers, and a number of small Filipino restaurants have opened within the vicinity of the church and Centre. Filipino migrants attend these places on a Sunday and socialise with their *kakabayan* (lit. countrymen, in Tagalog). Those with health, migration or labour problems flock to the Centre after mass to seek assistance and advice, and on any given Sunday the number of Filipinos waiting for assistance at the Centre can reach up to one hundred.

What is notable about these social, support and advocacy activities for our purposes is the almost complete absence of migrant entertainers. Father Glenn provides direct assistance to individual women, and they sometimes shelter at the Centre, but otherwise the involvement of the Centre and its volunteers with entertainers was highly circumscribed. One Sunday about nine months after my arrival in Korea I was invited to participate in a volunteers' meeting held at the Centre. There were nineteen women and men in attendance, as well as Father Dong. I was the only foreigner present but was invited because I was, according to Father Glenn, "the only one who knew anything about the situation of the entertainers". This admission surprised me greatly because Father Glenn knew many runaway entertainers *themselves* who clearly held the authority of experience and insight into their problems. Father Glenn had perhaps subconsciously begun to view entertainers as 'to be helped' rather than 'helpers' themselves. This of course was not particularly surprising since Father Glenn encountered entertainers when they had reached the limits of their ability to overcome their situations, including by seeking shelter at the Centre or by making claims for unpaid salaries.

At the meeting that day the group wished to address the issue of advocacy for migrant Filipino workers in Korea and develop strategies to better raise the main concerns to the Filipino Embassy in Seoul, local NGOs in Korea and international NGOs, including those from the Philippines. With the exception of Jane, the Filipinas who ran the women's arm of the Filipino migrant support group KASAMAKO were all working in factories and had little understanding of the problems facing entertainers. But what was notable at the meeting was the *unwillingness* of these volunteers to embrace the problems that entertainers faced or to attempt to include these issues in their work and indeed the entertainers themselves in their meetings and activities. This was evidenced when discussion at the meeting turned to entertainers:

PRESIDENT OF THE YOUTH VOLUNTEERS GROUP: Do we need to think about entertainers' problems?
PARTICIPANT 1: Why should we include them? Don't you think that if we include their problems we might not be taken so seriously?
SALLIE: Why would that be the case?
PARTICIPANT 1: Well, you have to think about what we are trying to do here. We want migrant rights to be respected in Korea. That is our goal. The entertainers aren't really migrant workers [some snickering from other members of the group].

PARTICIPANT 2: But don't these women sometimes come to the Centre for help? And anyway the mail order brides [*sic*] aren't workers either, but we support them.

PARTICIPANT 3: Yes, I've seen the entertainers in Father Glenn's office doing affidavits about their situations. Some of them have been beaten up, and some of them are pregnant.

PARTICIPANT 1: I think the issue of the mail order brides is different. They are abused by Korean men in their marriages. Some of them are also forced to work for their husbands for nothing, so it's a labour issue as well. This is about what happens in Korea and by Koreans.

PARTICIPANT 4: [Ignoring Participant 1] So if we include entertainers in our advocacy, what would we say about them?

[Protracted silence]

FATHER DONG: Sallie knows. Why don't we leave it to her, and we can see where it fits in our broader advocacy after we get the main issues of the factory workers sorted out?

PARTICIPANT 2: And the brides.

PRESIDENT: Yes, of course, the brides too.

The meeting revealed that the Filipino migrant community has a narrow interpretation of the problems faced by entertainers in Korea. They are assumed to be issues of (sexual) violence, including pregnancy, and as an American rather than Korean issue because of the location of women in *gijich'on*. Despite the multiple sites of exploitation to which many entertainers were subject, and the prominence of salary and worker entitlement claims amongst these problems, factory workers clearly had the authority of representation over migrant *workers'* issues in Korea. An undercurrent to the meeting that day was the unarticulated fear that the inclusion of entertainers' problems would undermine the legitimacy of the group's advocacy work. This came most closely to the surface when Participant 1 stated that the group might not "be taken seriously" if entertainers' problems were to be included in their efforts. I had spent enough time at the Centre to know that many Filipino migrants regarded entertainers as not really deserving of assistance, since they came to Korea to 'do prostitution' or 'marry an American'. However unjustified, in the absence of entertainers to speak for themselves about their concerns and experiences, this view only received further momentum in the meeting that day.

One of the key outcomes of the meeting was the scripting of a short play in which the Centre volunteers were to be the main performers. The play was to highlight the plight of Filipino migrants in Korea, with the performance to be given at any appropriate opportunity. Watching the performance of this play at one migrant workers human rights event in Seoul a few weeks after the meeting revealed the discursive limits of migrant worker advocacy and activism to the problems encountered by factory workers and migrant brides married to Korean men. Not surprisingly given the advocacy meeting at the Centre, the plight of entertainers and the specific concerns they faced in the clubs and in subsequent factory work and transnational marriages did not figure at all in the play. The issue of factory work was constructed as one of physical and verbal abuse from bosses, salary delays and non-payments and the demands of excessive overtime. The specific concerns of women who run away from clubs to work in factories, like Jane and Cecile, were not covered in this presentation. Migrant brides' problems were presented as exclusively a concern relating to Filipinas who married Korean men through transacted/market mechanisms, with runaway entertainers who married GIs absent from the play, despite the fact that many of their negotiations around violence, children and economic, social and sexual censure by their husbands were commonplace.

Local and religious third-sector organisations in Korea

Unlike the Centre and its migrant workers' advocacy group, some Korean women's NGOs and religious support workers were embracing the issue of trafficking to *gijich'on* areas. In particular Turebang, which is based outside Camp Stanley near Uijongbu, and Saewoomt'uh, with its main office in American Alley in TDC and a subsidiary office in Songtan, have been working with Korean women deployed in *gijich'on* areas for many years, including prior to the naming of entertainers' problems as trafficking. However, there were two notable undercurrents to the support offered by these stakeholders which acted to limit their potential to support women appropriately. The first concerned the construction of problems entertainers faced as deriving from what we might call the military-prostitution nexus (see Chapter 2 for further discussion). Those individuals and organisations working from understandings of the trafficking issue according to this nexus – such as Saewoomt'uh and Turebang – assumed that these problems could all be located in and attributable to the extension of a system of transnational militarised prostitution that puts women into situations of forced prostitution and in which GI customers and Korean club bosses are depicted as the instigators of violence, coercion and exploitation of these unwitting victims. Notably their efforts did not accommodate important concerns articulated by women themselves, such as romance with or marriage to an ex-customer or salary claims. Assistance with documentation required for marriage, for example, was something that, in the absence of the provision of information by a third-sector organisation, was left to anecdotes and advice circulating amongst the women themselves. Similarly, although job opportunities in factories were made available to runaway entertainers who sought support at the Centre, women's NGOs in Korea normally advised women to return to the Philippines, thus creating anxieties for women about unfulfilled financial responsibilities and their failure as labour migrants.

Support also failed migrant entertainers when some local NGOs in Korea attempted to position themselves as anti-trafficking organisations. In these cases organisations attempted to adopt 'sex trafficked entertainers' as clients in order to bolster their funding and credibility in anti-trafficking work. Other have noted that trafficking, particularly in the sex and nightlife entertainment sectors, is an attractive conduit for availing funding opportunities at the present time. Commenting on anti-trafficking amongst NGOs in the Indonesian context, for example, Johan Lindquist (2010) has suggested that "auditable victims" – those who can be counted – are important in justifying interventions which in turn underscore the need for funding. The legitimacy of claims by NGOs such as Turebang and Saewoomt'uh to funding for anti-trafficking work in Korea, particularly direct case work, is inexorably tied to evidence of need, which in turn is based on the number of victims who may be helped, or indeed who are already being helped, on a shoestring budget. Put simply, the more cases the greater the possibility of enhanced funding. Although we might think that better funding would enhance, rather than dilute, the support work of NGOs by enabling them to better understand the *actual* needs of women they supported, this turned out not to be the case for *gijich'on* entertainers. This was demonstrated to me on many occasions, and I share two of these that illustrate the perils of professionalisation of anti-trafficking amongst some NGOs working in Korea's *gijich'on*.

The first episode involved Jane, whose case was discussed in the previous chapter. After her arrest and placement in Mok-dong Immigration Detention Centre Jane was without her possessions and money. Detainees were allowed one phone call a day on the public phone located in the main office. Jane used her call to phone me and ask if it would be possible for me to collect her belongings, including some money owed to her, from her friend's apartment in TDC and bring them to her at the detention centre. I told her I would do my best, as I had never visited the detention centre before and was unsure if I would even be allowed to see Jane. The following evening, approaching the designated visiting time, I made my way to the detention centre with Jane's bag in hand. Emerging from the subway station I noticed Sister Jasmine, a Filipina support worker for the NGO Turebang. To meet the support needs of the changing clientele of Turebang, the director had employed Sister Jasmine, a Filipina who spoke both Tagalong and Visayan, to better assist the Filipinas in the clubs around Camp Stanley near Uijongbu. Sister Jasmine and I exchanged pleasantries, after which she related her intention to also visit Jane. I thought this would enhance my chances of seeing Jane since a Catholic sister would impress the detention centre staff far more than I, with no organisational backing, probably would.

The detention centre rules for visitation of a detainee are meticulous in their regimentation and surveillance. Both Sister Jasmine and I had to fill in a two-page form which included our passport and alien card details. The rules of visitation were explained by an officer who made it clear that we had ten minutes with Jane, after which she would be taken back to her room. Signing an agreement to respect these rules, we sat on two chairs facing a glass partition with a chair placed directly opposite on the other side of the glass. The visiting space was only about four metres from the counter where we completed the forms, and the officer was well within earshot of our conversation. Jane emerged with the officer through a door on the other side of the glass with a look of relief on her face as she saw us sitting there. As she sat down Sister Jasmine said to me, "I will talk Tagalog with her, Sallie. It is quicker that way and because we don't have long with her". Their conversation proceeded thus:

SISTER JASMINE: Jane, why did you not call me or Turebang for assistance earlier? Why did you call the Anyang Migrant Workers Centre for help? They only help factory workers. They are not interested in women like you.

JANE: I was arrested by the police and they brought me here. I didn't really know what to do. I knew from my work in the factory and for KASAMAKO about the Anyang Centre. They are sending me back to the Philippines anyway, so there isn't much anyone can do to help me now.

SISTER JASMINE: Yes, but you were beaten by your boyfriend, so why didn't you call us first? We are the ones to help women in your situation.

JANE: I am sorry, Sister.

SISTER JASMINE: Why were you staying with that man from Peru? You should have gone to a different factory to work. You have kids to support back in the Philippines and you are here playing with guys. This is what has got you into this situation. Now you are going to be sent back to the Philippines and for what? You have nothing to take back to your kids and you are going to be blacklisted from Korea. Do you understand the position you have put yourself in?

JANE: [Looks at me and then down at her hands] Yes, Sister.

SISTER JASMINE: Okay, we have one minute left, so is there anything you need?

IMMIGRATION OFFICER: Your time is up. If you wish to continue this interview you must fill in another form please.

Jane was hoisted from her chair and escorted back to her room on the verge of tears. Visiting hours had almost finished for the night, and I felt no desire to see Jane again whilst Sister Jasmine was still there. As we left the detention centre I fell silent, feeling that if I spoke it would be impossible to conceal my frustration at the meeting that had just taken place. As we walked to the subway station my phone rang, and it was Jane. She said she never asked Sister Jasmine to come and hoped I could do a couple of things for her before she was deported, if I had time. She said she didn't have time to ask me those things during my visit to her. When I ended the call Sister Jasmine suddenly broke the silence, "You know the way I work, Sallie. I only help women who help themselves". I did not respond, and as we neared the subway station entrance we said our good-byes.

This incident clearly exemplifies the claims NGOs make over individuals they perceive as 'their clients'. But there were two even more striking aspects to Turebang's claim over Jane concerning the emerging politics of anti-trafficking in Korea. The first related to the way ownership of Jane's case took precedence over the provision of support that might have assisted her in her current predicament. The second related to the important issue of consent. Turebang felt it not only their responsibility but also their *right* to assist runaway entertainers, and this often meant intervening in their lives without their consent. As Jane had told me on the phone only a few moments after the meeting at the detention centre, she had not asked Sister Jasmine or Turebang for help. Finally, I considered Sister Jasmine's chastising of Jane not only to do with Turebang's ownership of her case, but also and perhaps equally due to the fact that helping Jane now, when she was already in detention and had a police case pending, would expend too many resources and too much of Sister Jasmine's time. Sister Jasmine had implied this to me when she had said that she only helped women who helped themselves – women who could be counted amongst the number of support cases served by Turebang but who simultaneously did not fall outside the parameters of accepted and easily administrable interventions on their behalf.

A few weeks after the incident with Jane and Sister Jasmine, I met with Sister Theresa, a Catholic nun who conducted outreach with the women in the clubs in TDC, Uijongbu and Songtan. One of the women I knew in TDC, Monica, had a dilemma that was proving difficult for her to resolve. and I wished to discuss her situation with Sister Theresa and possibly seek her assistance. Monica came to Father Glenn's mass in TDC specifically to talk to me about her situation. It turned out that she had been deployed in Harley's Club ten months previously and had developed a relationship with a GI, to whom she had become pregnant. Monica was five months pregnant when she related her problem to me and had managed to conceal the pregnancy from the Korean bar manager and the owner of Harley's Club. Monica knew it would be more and more difficult to continue the pregnancy whilst working in the club. She was certain that if her pregnancy was revealed the owner of Harley's Club would force her to have an abortion or send her straight back to the Philippines, and she feared her boyfriend might lose interest in her should there no longer be a baby to consider or should she no longer be in Korea. She had planned to run away in order to marry her boyfriend but had entered Korea on a false passport. I knew from conversations with other Filipinas that this would make it extremely difficult for her to marry in Korea. I discussed Monica's situation with Cherry, who seemed to know the right course of action for almost any problem encountered by an entertainer. Cherry confirmed what I had also suspected; it would be easiest if Monica returned to the Philippines and waited for her boyfriend to join her there to marry.

But Monica was extremely reluctant to leave Korea. She harboured a well-founded suspicion that her boyfriend would not keep his promise and that she would end up as a single mother in the Philippines. Such as situation, especially when it involved a liaison with a foreign man in the context of working abroad, would undoubtedly emerge as source of stigma for Monica once she was back home. Whilst Rafael (2000) has recognised the preoccupation of Filipinas with "white love", Espiritu (2003) and Tadiar (2004) have both noted the discourses of shame (*hiya*, in Tagalog) that can equally accompany non-conjugal transnational expressions of such love. I related all Monica's information to Sister Theresa because I thought that as a migrant worker advocacy officer she would be best placed to assist. I was therefore surprised by her response:

> Well, we don't want too many people involved in one case because then we are wasting all our energy on one person. It's better that you handle it. Why don't you try and get some advice from Father Glenn? You know I have a lot of other cases and they probably have more need than your friend. [I look questioningly at Sister Theresa.] I mean they get pregnant because of force,

not because of their boyfriend. Anyway your friend has a good option to go home, but she is choosing to put herself at risk by staying here [in Korea].

I persisted and asked Sister Theresa if she had at least come across a similar case so I might know what to do. "No", she replied, "You learn by doing". Sister Theresa's advice to me underscored that of Sister Jasmine; some women are worth helping – not only because their problems are more manageable, but also because they approximate the victim of trafficking far more readily than others. This observation has also been made by Jo Doezema (1998: 46–7), who suggests,

> The most frightening division created by the voluntary/forced dichotomy is that it reproduces the whore/Madonna division within the category of "prostitute". Thus, the Madonna is the "forced prostitute" – the child, the victim of trafficking; she who, by virtue of her victim status, is exonerated from sexual wrong-doing. The "whore" is the voluntary prostitute: because of her transgressions she deserves whatever she gets.

Taking Doezema's observation about deserving and undeserving victims further, what I witnessed developing amongst the women's, migrant workers and religious support organisations in Korea were the extant effects this demarcation was beginning to have on the lives of some – ostensibly deviant and undeserving – runaway entertainers. Sister Theresa's suggestion that it would be better for Monica to return home and that, more broadly 'force' rather than choice in sexual encounters leading to pregnancy held more legitimacy in labelling a 'victim of trafficking' and supporting her was telling of the disciplinary potential of this divide.

Even Father Glenn was not immune to such distinctions between who deserved and who did not deserve help. Vivian, the runaway entertainer who showed up at the TDC mass for some advice on the day when the Korean bosses were all there, was one of the entertainers subject to this impulse to divide. After running away to marry her long-time boyfriend from Yes Club, she was confronted with his admission that his tour in Korea was about to finish and he must return to the US. He told Vivian he would return to Korea for her and was hoping he would be able to extend his tour there after taking home leave. Vivian was devastated, having run away solely for the purpose of marrying her boyfriend. He gave her enough money to survive in TDC for a few weeks, so she rented a room in one of the cheap hotels on the outskirts of American Alley, where she was now residing illegally. She did not want to rent an apartment in her boyfriend's absence but wanted to wait for her boyfriend's return so they could choose a place together. Besides, she did not have enough money for the deposit on even a small apartment in American Alley. One month had come and gone and still Vivian's boyfriend had not returned. She reflected, "He might not come back. Maybe I should look for a second option now. But the problem is I'm illegal and I can't go downrange or out much. If I go back to the Philippines I've lost everything. I think I need to talk to Padre [Father Glenn]". A few days after Vivian's failed attempt to talk to Father Dong at the TDC mass she was picked up by Immigration officers who were on a compliance check in TDC.

The officers searched the clubs, as well as apartments and hotels in American Alley and downrange. Vivian was taken to Mok-dong Immigration Detention Centre, where Jane had also been taken, in what emerged as the most extensive immigration compliance check ever to occur in TDC, with twenty-two women being detained that day. Vivian called Father Glenn from the detention centre to ask if he could help her, to which he had replied that he could not. Discussing the immigration check in TDC and Vivian's phone call later that day, Father Glenn explained to me, "If Vivian wanted help she should have come to me straight away [after running away]. She just stayed in TDC and in that hotel and didn't help herself at all. I don't have time to run around after women like that". Time, resources and the distinction between those who deserved help and those who did not were meshed together in Father Glenn's explanation as to why Vivian was not to be assisted. It seemed deeply ironic that Father Glenn had played an instrumental role in having the E-6 visa suspended several months earlier. Contrary to Sister Jasmine's view of runaway entertainers as "not helping themselves", I found that women such as Jane and Vivian used diffuse, imaginative and courageous efforts to move on with their lives and secure their transnational aspirations through manoeuvrings outside the infrastructure of anti-trafficking.

A place for hope: networking transnational support in *gijich'on*

Denise Brennan (2005) and Jennifer Lynne Musto (2008) have both suggested that it is vital for trafficked persons themselves to play a more central role in the anti-trafficking movement. Discussing the US context specifically, Brennan (2005: 38) states that "the sustainability of an anti-trafficking movement in the U.S. hinges not only on ex-captives telling their own stories, but also on taking their own active leadership role in its direction, agenda-setting, and policy-making". Although Musto (2008: 7) also embraces this suggestion, she argues that any effort to include trafficked persons in the anti-trafficking movement in the US must also confront the realities of the "NGO-ification" of this movement. This would mean recognising the ways funding for anti-trafficking work is tied to particular understandings of trafficking and definitions of trafficked persons which themselves have clear ideological underpinnings in, for example rights-based and/ or neo-abolitionist discourses. These constraints of professionalisation in anti-trafficking work can certainly limit the roles trafficked person may be able to play in such a movement. This led Musto (2008: 7) to suggest that

> the professionalization of the anti-trafficking movement . . . has contributed to asymmetrical power relations between NGO staff and the clients they 'serve', while restraining an anti-trafficking movement in the United States led by those who have firsthand experience in the process of irregular movement and exploitation.

As discussed earlier, the support offered to migrant entertainers in Korea demonstrates that growing professionalisation of anti-trafficking in Korea also raises issues of power, voice and participation of trafficked persons in the anti-trafficking movement. These issues are also embedded within particular agendas and approaches to trafficking, prostitution and, in the case of the Centre, the meanings attached to being a Filipino abroad. But simply because it is not easy for trafficked persons to play a more prominent role in an increasingly inaccessible and professionalising anti-trafficking movement in Korea, as elsewhere, we should not then necessarily presume the absence of other types of movements aimed towards the restoration of entertainers' transnational mobility projects. In this second part of the chapter I outline five expressions of the diffuse everyday politics of anti-trafficking in which (former) entertainers *are* the movement, the network and the hope.

To illuminate this politics I draw on prevailing approaches to "development-with-identity" in the global South, which might be understood as "embrac[ing] a wide set of understandings and divergent views about how to make development sensitive to . . . [local] needs . . . Development-with-identity treats indigenous culture as a flexible and dynamic resource, as a basis for creative thinking outside the standard 'box' of development solutions" (Laurie et al. 2005, see also Radcliffe et al. 2005). Filipina entertainers' expressions of anti-trafficking in Korea's *gijich'on* areas suggest that we might usefully unbind this approach to development from indigeneity, which presumes containment within the nation-state or a geographically stable and essentialised ethnicity, and extend it to sites of transnational migration. Several geographers have made similar suggestions about the transnationalisation of ethnic networks of support in migrant destinations (for example, Bunnell 2007), though notably not in relation to trafficked women where presumptions of lack of agency tend to prevail. Yet the women in TDC, Songtan and other *gijich'on* areas in Korea have drawn on cultural resources such as shared language, food and friendship networks established 'at home' to resist their marginality and victimology and create possibilities for the reworking of their mobility projects.

The diffuse expressions of support networks that exist beyond these institutional actors/actions and, in particular, the initiation and involvement of trafficked persons in such supports have not been well documented in the burgeoning critical scholarship on anti-trafficking. Whilst co-ethnic/national networks in transnational locales have been documented by several geographers recently (for example, Bunnell 2007, Law 2001), fulfilling multiple roles of providing information, affirming shared (national) identity and offering direct supports to co-nationals/co-ethnics, none of this literature addresses migrant/trafficked entertainers, thus perpetuating assumptions about these women's lack of ability to be involved in any significant way in transnational community formation and support in migrant destinations. Several scholars have nonetheless noted the spaces Filipina migrants form in destination countries in order to 'manage' transnational lives (Yeoh and Huang 1999, Zontini 2009, Barber 2000). But any investigation of such management involves a thorough ethnographic engagement with the everyday of migrants' movements against marginalisation in a transnational locale as well as migrants' encounters with a professionalising third sector.

142 *Anti-trafficking by NGOs and entertainers*

Expression I: circulating support

When I arrived at Lisa's place she was sitting at the dining table with a stack of business card–sized papers on her right and a scattering of blank ones on her left. She was writing on each card, by hand:

> Mass in Tagalog every Thursday at 2 pm in TDC Catholic Church.
> All are welcome and if you have any problems you can discuss with Father Glenn afterwards.
> If you need any other advice or help you can call:
> Lisa [phone number inserted]
> Father Glenn [phone number inserted]

Lisa and I walked around all the back streets and knocked on all the doors of all the apartments to distribute the cards to those who had run away and were living in TDC. It took the entire day. The following night Lisa and David and I went into several clubs and gave one card to a woman she or we knew. Father Glenn had given up driving to TDC every Thursday to deliver mass to a group of usually less than five women, especially after the drama of the club bosses' 'human rights performance' described in the opening of this chapter. But I urged Father Glenn to come back and try one more time. Lisa's efforts at circulating details of the mass and of Father Glenn's availability to talk with women about their problems boosted the numbers of parishioners up to more than twenty in most weeks. Every month Lisa would distribute cards this way to catch the high turnover of occupants in the apartments and women in the clubs. Sometimes Lisa wrote her number and Father Glenn's on the back of one of the stalls in the women's toilets in the clubs where it was harder to talk with women openly.

Expression II: making a space

After running away from Peace Club, Beth married her GI boyfriend and, against the grain of the common practice of runaway brides, gained work in a phone card shop on the main strip downrange in TDC. This was, as Beth explained, a "strategic move". Nearly all the women in TDC used this phone card shop to buy phone credit since it was the only store on the strip to sell phone cards for Korea and the Philippines, as well as significant other international destinations, such as the US. Beth used her location in the store not only as a way of earning money and thereby asserting her independence, but also to meet women in the clubs and check on what was going on downrange. Beth's ability to craft a legitimate position in the main strip was a point of inception to connect with women who wished to run away or needed some other type of help. Beth befriended a Bangladeshi migrant worker named Bobby who had previously frequented the clubs as a customer but had fallen in love with a Filipina entertainer and helped her escape, also with Beth's assistance. Since then Bobby was utilised by Beth to enter particular clubs under the guise of a customer and make arrangements with women who wanted to leave. Twenty-one women in all had sought Beth's assistance to run away and then refuge at her house whilst she helped make inquiries with former entertainers in factories about the availability of factory work. Women came and went from Beth's house, often – like Cecile – leaving possessions there until they had other accommodation.

Expression III: dance moves

When Cherry returned to TDC to live as the legal spouse of her GI husband, she took up residence in an apartment on the edge of American Alley. After several visits downrange to the clubs with either myself or her husband she encountered a large number of women who, she recalled, "did not know how to dance at all". In fact Cherry had meant that these women did not know how to perform the erotic dances required for work in some clubs. Around half the clubs in TDC and nearly all in Toka-ri promoted live strip and erotic dances for customers, whilst the others – such as Harley's and Silver Star – did not expect women to perform on stage at all. The clubs that promoted live shows were different in their expectations about women's dancing, with some expecting women to perform as part of their normal duties, and deducting salary or points if women refused to dance or danced badly, and others expecting women to perform for bonus cash from their boss. Women who chose to perform also generally had a greater chance of attracting customers for drinks and bar fines and therefore additional points/ money.

After talking to many of these women in the clubs with live shows, Cherry became aware of the anxieties of dancing on stage for these women. An erotic dancer in the Philippines prior to migrating to Korea, Cherry was a seasoned performer, and she decided to take it on herself to teach new arrivals to dance. She focused on the clubs where women were punished for not dancing and where she was able to gain the agreement of the owner or manager of the club to spend time with the women. Cherry's husband approved of her doing this, and so Cherry became a volunteer dance teacher to fifty or so women at any one time in a range of different clubs. This assistance was crucial in lessening oppressive working environs for many women, who gained more money and less rebuke from their bosses during the time they remained in the club. Cherry was able to turn erotic dance, at least to some degree, from a site of exploitation and source of anxiety for some women in the clubs to a locus of power for the women who availed themselves of her lessons. For the women, joining Cherry's lessons enabled them to insert some fun into the work of dance.

Expression IV: home cooking

Janice was one of the best cooks of Filipino cuisine I had ever met. When I first met Janice she emerged from the kitchen of the apartment I was visiting with Cecile wearing an apron and inviting us to try her latest creation. After the meal she began to tell us about her work since running away from Peace Club:

> I had this idea for a business. When I was in Peace Club we could only eat instant noodles or sometimes sardines if we had some money. The food was

awful and I was always hungry and tired because I'm not eating properly. Papa-san said that we had to cut our food and no more rice or meat, because it made us fat. So when I ran away from Peace Club I decided to start a mobile cafe. I cook for women in the clubs and they give me whatever money they can. Sometimes it's just one or two dollars, and sometimes nothing at all. That's funny; I guess I'm a better cook than a business woman.

Janice's food was always in demand, and, despite her generosity in giving some food away, she still made a considerable sum each week from her business. On average she served a meal to forty women in the clubs every day using the tiny kitchen in her apartment to prepare all the food. Lisa Law (2001) has also explored the role of culinary culture amongst Filipina domestic workers in Hong Kong, suggesting that food is a site for the reaffirmation of shared community and connectedness to the nation in diaspora. Although this was also true for the entertainers in the clubs of TDC and Toka-ri where Janice served her food, these cultural meanings were also inseparable from the practical needs of women in the clubs, where food was interminably both cultural glue and basic need.

Expression V: visiting friends

Once Honey had moved to her new factory job in Songtan she managed to contact a friend, Eliza, with whom she trained as a dancer at Villa Flor's talent studio in Manila. She found that Eliza was deployed in a club in Anjoyng-ri, about thirty kilometres from Songtan and completely isolated from NGOs. On her day off Honey visited Eliza and her co-workers, all of whom made protestations about the paltry salary and the nature of their work. Honey and I stayed with Eliza and her workmates in their room upstairs from the club that night, and they promised to keep in touch with us should they need anything. Two weeks later Father Glenn called me and asked me if I could go with him to "a place called Anjongli" to help bring some women back to Seoul. When we arrived I was surprised to see Eliza and two of her co-workers sitting in the Pinoy Cafe, two blocks away from their club. They smiled in recognition when they saw me and told me that Honey had given them the idea that there was something better in Korea outside the club work. Whilst I thought Honey and I were just visiting Anjongli to see her friend from Manila, she had left these women with a strong, positive impression of life beyond the club. Unlike the NGO workers who were either refused entry into clubs (because the owners knew they would influence their entertainers to run away) or who had difficulty talking to the entertainers, Honey did not have to work at developing a trusting relationship with these women. For Honey it was a form of post-feminist body politics where being a 'modern women in Asia' (as in Munshi 2011) entailed the bodily projection of financial autonomy, social freedom and familial responsibility simultaneously enacted in the position of irregular Filipina factory worker. As Chandra Mohanty (1987) reminds us, a feminist politics of location helps illuminate the contextual specificities of representations of women. Honey was able to simultaneously embody the Filipino ideal of the traditional delineation of a filial daughter *and* a modern, liberated women working abroad. She continued doing this in Anjongli until she returned to the Philippines nearly two years after running away.

The support provided by third-sector organisations and the support provided by friends and compatriots like Lisa, Honey, Janice, Cherry and Beth in *gijich'on* areas were utterly distinct in both their orientation and, arguably, in their impact. At the risk of stating the obvious, women who had been deployed in *gijich'on* clubs knew what support entertainers needed whilst still in the clubs, both to ameliorate the immediate everyday circumstances of their marginality – as in Cherry's and Janice's interventions – and to help craft longer-term transformative projects of women through exit from the clubs – as in Beth's, Honey's and Lisa's interventions. Sex worker rights advocates have long recognised the value of employing sex workers and former sex workers as peer educators, particularly in the delivery of health-related interventions with women. In Korea, neither NGOs oriented to prostitution, especially those around US military bases, nor migrant worker NGOs include former migrant entertainers as service providers or advocates in their programmes. Nor, despite the feminist overtones of many of these organisations, do they offer participatory activities which might enable the inclusion of the perspectives or insights of migrant entertainers in Korea. As Musto (2008) has suggested in relation to the US context, these difficulties of inclusion reflect broader concerns about the ways funding is tied to particular constructions of trafficking, so constraining and directing NGO relations with trafficked persons to well-accepted roles of client and service provider with their attendant scenarios of support, such as counselling, alternative livelihoods support or assistance with migration issues, especially where this might portend a return to the Philippines.

Conversely, in the emerging rhetoric of support amongst the various NGOs attending to entertainers' problems in Korea it would have been an anathema to suggest teaching women to perform erotic dances or providing them with food so they could remain healthy whilst working. These interventions would simply not be considered as legitimate amongst support organisations because they would endorse the legitimacy of club work by, as Sister Theresa once put it to me, "encouraging women to see that work as normal". Arguably support that facilitated or encouraged women's departures from the clubs, such as those offered by Beth, Honey and Lisa, would be viewed favourably by comparison. But I also found this was not the case, principally because these measures were not oriented to the subsequent provision of standard post-exit interventions, primarily in the form of counselling and/or the organisation of the return of women to the Philippines. Honey's and Beth's activities were viewed particularly unfavourably by *gijich'on*-based women's organisations because these two women were, in the words of one representative from Saewoomt'uh, "making illegality an attractive option". Saewoomt'uh, like Turebang, has been relatively successful in providing Korean entertainers in *gijich'on* clubs with alterative livelihoods support, counselling and health-related services and indeed had been engaged in these support interventions long before the coming of trafficking to *gijich'on* areas. But what Saewoomt'uh failed to appreciate in its admonishment of Beth's and Honey's interventions was the particular challenges facing *migrant* entertainers and their desire to fulfil their mobility projects transnationally in/through Korea. The Centre was the only support organisation that normalised and supported irregular labour migrants in Korea through its various efforts but, as suggested earlier, largely excluded migrant entertainers for their failure to conform to the ideal of the irregular migrant worker because ostensibly they engaged in 'prostitution' and married 'foreign men'.

Beyond the formal organisational milieu of anti-trafficking, militarised prostitution and irregular migrant labour amongst third-sector organisations in Korea, *gijich'on*-based social networks and the imaginative support projects developed by some women situated within these networks fulfilled a vital role: they conferred unconditional, flexible and immediate support. Recognising this enables us to expand our considerations of transnational social movement networks in anti-trafficking to the scale of the locale and the site of culture. Most recent work on global civil society and global social movements, including in human trafficking, focuses on the ways global networks transform local and national activism and on the iterations between local, national and global activism (as in Della Porta and Tarrow 2005). But absent in this territorial reductionism in which 'local' can be read as citizen, ethnic or indigenous, there is little recognition that transnational migrants also make significant contributions to transnational social movements, often in marginal localised spaces. In her focus on global cities and diasporic networks Saskia Sassen (2002: 217) is one of the few to recognise global cities as "thick enabling environments for these types of activities even though the networks themselves are not urban *per se* . . . They enact global civil society in the micro-spaces of everyday life rather than on some punitive global stage". Although Korea's *gijich'on* are a far cry from a global city in many respects, they nonetheless illustrate Sassen's key point that diasporic networks in migrant destinations are important conduits for conducting a critical transnational politics and that (re)grounded networks amongst migrants themselves are the key resource by which new social movements are sustained.

Conclusion

Women who are trafficked negotiate the position of marginalised migrant entertainer after running away from exploitative work in *gijich'on* clubs through mechanisms and projects that exist entirely outside the state and third-sector infrastructure of anti-trafficking and outside of existing supports for migrant workers in Korea, including those offered by the Filipino community. Outside this infrastructure and beyond their efforts to secure better relational and financial situations for themselves through marriage or factory work, women also form support networks to help each other. The communities of *gijich'on* thus become communities of reworking mobility projects *and* resistance to the disciplining gaze of anti-trafficking and of the wider Filipino and NGO community in Korea. Indeed, at the time of the fieldwork for this study anti-trafficking as discourse and practice in Korea was still in its early stages, but, as discussed earlier, the Filipino community and women's NGOs – including those concerned with (militarised) prostitution – were both well established, particularly in Seoul. Both these groups had also begun to form networks with third-sector women's organisations in the Philippines, including the Coalition Against Trafficking of Women and the radical feminist group Gabriella. Representatives from Gabriella and CATW had both made visits to the Centre on 'exposure trips' to Korea in 2003 to assess the problem of trafficking of Filipinas there but never once visited the women providing supports in *gijich'on*.

8 Home is where the hurt is

> When I came back home it was very hard for me. My family was embarrassed and a little angry with me too, and my friends who have never been abroad treated me differently. It was difficult to understand why they treated me this way, because my experience abroad was very bad and they all know that. It's strange to think that when I was abroad even though it was very hard for me in many ways when I came home it was just as hard – but of course in a different way. You know the saying "home is where the heart is"? Well my version is different: "home is where the hurt is". Do you like it? (Charie)

Charie, who was rescued by the Philippines Embassy in Seoul from a club in TDC just after I commenced my fieldwork in Korea, made this comment when we met again a few months after her return to the Philippines. As her remark suggests, home and homecoming were not occasions filled with promise, hopeful anticipation or happiness. Many of the women I came to know in Korea expressed similar sentiments. Home, which I understand as a multi-scalar construct encompassing nation, community and family, was rendered time and again as problematic – a site for the production of anxiety, shame, sadness and, in Charie's words, "hurt". The reason for this is startlingly simple: trafficking, as a form of failed labour migration, produces moral responses at home because it deviates from dominant discourses about the financially successful migrant worker cast as the new 'hero' of Philippines development and, additionally, for women, the sexually chaste migrant. This rendering, I argue, operates to compound – rather than diminish – the negative aspects of women's experiences whilst in Korea. Thus, for Charie, coming home to Tarlac in Central Luzon was "just as hard" as being in a trafficking situation in Korea, albeit for reasons that were not entirely the same. The ways the tropes of the sexually suspect ('the prostitute') and the financially failed ('the anti-hero') migrant were invoked for women like Charie in the site of home, and the experiences and consequences of this are the subject of discussion in this chapter.

The limited research so far conducted on returned trafficked persons has focused almost exclusively on those who are formally 'detected' and submit to recovery or rehabilitation programs and almost exclusively within the context of sex trafficking. Experiences, anxieties and trajectories of those outside this framework – often referred to as 'undetected victims' in prevailing anti-trafficking discourses – remain, by contrast, almost entirely absent from research (for exceptions see Richardson et al. 2009, Lisborg and Plambech 2009). In this chapter I offer some insights into the ways the label and perception of sex trafficking within the space of return home renders return different from that of many other non-trafficked labour migrants and consequently difficult in ways not well documented in the literature on return migration in the Philippines more broadly. In exploring how this is manifest I focus on the way prostitution and heroism are invoked as moral tropes that the women in my study encountered and subsequently negotiated upon their return home. The chapter problematises home as a place that is safe, supportive and empowering for these returned women, despite the central importance given to returning home in prevailing anti-trafficking discourses. This is because home represents the most intense and immediate environment in which women manoeuvre these tropes of heroism and prostitution. These moral geographies provide significant conceptual import in illuminating the experience and perception of return from so-called failed migrations, of which trafficking must be one of the most exemplary forms.

Only a few studies have appeared on the experiences of return in the context of human trafficking, and these are often rather uncritically situated in prevailing anti-trafficking ideas about rehabilitation and reintegration (see for example, IOM 2006, Shigekane 2007, Richardson et al. 2009). Shigekane (2007: 136), for example, acknowledges that "further research is needed to understand the process of survivor rehabilitation and community integration to develop more effective and far-reaching services", thus framing analysis within discussions about the effectiveness and extension of rehabilitation programs through an evaluation of clients' experiences. This type of focus also means emerging research on the subject of return from trafficking is largely restricted in its coverage to trafficked persons who actually avail of such programs, leaving a large number of persons returned from situations of trafficking absent from discussions (an exception is Lisborg and Plambech 2009). It is these latter cases that provide the focus for discussion in this chapter.[1]

The chapter begins with a brief discussion of the conceptual underpinnings concerning gender, identity and transnational migration as they relate to the space of home. The main part of the chapter discusses the ways anxieties are produced through the moral tropes of heroism and prostitution. In this part of the chapter I explore the ways the act of return brings these moral tropes into play. I draw more fully on the experiences of three of the women from VIP Club in Songtan – Maricel, Amy and Eva.

Return: gender, transnation and moral (b)orders

Home in prevailing anti-trafficking discourses is viewed as the ideal location for return.[2] This would generally include return to the home country and to the home community. For younger trafficked persons (children) especially, but also for women, return to the natal or marital family through formal reintegration is still considered the most effective option by most anti-trafficking organisations for recovery and for breaking the cycle of vulnerability of trafficked persons. Many of the women in my research also shared this view prior to actually going home, with many stating that they missed their families and especially their children. Yet precisely the fact of these women's experiences abroad meant that their encounters with home were markedly different than prior to their migration but almost universally in ways that fuelled anxiety, stress and depression. In taking home as problematic in the context of my research in Korea, I find discussions by feminist geographers who see the home as a site of oppression and containment for women particularly useful. I draw on two strands of these discussions in this chapter. The first concerns the distinction between the public and private realms as women are (differentially) situated and contained within them. Reid (2007: 936), for example, suggests that

> the confinement of women to the supposedly private realm was meant, in the nineteenth century, to distinguish 'respectable femininity' from the prostitute or 'public woman'. . . . an operation of power which facilitated the categorisation and therefore control of a disenfranchised population".

The fact that 'moral women' occupied the private space of the home meant – and in many places still means – that women in public spaces become subject to moral censure and suspicion. In discourses of gender in the Philippines, Filipinas are often constrained by the ways they are positioned in relation to normative models of sexuality and femininity, with the home figuring as the normative site for the articulation of sanctioned roles and models of the 'good Filipino woman'. In this vein, Filipinas are often marked according to the dominant divide between the virginal, family-centred woman and the sexually deviant women, with the latter symbolized by Mary Magdalena (Roces 2009, Law 1997). Following this division, as Espiritu (2003) and Tadiar (2004) both suggest, sexuality and family can become markers of otherness. The failure to live up to standards of sexuality or femininity can be productive of moral geographies of "outsiders in society and space" (cf. Sibley 1995).

Tyner (2002, 2004), Chang and Groves (2000) and Suzuki (2004) all have suggested that Filipinas must also negotiate these gendered discourses in the migration context as well as in the Philippines itself. In particular, Chang and Groves (2000) have documented the ways that Filipinas in Hong Kong who fill low-valued labour functions outside the nightlife entertainment sector, such as in paid domestic work, are subject to the same scrutinising gaze focused on their suspect sexuality. These finding are not unique to Filipinas. Lindquist (2004: 490), similarly, found that internal migrant women on the Indonesian island of Batam experienced anxieties concerning sexuality, "for factory workers in relation to premarital sexuality, and for prostitutes with regard to selling sex for money". These types of studies of female labour migrants recognise the anxieties that emerge as real or imagined transgressions of women in public space are extended to *global* space through more rapid and intense transnational migration processes. As Ferguson et al. (2008: 9) suggest,

> Anxieties about change and control often focus on women's bodies . . . In more and more places around the world . . . mechanisms to control [women's] sexuality seem to be on the increase. At the same time, global conditions of labour, persistent wars, and transnational family structures require/allow/force women to move around.

Remittances can offer a way to manoeuvre sexual censure because they embed women in normative constructions of home, family and sexuality through material contributions to the domestic sphere. Thus, the celebration of Filipino/Filipina migrant workers as 'modern day heroes and heroines' in popular and governmental discourses in the Philippines is itself embedded in broader constructions of gender and family (Rodriguez 2010). In a speech to the Commission of Population at the United Nations in 2006, for example, the Philippines representative reiterated a well-known fact:

> Filipino migrant workers continue to be regarded as the unsung heroes of the nation essentially because of their contributions to Philippine development. The huge amount of dollar remittances estimated by the UN to have reached USD 11.6 billion last year has given a boost to the Philippine economy, contributing 18% of GNP.
>
> Asia 2006

The role of remittances in Philippine national development has been subject to extensive academic treatment (for example, Semyonov and Gorodzeisky 2005, Parrenas 2001), but what is important here is the normative status that the discourse of heroism achieved as part of this development strategy.

The second and related strand of discussions about home in feminist geography on which this chapter draws concerns home as a site that is productive of, and container for, particular values about gender roles and positions of women/girls in the family. Drawing on this premise, Koning (2005: 165) describes the ways young internal migrant women in Java, Indonesia, find return to their home villages difficult because they have developed "divergent values" during their absences which lead to clashes in values and changing relationships, particularly with older generations of women, when they return home. Although Koning (2005) tends to fix the home village as an unchanging and timeless container of traditions, her discussion nonetheless provides useful insights into a little explored subject – namely, how experiences during circular migration affect women and their relationships with family and community at the point of return. For young internal migrant women in China, Gaetano (2008: 631) also found that "return will be interpreted as readiness to marry", which she further argues will be difficult precisely because of the experiences and subjectivities accrued through migration.

These reflections on home in the context of transnational migration of women help us think productively about how embodied experiences of returnees can be understood and the subjectivities they produce explained. In tracing women's experiences of returning home from trafficking in this chapter it is therefore helpful to conceptualise a moral geography of return. Moral geography rests on the premise that the normal (moral) can best been seen when the pathological (immoral/ abnormal) becomes evident (Canguilhem 1989 in Creswell 2005). According to Tim Creswell (2005: 130), "it is clear that the study of forms of transgression in geography points towards the often unspoken existence of normative mappings of human groups and behaviours into those that are 'in place' and those that are 'out of place'". Of different groups considered to be 'out of place' because of their deviance from the spatial norms, work in geography has focused variously on gypsies, vagabonds and homeless people, amongst others. These groups threaten the moral order through their mobility, which challenges the disciplining governmentality of institutions that rest social groups remaining 'in place'. Arguably – although hitherto little explored by geographers – transnational labour migrants disrupt the moral order upon their return home when they deviate from the culturally and institutionally accepted norms of return migration. 'Sex trafficking' is one such locus of deviation since returnees are perceived to be morally suspect (sexually deviant) and economically abnormal (financial failures).

A moral geography of return: manoeuvring discourses of prostitutes and heroines

The process of return in migration has been relatively under-researched compared to other stages of the migration process (King 2000). Return migration in trafficking presents some similarities to broader processes of return for migrants, such as negotiations of home after having been away – often for long periods of time – of changing identities and relationships as a result of their migration experiences, and of concerns around employment and family responsibilities. Nonetheless, there are four characteristics that arguably mark the return from trafficking as distinct from other labour migrants. First is a general lack of choice about conditions of and decisions to return home. Women may run away and seek assistance from the embassy or an NGO to assist them in returning home, or, if they are rescued or detained by the police or immigration authorities, they are normally deported to their home countries at the earliest convenience. Second, return from trafficking can be highly regulated and subject to institutionalised practices and processes of the state and international organisations, often in concert. This is the case where women are recognised as 'victims of trafficking'. Third, unlike other returned migrants, those who are trafficked very rarely fulfil their migration goals in terms of remittances, economic security or financial/ personal advancement (see 'Failed heroines', following). Finally, it has been well documented in the emerging literature on trafficked persons within nongovernment organisations in particular that, beyond economic concerns, some of these migrants also experience problems associated with psychological and physical health as a result of (gendered) violence, abuse and sexual exploitation during their trafficking experiences, in addition to various difficulties in relating to others, such as a breakdown of trust (see, for example, United Nations Inter Agency Project [UN-IAP] 1998). Practices governing and processes guiding return, as well as programs for returned victims of trafficking, are built on the recognition of these problems (IOM 2007).

Charie and many other women I traced in the Philippines after they returned home disclosed that they experienced stress, loneliness, anxiety, boredom and depression at least some of the time since returning. The problems they encountered after returning that brought on these feelings fell into three main areas: financial problems stemming from their failure to remit money and returning without any substantial sum of money, family disruptions brought on by both these financial issues and stigma over suspicions around their sexuality abroad. These findings echo those of Lisborg and Plambech (2009: 63), who noted that "'financial difficulties' was mentioned most frequently, with 'family issues' second, but 'stigma' was the problem that was chosen most often as the most pressing problem by a wide margin". Of course stigma cuts across both these other problems in complex and manifold ways.

In this part of the chapter I locate the anxieties of return for women like Charie, Amy, Maricel and Eva within the prevailing discourses of Filipino migrant workers as heroes and prostitution as moral deviation. The interplay of these tropes helps explain how and in what ways return produced emotions of shame, guilt, frustration, stress, depression and anxiety amongst the women in my research. These problems led to concrete decisions and actions by women that circulated around the need to earn money or assume other responsibilities in the context of the family, minimising the risk of their experiences being disclosed to either their families or their home communities, plans set in motion to move elsewhere and the related desire by many participants to go abroad again.

Failed heroines

Whilst many women brought home some money, which ranged from PHP 3,000 to PHP 100,000 (USD 65 to 2,140), none of the participants I focussed on in this return section had actually managed to remit any whilst they were abroad. Those participants who were eventually given salaries – usually after a long period of debt repayments had ended – had managed to save a little from their salaries to bring home, whilst others who lodged a complaint or filed a case had some compensation money (although this came more than a year after they returned home). Nonetheless, nearly all the women had substantial debts (ranging from PHP 5,000–85,000, or USD 105–1,800) to pay upon returning to the Philippines. These debts were both to family members or friends and/or to an agent or informal creditor who helped facilitate their migration. After paying these debts none of the women had any money left over. Also cutting into the little money they may have managed to accrue whilst abroad was the cost of the airfare home. Half the participants had to pay their own airfares, even though airfares were supposed to be provided by their managers in Korea. One of the main problems for women here was that their managers would hold all their documents, including air tickets, during their sojourns. This meant that if they ran away, for example, they normally would not have their original air ticket with them.

Only three of my participants reflected that their financial goals had been achieved despite their largely negative working conditions, whilst the rest said they were no better off financially – indeed for some they were much worse off – than they had been prior to migrating. Those who had some money after their debts were paid either spent the money quickly on family members and personal items for themselves, such as cell phones and clothes – which at least acted to give the illusion of their success abroad – or gave their money to their parents. Lisa put all her small savings into a college insurance plan for her child. Maricel paid for medical expenses for her parents, which exhausted the little money she brought home. Eva was the one exception to the rest of the women; she managed to build a house in her province. But she was receiving a monthly sum of USD 500 from her American fiancé abroad, and it was this money, rather than money accrued through her sojourn in Korea, that financed the building of the house. Five other women I contacted upon their return home also received regular remittances from boyfriends abroad (ranging between USD 300 and USD 500 per month). This source of money, as will be discussed in more detail in the following, held contradictory implications for the women who received it; on the one hand it worked to negate the pressure to earn money and support family members, but on the other it acted to exacerbate the suspicion and stigma of the women concerned as having 'been prostitutes' whilst abroad.

Having returned without a substantive sum of money, all the women except Eva were under pressure from their families to compensate for this by getting a job quickly back home. Despite this, the vast majority of the women had failed to gain employment. Only three managed to get casual or short-term jobs – in these instances as a vendor, a cashier and a medical secretary – which paid between PHP 4,000 and 6,000 per month. Eva was the only one to state that she had or was 'earning' enough money to cover her living costs and that she was not compelled to try to find a job.

Maricel, who was twenty-two years old when she returned from a twelve-month stint in VIP Club in Songtan, was unemployed for more than a year between the time she returned home and when I met up with her again in Manila and then again in her home town in Bulacan a few days later. She was single before she left for Korea and upon her return, and she moved back in with her parents, her younger brother, and her sister and her family. When Maricel left Korea in late 2003 she had hardly any money in her pocket because the first six months of her salary was deducted for agency fees and other dubious costs. When she finally started to get some money from the bar most of it was spent on simply covering her expenses, like accommodation, clothes, personal items and so on. In fact the salary she did eventually receive in Korea was USD 250 below what she had been promised before migrating as an entertainer. She therefore received exactly half of her promised salary at USD 250 and for only half of her sojourn. Although Maricel had been deceived about both the work she was to perform in Korea and the salary and financial arrangements, she chose to remain quiet about her situation and hold out for the time she could return home. When her contract finished it was with some trepidation that she returned to her family in Bulacan in central Luzon. Her family was disappointed at her failure to return with money or to send money back to them whilst she had been away. She confided to me that since coming back:

> I feel so much under pressure to get a job coz I didn't bring enough money home with me. I tried an interview at Jollibee [local fast food chain] but part time so not enough money. What can I do to make up for the all the time I'm away and not sending anything back?

Attempting to earn money was a key means by which Maricel and some of the other women made up for the shame associated with their failure to earn/remit money whilst abroad. I witnessed both Maricel and other women I came to know through the research devote considerable energy towards looking for work to make up for lost remittances and for the futile absence of their labour in the Philippines during their sojourns abroad. This pressure was doubly felt in the context of the celebration of Filipino migrant workers abroad as 'national heroes' and my participants' failures to live up to these nationally embedded and popularly consumed expectations.

Maricel had become an additional burden on her family since returning home – another mouth to feed in an already stretched household. She spent much of her time out of the house on the pretext of looking for a job because of her embarrassment to her family. As a high school graduate without a college education and at twenty-three years of age – and therefore above the normal entry age for factory work – Maricel's prospects were extremely limited. Her father in particular accentuated her feelings of embarrassment on an almost daily basis:

> I hate being at home because my dad always says to me that he feels embarrassed when our family friends or relatives meet him. They joke about why we haven't got an extension on our house or opened a small business since I'm back already. He says he has to make up a story about me coming home because I got sick and the money had to pay the medical bills. It's a good story, but his telling me this doesn't make me feel any better about things. I just feel guilty and guilty.

In discussing the impacts of overseas Filipino workers on local – and specifically rural – development, McKay and Brandy (2005: 92) emphasise the material expressions of success within the landscape:

> A neighbourhood with many workers overseas could be distinguished by the newness of its houses, cars, exotic appliances, as well as commercial crops. Thus, the circular migration of female OFWs [overseas Filipino workers] to and from 'abroad' transforms rural landscapes in material ways.

The effects of women who are working abroad but not remitting money to contribute to these material landscape transformations and development strategies are equally conspicuous by their absence, as Maricel's experiences with her father attests.

This is the key point here; women leave the Philippines as migrant workers with all the expectations this creates around remittances and the enhancement of family welfare. However, their trafficking precludes their financial success as migrant workers and precipitates their erasure from the discourse of heroism that celebrates the *balik bayan* (lit. homecoming, in Tagalog) of other migrant workers. Thus, whilst McKay and Brandy (2005: 93) claim that "communication and remittance practices continue and even intensify, rather than attenuate, social immediacy between migrants and sending localities", the opposite must also hold: for those who cannot remit during their sojourns abroad, failure to remit can strain, rather than strengthen, these same relationships. This in turn induced nearly all the women in my research to devote considerable effort to making up for their lack of remittances and lost income/labour by looking for work locally – or at least getting out of the house on the pretext of looking for work – or initiating plans to go abroad again. Home thus becomes a site of social disarticulation and stress, rather than confirmation and support.

Prostitution or trafficking?

In academic discussions of trafficking there is a debate around whether and to what extent migrant women in sex industries globally are voluntary sex workers or victims of trafficking (for example, Agustin 2003, Doezema 1998). This debate occupies considerable space in the body of literature related to trafficking and is preoccupied with determining whether women fall into one or the other category. Yet, for the most part, this debate engages very little with how regimes of morality within home communities situate women as 'prostitutes' no matter what the actual work as an entertainer involves. This was the case for virtually all the women in my research. In other words, the fact of whether they were trafficked or voluntary sex workers mattered very little within their home communities, which, in the absence of some formal outside intervention like awareness raising or the women's own ability to make this distinction clear, failed to grasp the difference between the two categories. Chang and Groves (2000: 74) assert that even Filipinas who are paid domestic workers in Hong Kong are subject to moralising discourses that centre on women's sexuality and specifically invoke prostitution as means of rendering Filipinas 'morally suspect' (see also Constable 1999, Aguilar 1996). These are what we might call the 'transnational effects' of national discourses concerning morality/prostitution (Cannell 1999).

This has meant that many of the women I encountered upon return felt they could not relate to those in their home environments because of their experiences abroad and so became alienated from their communities. Whilst some women did disclose financial exploitation, details of rape or physical and sexual abuse are often not recounted due to shame. Women who discussed the full extent of their experiences to family or friends were often not met with a sympathetic response. Tensions arose, particularly with husbands and boyfriends, often leading to relationship break-ups. Partners often left women who had been working in clubs in Korea because they had difficulty understanding exactly what the women did in the clubs.[3] Merle, who returned from Korea in 2002, exemplified this dilemma.

Merle returned to Angeles at the age of twenty-five, at which point her family life was profoundly negatively affected by her experiences in Korea. Merle had left a husband and three children behind when she migrated to Korea with Charie as an entertainer and was motivated to go abroad solely to earn money to support her family. When she returned home she disclosed to her parents and her husband what had happened to her in Korea, including details of financial exploitation and sexual and physical abuse. Merle's husband's reaction was unexpected; he told her he could no longer accept being married to her and subsequently abandoned her.

After this Merle became solely responsible for the welfare, including financial support, of her three children. She managed to get a short-term job as a sales lady in an appliance store in Dau, near Angeles, but after a three-month contract she became unemployed again. She said that she found it very hard to secure a job because, like Maricel, she was only a high school graduate and not skilled or qualified for any particular profession. Until the time of writing Merle has had only casual employment and been mostly unemployed. She was planning to migrate abroad again but, she stressed, not as an entertainer. In complex and sometimes unexpected ways, then, disclosures of their experiences abroad can cause family disruptions which, in turn, can also have negative financial consequences.

Because Merle was one of the group of women who had filed a case against their employer in Korea through the Philippines Embassy in Seoul for fraudulent employment contracts and forced prostitution, there were further consequences. Some of the details of this group's experience emerged through the context of this case and newspapers, initially in Korea and then in the Philippines, since this was one of the first such cases of 'sexual slavery' of foreign women in Korea involving a compensation claim. As Charie later told me, "We don't mind so much if the newspapers interview us in Korea because, you see, the story will stay there. But if it is in the Philippines it is a big problem because someone we know might see our pictures or recognise our names. What if my mum finds out? She will be shock[ed]". The fact that the case received some media attention back in the Philippines was, Merle felt, the real reason her husband had decided to leave her:

> I think it's not that he couldn't accept what happened to me in Korea – even though he said he didn't want to [have] sex with me anymore because I'd been with other men. No, I think the more important thing was the embarrassment when the case came out here [Angeles] because his friends saw it and his family too. He said his mum gave him a lot of trouble about me after that. How could he defend me when underneath he felt the same way too? It was just easier for him to leave that deal with this problem I guess.

The fact that Merle's 'being with other men' was not entirely consensual was certainly something her husband understood, but it appeared not the most important factor influencing his decision to leave her. He was more concerned with the pressure from his own parents and the ridicule of his friends about his wife having been "a prostitute in Korea". It was difficult for Merle, who was still – perhaps more than many of the other women I met upon return – deeply affected by her experience in Korea, to attempt to work towards redressing this.

Double jeopardy: financial failure and the stigma of prostitution

Some women experienced ruptures and tensions in their home lives upon return because they had failed to earn and remit money as they had intended *and* because they were subject to moral censure around prostitution. Eva was in such a situation since, despite having quite a bit of money, she had not earned this through supposedly 'legitimate work' in Korea, but through remittances from her American boyfriend. Eva had been married prior to departing for Korea, and her husband was a drug addict and was serving a prison term when Eva departed for Korea; it was this family breakdown that had supplied her main motivation for going abroad as she had become the sole breadwinner for her children, who lived with her sister and her aunty whilst she was abroad. Eva's parents had both passed away, so there was no other immediate family support available for her. Subject to the same financial exploitation as Maricel whilst in Korea, Eva decided it was in her best interests to develop a relationship with a customer. As Eva stated,

> If I did not meet my boyfriend when I'm in Korea I come back here with nothing. My sister and aunty are the ones to look after my kids and they expect a lot when I come home coz they do it [care for her children] for nothing.

In the context of her sexual and financial exploitation in Korea, Eva's American boyfriend became her transnational strategy for economic stability and upward mobility. The chosen customer was a civilian staff at the nearby air force base in Songtan. He lived in Alaska and had returned there before Eva's own contract had expired. He had another family in Alaska with another Filipina, and, despite my subtle probing, it was unclear whether he was divorced or separated from this other woman or indeed whether they were still together.

I visited Eva in Bulacan with Maricel. She was ecstatic to see me because, since her return, her American boyfriend had paid for the construction of a new, two-story dwelling near her aunty's house, and she was keen to show it off. The dwelling was elaborately furnished, with a massive television and karaoke taking up an inordinate amount of space in the lounge room. Her two children were back with her, and her American boyfriend was also visiting from Alaska at the time I was there. Although much thinner than she was in Korea it was clear that Eva was pregnant, and it turned out her baby was due in four months. Her boyfriend would not be around for the birth as he had to return to Alaska – whether for family or work reasons was unclear. When I asked why she was so skinny even when she was five months pregnant (she ate virtually nothing when we went out for lunch at a nearly restaurant), she responded that she feared her boyfriend would find another Filipina if she didn't look 'sexy'.

Eva's aunty and sister were notably absent from the scene when I visited her new home, and apart from us the large house was empty. Eva was not keen to discuss her aunty and sister, and I could see the distress it was causing her and her boyfriend to raise the subject. When we were alone in her kitchen she said:

> They don't come here to my house coz they don't like how I got the money to build it, even though we still have communication and they still accept money I give them. Even some of my old friends from before don't come round coz they think I'm a prosti [prostitute] abroad. I sell my pussy when I'm in Korea coz I have no choice; my kids don't eat, my aunty and my sister have nothing. I get my boyfriend and I can come back with something. I have a boyfriend so no need to use my pussy anymore. It's not the way I want but that's the way it is.

Whilst still situated transnationally Eva could easily proclaim that the money she returned to Bulacan with was from her salary, but when she returned and continued to receive money from abroad questions about the origins of this money were raised. With the appearance of her American boyfriend there was no choice but to reveal her source of support. At home she was no longer able to manage the techniques of distancing that she had developed whilst in Korea. Eva's family life suffered as a result as her two closest relatives distanced themselves from her. She said she thought that her aunty, whom she described as "old-fashioned", had influenced her sister because of fear that her sister might also "try for a foreign boyfriend". I felt sad as we left Eva that day because she would probably be alone when her new baby was born and would have to continue to live in a community in which she was not entirely accepted or wanted. Unable to join her boyfriend in Alaska because of his pre-existing family, Eva experienced anxieties of return like Maricel, but also the contradictions of sexual censure that accompanied her strategy for meeting the demands of financial 'success'.

Conclusion

Return migration for women like Eva, Grace and Maricel is markedly different in many respects – and negatively so – from that of returned migrant workers more generally. The specific circumstances that are likely to negatively influence trafficked women's experiences of return include poor financial status and moral censure centring on suspicions about prostitution. These factors were variously evident for the women in my study, and I witnessed women's stress, anxiety, sadness, boredom and shame at home. Some commissioned research has provided insights into the experience of return from trafficking in Southeast Asia (Lisborg and Plambech 2009), with Lisborg and Plambech's study of women who returned to the Philippines and Thailand from exploitative work situations in the sex/entertainment industry and from domestic servitude a particularly notable study.

This is because it calls into question the prevailing architecture of return under an anti-trafficking framework and the assumptions that guide the responses inherent in this framework. They argue for a re-thinking of reintegration, suggesting that

> often, returned victims of trafficking are understood and treated by external observers, such as policy makers, journalists and even involved organisation staff, as one homogenous group of people sharing a common wish to go back to where they started. However, in seeing all returnees as sharing the same difficulties and wishing to go 'home', crucial questions are not asked and the different needs and aspirations of returnees are not fully understood and addressed.
> (2009: 17)

Drawing on the tropes of migrants as heroes/heroines and prostitution as moral deviation – both of which receive much discursive attention in the Philippines – helps explain the anxieties of those women who return from Korea as entertainers.

The problems experienced by many of the women I knew upon their return to the Philippines point to some marked differences in narratives of return from those of migrant workers who were not trafficked or exploited. Recent discussions of these return migrants' experiences tend to focus on issues around exposure to cosmopolitan attitudes and lifestyles in making it difficult to readjust to life back home. In these cases migrants return as different from before they left, but their difference is marked by positive associations with new attitudes, possibly education and exposure to new experiences, places and people – all notable components of 'cosmopolitanism' (as in Vertovec and Cohen 2002). In addition, 'success' in an economic sense confers immediate respect and gratitude on these other migrants in a way that returned victims of trafficking are unable to command. This is particularly acute in the Philippines where the discourse of migrant heroes/heroines is constructed through state and popular discourse.

All the women who participated in my research, as well as the anecdotes I heard of others through these participants, desired to take their chances in going abroad again or at least to move to another place in the Philippines, and whilst they located their decisions in the need to make up for their inability to remit money when they were in Korea, it was clear that coming home had not been a positive and enabling experience emotionally for them. Understanding the role of morality – in this case in the experiences of trafficked persons – requires us to think about relationships (with family and friends), subjectivities (of being heroines, trafficked persons, prostitutes or wives and mothers) and places where these are played out, including 'home'.

Notes

1 Anecdotal evidence gathered through discussions with various organisations in the Philippines, including Scalabrini Migration Centre and Coalition Against Trafficking of Women, Asia-Pacific, suggests that approximately 70–80 per cent of trafficked persons return to the Philippines undetected.

2 The fact that many trafficked persons, including children, are unable to return home because of unconducive family environments (family dissolution, domestic violence and other forms of stress) is recognized and accepted widely amongst the anti-trafficking organizations, but this has nonetheless failed to dislodge the view of return home as the ideal scenario for reintegration.
3 Although not discussed in detail in this chapter, returned victims of trafficking can also undergo change in attitudes and perceptions which can affect how they relate to, and interact with, others. At the heart of human trafficking is a breach of trust that occurs when a victim is tricked or coerced by a person who claims to be providing legitimate opportunities to migrate and/or is sold by a relative or friend. This breach of trust is carried throughout a victim's deployment abroad and constantly reinforced by interactions with clients/customers, bosses and, in many cases, law enforcement agencies and immigration authorities. When victims return home they often have developed a deep distrust of police, which can affect their opportunities for seeking legal redress for their trafficking. They may also fear retaliation from traffickers, especially if they ran away from where they were deployed abroad or made a complaint to authorities.

9 Conclusion

The goal of this ethnography was to explore the trajectories, anxieties, vulnerabilities and aspirations of Filipinas who migrate to Korea's *gijich'on* as entertainers. The book examined these constrained mobilities both in the context of women's working lives in the clubs and in Korea and the Philippines after they left their initial workplaces. I was particularly concerned to detail women's trajectories in Korea after running away from the clubs, since these sites are often overlooked in accounts of migrant entertainers, including Filipinas. Most discussions of migrant entertainers and migrant sex workers tend to presume that after club work women will either go back home of their own accord or under the directorship of a government authority or that they will be subject to rehabilitation measures in the context of anti-trafficking interventions. Yet in Korea post-club manoeuvrings and re-workings constitute a pivotal and formative period in these women's lives and one where – as with working in the club – their agency is always visible, even where its transformative potential is often opaque and elusive.

I have attempted to engage with the discourse and experience of trafficking in elaborating these women's mobilities. When discussing the lives of migrant sex workers and entertainers existing scholarship tends to dismiss the experience of trafficking because, it is often argued, such women migrate knowing what kind of work they will do. Indeed, this argument has been made both in relation to Filipina entertainers in Korea (Cheng 2010) and Japan (Parrenas 2011). Such arguments are of course a reaction to the 'sex slave' rhetoric outlined in chapter 2, and in that respect Cheng and Parrenas are right in contesting this characterisation. Rosie, Cherry, Lisa, Grace and the other women whose experiences figured in this book are not 'modern day comfort women', nor are they victims of sex trafficking in the ways the media, governmental organisations and NGOs in both Korea and the Philippines have described them. Indeed, my hope in part in describing these women's lives in Korea is to contest the appropriateness of such as classification. Of the over 100 women I came to know in TDC, Songtan, Anjongli and Kunsan, not one described herself according to the 'sex slave' or 'comfort woman' labels.

Most of these women were open to performing some form of sexual or intimate labour during their sojourns in the clubs, even where they had not been expecting to do so prior to their migrations to Korea. Undoubtedly this produced anxieties for many of the women I came to know, like Honey, who talked at length about her creative tactics for avoiding the advances of customers whilst simultaneously avoiding the admonishment of the mama-san in her club for threatening clubs profits by not performing her 'work' properly. Other women, like Cherry, Lisa, Rosie and Grace, performed sexual intercourse and other forms of erotic labour both within the club and in the context of bar fines. They needed the money because they weren't paid their correct salary, and so commissions from sex and ladies drinks became the *only* way of surviving in the club and being able to remit much-needed funds back to the Philippines. Did they see themselves as sex workers as a result? The simple answer – and the one Lisa gave to me often when we discussed the subject – was that she did what she had to do and that was all there was to it. Sexual labour was a means to an ends and certainly not a career path.

So if sex trafficking is not a relevant interpretation of these women's migration experiences, why then do I continue to argue for the significance of trafficking in understanding their lives in Korea? Foremost, all the women I knew were deceived about key aspects of their work that had to do with salary, working hours, duties in the club, penalties and punishments, humiliations and abuse, surveillance and controls over their movements and their ability to easily extricate themselves from these situations. Even where the women's contracts clearly stipulated that they could break their contract at any time for valid reasons and without penalty, this was simply untrue for all the women I knew. They could not leave their work unless they found a boyfriend or customer willing to pay out their contract or unless they took the dramatic step of running away. In other words, their self-articulated concerns about their work as entertainers in the clubs had to do with exploitative relations and practices that were not centred around sexual or intimate labour, or in some instances this may have been a secondary concern. But here is where the paradox of trafficking lies for these women: Filipina entertainers are subjects pre-figured as sex trafficking victims, which leaves redress for labour violations under the rubric of labour trafficking foreclosed as an option or a frame for understanding their situations. Further, and as Parrenas (2011) took pains to point out, the migration regime in the Philippines that ostensibly helps protect female migrants creates massive and debilitating debts that bind these – and many other – Filipino migrants to oppressive and exploitative workplaces abroad. Debt bondage, or what Parrenas (2011) labels "indentured mobility", was undoubtedly a factor weighing on the minds of all the women in *gijich'on* clubs, and one which bound them to their workplaces. These conditions, I have argued, mark women as falling within the ambit of *labour* trafficking.

What recourse is available to migrant labourers like *gijich'on* entertainers who are caught between trafficking classifications? I have argued in this ethnography that key to women's experiences in Korea was their productive engagement with trafficking not just as a discourse, but as an *experience* of labour exploitation that framed their post-club trajectories. Women strategized and planned for their futures in ways that would re-centre their aspirations in positive ways. These strategies could not be anticipated prior to migration, echoing scholars who document the importance of understanding the ways migration destinations – or indeed transit points – become significant sites for re-working and re-imagining mobility in which new options, trajectories and plans are continually mapped out and pursued. This re-working in situ enables *gijich'on* entertainers to act in ways that restore, to varying degrees and with varying levels of success, their agency in crafting their futures. I also suggested that, as with any migrants, this re-crafting is highly volatile and contingent. In this vein, intimate and sexual labour in the clubs, for example, began to drift into the murky waters of love, romance and the possibility of marriage. Customers became boyfriends and husbands in the context of the desire to re-craft positive post-club futures that did not necessarily entail going back to the Philippines, as homecomings, as I suggested in chapter 8, are not always the fulfilling and celebratory occasions they should be. But, as chapters 4 and 5 suggested, romance as a strategy is often fraught precisely because of women's prior positionings in the clubs, which situates them in relation to their prospective partners in ways that are difficult to move past. The same holds true for women who run away to work in factories as irregular migrant labourers. As Jane's and Charie's experiences illustrate, these women often find themselves subject to gossip and ridicule outside the clubs and beyond *gijich'on* communities. Club work casts women in social relations where they must continually navigate the stigma of the club and where they continue to be yoked to their prior work in the clubs despite their ardent efforts to move on and re-craft their mobility according to more positive relational and material frames.

Collectively, as I suggested in chapter 7, women also craft futures that are not exclusively tied to their own individual betterment, as Cheng (2010), for example, would have it. Women support each other in surprising and creative ways through material, symbolic and practical means. Although they would rarely call these support anti-trafficking measures, at least in the context of *gijich'on* these measures have a far greater immediate positive effect in minimising harms and vulnerabilities of entertainers than any intervention proffered by the anti-trafficking stakeholders who claim to know what trafficked entertainers need and how to deliver effective 'protection'. Indeed, as we saw in chapter 7, these anti-trafficking stakeholders are often at odds with, and can sometimes undermine, women's own projects to this end.

By turning our gaze to the ways one moves on from trafficking outside the architecture of anti-trafficking interventions – either individually or collectively – one can gain a sense of these women's resilience. One of the most persistent and largely unanswered academic criticisms of anti-trafficking work is that it diminishes, rather than enables, the agency of migrants. The ultimate goal of anti-trafficking interventions should be to realise victimised and exploited migrants' potential to become empowered to take control of their own lives. In this sense *gijich'on* entertainers are political subjects with the potential to disrupt the disciplinary impulses of anti-trafficking and proffer their own interpretation of where their vulnerabilities lie and how these may be transformed.

References

Adams, Vincanne and Stacey Pigg 2005. "Introduction: The Moral Object of Sex". In Vincanne Adams and Stacey Pigg (eds.), *Sex in Development: Science, Sexuality, and Morality in Global Perspective*. Durham, NC: Duke University Press.
Agathangelou, Anna M. and L.H.M. Ling 2003. "Desire Industries: Sex Trafficking, UN Peacekeeping and the Neo-liberal World Order", *Brown Journal of World Affairs* 10 (1): 133–148.
Aguilar, F.V. Jr. 1996. "The Dialectics of Transnational Shame and National Identity", *Philippine Sociological Review* 44: 101–36.
Agustin, Laura 2007. *Sex at the Margins*. London: Zed Press.
Agustin, Laura 2003. "Sex, Gender and Migrations: Facing up to Ambiguous Realities", *Soundings* 23: 84–98.
Agustin, Laura 2002. "The (Crying) Need for Different Kinds of Research", *Research for Sex Work* 5: 30–32.
Air Force Times 2002. "Sex Slaves and the US Military", *Air Force Times*, August 12. Retrieved May 22, 2008, from http://airforcetimes.com/channel.php?.
Al-Ali, N.R. Black and K. Koser 2001. "Refugees and Transnationalism: The Experiences of Bosnians and Eritreans in Europe", *Journal of Ethnic and Migration Studies* 27 (4): 615–634.
Andrijasevic, Rutvica 2007. "Beautiful Dead Bodies: Gender, Migration and Representation in Anti-trafficking Campaigns", *Feminist Review* 86: 24–44.
Andrijasevic, Rutvica 2003. "The Difference Borders Make: (Il)legality, Migration and Trafficking in Italy among Eastern European Women in Prostitution". In Sara Ahmed, Claudia Castaneda, Anne-Marie Fortier, and Mimi Sheller (eds.), *Uprootings/Regroundings: Questions of Home and Migration*. London: Berg, pp. 251–272.
Asis, M. 2006. *International Migration, Migrant Empowerment and Development Prospects: The Philippines*. Scalabrini Migration Center-Philippines.
Associated Federated Press (AFP) 2007. "South Korea Gets Tough on Sex Tourism", September 20. Retrieved November 12, 2009, from http://www.humantraffickingorg/updates/723.
Barber, P.G. 2000. "Agency in Philippine Women's Labour Migration and Provisonal Diaspora", *Women Studies International Forum* 23 (4): 399–411.
Battistella, G., & Asis, M.M.B. (1999). *The Crisis and Migration in Asia*. Manila: Scalabrini Migration Center.
Boris, E., S. Gilmore and R. Parrenas 2010. "Sexual Labors: Interdisciplinary Perspectives towards Sex as Work", *Sexualities* 13 (2): 131–137.
Brennan, Denise 2005. "Methodological Challenges in Research with Trafficked Persons: Tales from the Field", *International Migration* 43 (1–2): 35–54.

Brennan, Denise 2004. *What's Love Got to Do with It? Transnational Desires and Sex Tourism in the Dominican Republic*. Durham, NC, and London: Duke University Press.

Brennan, Denise 2002. "Selling Sex for Visas: Sex Tourism as a Stepping-stone to International Marriage". In Barbara Ehrenreich and Arlie Russell Hochchild (eds.), *Global Woman: Nannies, Maids and Sex Workers in the New Economy*. London: Granta Books, pp. 154–168.

Brown, Louise 2000. *Sex Slaves: The Trafficking of Women in Asia*. London: Virago Press.

Brunovskis, Anette and Rebecca Surtees 2010. "Untold Stories: Biases and Selection Effects in Research with Victims of Trafficking for Sexual Exploitation", *International Migration* 48 (4): 1–37.

Brunovskis, Anette and Rebecca Surtees 2007. *Leaving the Past Behind? When Victims of Trafficking Decline Assistance*. Oslo, Norway: Allkopi AS.

Bunnell, Tim 2007. "Post-Maritime Transnationalisation: Malay Seafarers in Liverpool", *Global Networks* 7 (4): 412–429.

Cabezas, Amalia L. 2009. *Economies of Desire: Sex and Tourism in Cuba and the Dominican Republic*. Philadelphia: Temple University Press.

Canguihem, Georges 1989. *The Normal and the Pathological*. Brooklyn, NY: Zone Books.

Cannell, Fenella 1999. *Power and Intimacy in Christian Philippines*. Cambridge: Cambridge University Press.

Caouette, T. and Y. Saito 1999. *To Japan and Back: Thai Women Recount Their Experiences*. Geneva: International Organisation for Migration.

Capdevila, Gustavo 2002. "Korea's New 'Comfort Women' ", *Asia Times*, Retrieved June 6, 2011, from http://atimes.com/atimes/Korea/DI05Dg01.html.

Castles, Stephen 2000. "International Migration at the Beginning of the Twenty-First Century: Global Trends and Issues", *International Social Science Journal* 52 (165): 269–281.

Chang, Kimberley A. and Julian McAllister Groves 2000. "Neither 'Saints' nor 'Prostitutes': Sexual Discourse in the Filipina Domestic Worker Community in Hong Kong", *Women's Studies International Forum* 23 (1): 73–87.

Chapkis, Wendy 1997. *Live Sex Acts: Women Performing Erotic Labor*. New York: Routledge.

Cheng, Sealing 2010. *On the Move for Love: Migrant Entertainers and the U.S. Military in South Korea*. Philadelphia: University of Pennsylvania Press.

Cheng, Sealing 2008. "Muckraking and Stories Untold: Ethnography Meets Journalism on Trafficked Women and the U.S. Military", *Sexuality Research and Social Policy* 4 (5): 6–18.

Cheng, Sealing 2004. "Korean Sex Trade 'Victims' Strike for Rights", *Asia Times Online* (Speak Freely Forum).

Cho, Grace M. 2006. "The Diaspora of Camptown: The Forgotten War's Monstrous Family", *Women's Studies Quarterly* 34 (1/2): 309–331.

Choi, Chungmoo and Elaine H. Kim 1998. *Dangerous Women: Gender and Korean Nationalism*. New York: Routledge.

Chung, Ah-young 2005. "More Koreans Buy Sex Abroad", *Korea Times*, October 31.

Cloke, Paul, Phil Cooke, Jerry Cursons, Paul Milbourne and Rebekah Widdowfield 2000. "Ethics, Reflexivity and Research: Encounters with Homeless People", *Ethics, Place and Environment* 3 (2): 133–154.

Coalition Against Trafficking of Women–Asia Pacific (CATW–AP) 2002. *Women in International Migration Processes: Patterns, Profiles and Health Consequences of Sexual Exploitation*. Manila: CATW–AP.

Cohen, Erik 2003. "Transnational Marriage in Thailand: The Dynamics of Extreme Heterogamy". In Thomas Bauer and Bob McKercher (eds.), *Sex and Tourism: Journeys of Romance, Love, and Lust*. Binghampton: Haworth Hospitality Press, pp. 57–81.

Constable, Nicole 1999. "At Home but Not at Home: Filipina Narratives of Ambivalent Returns", *Cultural Anthropology* 14 (2): 203–28.
Cornwall, Andrea, S. Correa and S. Jolly 2008. *Development with a Body: Sexuality, Human Rights and Development*. Zed Books: London.
Crawford, Mary 2010. *Sex Trafficking in South Asia: Telling Maya's Story*. New York and London: Routledge.
Cresswell, Tim 2005. "Mobilising the Movement: The Role of Mobility in the Suffrage Politics of Florence Luscomb and Margaret Foley, 1911–1915", *Gender, Place and Culture*. 12 (4): 447–461.
Cupples, Julie 2002. "The Field as a Landscape of Desire: Sex and Sexuality in Geographical Fieldwork", *Area* 34 (4): 382–390.
Della Porta, Donatella and Sidney Tarrow 2005. *Transnational Protest and Social Activism*. Lanham, MD: Rowman and Littlefield.
Derks, Annuska 2008. *Khmer Women on the Move: Exploring Work and Life in Urban Cambodia*. Manoa: University of Hawaii Press.
Demick, Barbara 2002. "Off-base Behavior in Korea", *Los Angeles Times*, September 26: A1.
Doezema, Jo 2000. "Loose Women or Lost Women? The Re-emergence of the Myth of White Slavery in Contemporary Discourses of Trafficking in Women", *Gender Issues* (Winter): 23–50.
Doezema, Jo 1998. "Forced to Choose: Beyond the Voluntary v. Forced Prostitution Dichotomy". In K. Kempadoo and J. Doezema (eds.), *Global Sex Workers: Rights, Resistance and Redefinition*. London: Routledge, pp. 34–50.
Enloe, Cynthia 1989. *Bananas, Beaches and Bases: Making Feminist Sense of International Politics*. Berkeley: University of California Press.
Enriquez, Jean 1999. *Filipinas in Prostitution around U.S. Military Bases in Korea: A Recurring Nightmare*. Manila: Coalition Against Trafficking of Women (CATW).
Espiritu, Y. L. 2003. *Home Bound: Filipino American Lives across Cultures, Communities and Countries*. Berkeley: University of California Press.
Faier, Lieba 2009. *Intimate Encounters: Filipina Women and the Remaking of Rural Japan*. Berkeley: University of California Press.
Faier, Lieba 2008. "Runaway Stories: The Underground Micromovements of Filipina Oyomesan in Rural Japan", *Cultural Anthropology* 23 (4): 630–659.
Farley, Melissa (ed.) 2004. *Prostitution, Trafficking and Traumatic Stress*. Binghamton, NY: Haworth Maltreatment & Trauma Press.
Farley, Melissa, A. Cotton, J. Lynne, S. Zumbeck, F. Spiwak, M. E. Reyes, D. Alvarez, U. Sezgin 2003. "Prostitution and Trafficking in Nine Countries: Update on Violence and Posttraumatic Stress Disorder", *Journal of Trauma Practice* 2 (3/4): 33–74.
Ferguson, Kathy E., S. E. Merry and M. Mironesco 2008. Introduction. In K. Ferguson and M. Mironesco (eds.), *Gender and Globalisation in Asia and the Pacific: Method, Practice, Theory*. Manoa: University of Hawaii Press, pp. 1–14.
Ford, Michele 2004. "Organizing the Unorganizable: Unions, NGOs, and Indonesian Migrant Labour", *International Migration* 42 (5): 99–119.
Ford, Michele, Lenore Lyons and Willem van Schendel 2012. *Trafficking and Labour Migration*. London: Routledge.
Foucault, Michel 1990. *Discipline and Punish: The Birth of the Prison*. New York: Pantheon.
Foucault, Michel 1980. *Power/Knowledge: Selected Interviews and Other Writings, 1972–77*. London: Random House.

168   References

Franks, Katherine 2002. *G-Strings and Sympathy: Strip Club Regulars and Male Desire*. Durham, NC, and London: Duke University Press.

Frederick, John 2005. "The Myth of Nepal-to-India Sex Trafficking: Its Creation, Maintenance, and Its Influence on Anti-trafficking Interventions". In Kamela Kempadoo (ed), *Trafficking and Prostitution Reconsidered: New Perspectives on Migration, Sex Work, and Human Rights*. Boulder, CO, and London: Paradigm Publishers, pp. 127–148.

Fulton, Bruce 1998. "Nationalism and the Construction of Korean Identity". Edited by Hyung Pai and Timothy R. Tangherlini. *Korea Research Monograph* 26: 230. Berkeley: Center for Korean Studies, University of California.

Gaetano, Arianne 2008. "Sexuality in Diasporic Space: Rural-to-Urban Migrant Women Negotiating Gender and Marriage in Contemporary China", *Gender, Place and Culture* 15 (6): 629–645.

Glick-Schiller, N., L. Basch and C. Szanton Blanc 1992. "Transnationalism: A New Analytic Framework for Understanding Migration". In *Toward a Transnational Perspective on Migration: Race, Class, Ethnicity, and Nationalism Reconsidered*. New York: New York Academy of Sciences.

Global Alliance Against Trafficking of Women (GAATW) 2007. *Collateral Damage: The Impact of Anti-Trafficking Measures on Human Rights around the World*. Bangkok: GAATW.

Goldman, J. 2002. "Interview with Chris Smith". Fox on the Record with Greta Van Susteren, Fox Network News. Retrieved June 13, 2010, from http://www.foxnews.com/.

Gregory, Katherine 2005. *The Everyday Lives of Sex Workers in the Netherlands*. New York and London: Routledge.

Guevarra, Anna Romina 2009. *Marketing Dreams, Manufacturing Heroes: The Transnational Labour Brokering of Filipino Workers*. New York: Rutgers University Press.

Gulcur, Leyla and Pinar Ilkkaracan 2002. "The 'Natasha' Experience: Migrant Sex Workers from the Former Soviet Union and Eastern Europe in Turkey", *Women's Studies International Forum* 25 (4): 411–421.

Guy, Michelle Lee 2004. "Gossiping endurance: Discipline and Social Control of Filipina helpers in Malaysia", *Asian Journal of Social Science* 32 (3): 501–518.

Halliday, Jon and Bruce Cumings 1988. *Korea: The Unknown War*. London: Viking.

Hewamanne, S. 2009. *Stitching Identities in a Free Trade Zone: Gender and Politics in Sri Lanka*. Philadelphia: University of Pennsylvania Press.

Hicks, George 1995. *The Comfort Women: Sex Slave of the Japanese Imperial Forces*. Chiangmai, Thailand: Silkworm Books.

Hildson, Anne-Marie and Beena Giridharan 2008. "Racialised Sexualities: The Case of Filipina Migrant Workers in East Malaysia", *Gender, Place and Culture* 15 (6): 611–628.

Hoijer, Birgitta 2004. "The Discourse of Global Compassion: The Audience and Media Reporting of Human Suffering", *Media, Culture, and Society* 26 (4): 513–531.

hooks, bell 1990. *Yearning: Race, Gender and Cultural Politics*. Toronto: Between the Times.

Howell, Philip 2009. *Geographies of Regulation: Policing Prostitution in Nineteenth Century Britain and the Empire*. Cambridge: Cambridge University Press.

Hubbard, Phil 1998. "Sexuality, Immorality and the City: Red-light Districts and the Marginalisation of the Female Street Prostitute", *Gender, Place and Culture* 5 (1): 55–76.

Hughes, Donna 2008. "Response to Cheng", *Violence Against Women* 14 (3): 364–365.

Human Rights Watch 2010. *Off the Streets: Arbitrary Detention and Other Abuses against Sex Workers in Cambodia*. New York: Human Rights Watch.

Hutchinson, Jane and Andrew Brown 2001. *Organising Labor in Globalizing Asia*. New York: Routledge.

International Organisation for Migration (IOM) 2007. *The IOM Handbook on Direct Assistance for Victims of Trafficking.* Geneva: IOM.

International Organisation for Migration (IOM) 2006. *Life After Reintegration: The Situation of Child Trafficking Victims.* Phnom Penh, Cambodia: IOM.

International Organisation for Migration (IOM) 2002. *A Review of Data on Trafficking in the Republic of Korea.* Prepared by June J. H. Lee. Geneva: IOM.

Jhoty, B. 2001. "Trapped in Modern Slavery: Sex Trafficking Turns Russian Women into Korean Pawns", *Korea Herald*, November 2. Retrieved June 13, 2010, from http://www.koreahearald.co.kr/archives.

Joongang Daily 2007. "Enslavement of Women Still Persists Despite New Law", May 17. Retrieved March 14, 2010, from http://joongangdaily.joins.com/article/view.asp?aid=2875617.

Kapur, Ratna 2002. "The Tragedy of Victimisation Rhetoric: Resurrecting the 'Native' Subject in International/Post-Colonial Feminist Legal Politics", *Harvard Journal of Human Rights*: 1–37.

Kelly, Liz 2002. "Journeys of Jeopardy: A Commentary on Current Research on Trafficking of Women and Children for Sexual Exploitation Within Europe". Paper presented at the EU/IOM European Conference on Preventing and Combating Trafficking in Human Beings, September, London.

Kelly, Patty 2008. *Lydia's Open Door: Inside Mexico's Most Modern Brothel.* Berkeley and Los Angeles: University of California Press.

Kempadoo, Kamela 1999. *Sun, Sex and Gold: Tourism and Sex Work in the Caribbean.* Lanham, MA: Rowman and Littlefield.

Kempadoo, Kamela 1998. *Global Sex Workers: Rights, Resistance and Redefinition.* New York: Routledge.

Kempadoo, Kamela, J. Sanghera, and B. Pattianik 2005. *Trafficking and Prostitution Reconsidered.* New York and London: Routledge.

Kim, Hyun Sook 1998. "Yanggongju as an Allegory of the Nation: The Representation of Working-Class Women and Radical Texts". In Elaine Kim and Chungmoo Choi (eds.), *Dangerous Women: Gender and Korean Nationalism.* New York: Routledge, pp. 175–202.

Kim, H. S. 1997. "The Problems Faced by Women and Children in GI Camptowns". Retrieved July 11, 2005 from http://maria.peacenet.or.kr/i3.html.

King, R. 2000. *Return Migration: Journey of Hope or Despair.* Geneva: International Organisation for Migration.

Kloer, Amanda 2010. "Sex Trafficking High Around U.S. Military Bases Abroad". Retrieved March 20, 2010, from http://www.humantrafficking.change.org.blog/view.

Kondo, D. K. 1990. *Crafting Selves: Power, Gender, and Discourses of Identity in a Japanese Workplace.* Chicago: Chicago University Press.

Koning, J. 2005. "The Impossible Return? The Post-Migration Narratives of Young Women in Rural Java", *Asian Journal of Social Science* 33 (2): 165–185.

Korea Church Women United (KCWU) 2002. *Second Fieldwork Report on Trafficked Women in Korea.* Seoul: KCWU.

Korea Church Women United (KCWU) 1999. *Fieldwork Report on Trafficked Women in Korea.* Seoul: KCWU.

Korean Ministry of Justice Regulations 2001. Retrieved from http://www.moj.go.kr/HP/coun/bbs-034.

Laczko, Frank 2005. Introduction. In Frank Laczko and Elzbieta Gozdziak (eds.), "Data and Research on Human Trafficking: A Global Survey", Special Issue of *International Migration* 43 (1 & 2): 1–16.

Lainez, Nicolas 2010. "Representing Sex Trafficking? The Victim Staged". In Tiantian Zheng (ed.), *Anti-Trafficking, Human Rights, and Social Justice*. New York: Routledge, pp. 134–149.

Laurie, N., R. Andolina and S. Radcliffe 2005. "Ethnodevelopment: Social Movements, Creating Experts and Professionalising Indigenous Knowledge in the Andes", *Antipode* (37) 3: 470–496.

Lauser, A. 2008. "Philippine Women on the Move: Marriage across Borders", *International Migration* 46 (4): 85–109.

Law, Lisa 2001. "Home Cooking: Filipino Women and Geographies of the Senses in Hong Kong", *Cultural Geographies* 8 (3): 264–283.

Law, Lisa 2000. *Sex Work in Southeast Asia: The Place of Desire in a Time of AIDS*. London and New York: Routledge.

Law, Lisa 1997. "Dancing on the Bar: Sex, Money, and the Uneasy Politics of Third Space". In S. Pile and M. Keith (eds.), *Geographies of Resistance*. New York: Routledge, pp. 107–123.

Lim, Timothy C. 2008. *The Dynamics of Trafficking, Smuggling and Prostitution: An Analysis of Korean Women in the U.S. Commercial Sex Industry*. Report to Bombit Foundation, Seoul, July.

Limoncelli, Stephanie A. 2010. *The Politics of Human Trafficking: The First International Movement to Combat the Sexual Exploitation of Women*. Stanford, CA: Stanford University Press.

Lindquist, Johan 2010. "Images and Evidence: Human Trafficking, Auditing, and the Production of Illicit Markets in Southeast Asia and Beyond". *Public Culture* 22 (2).

Lindquist, Johan 2005. *The Anxieties of Mobility*. Manoa: University of Hawaii Press.

Lindquist, Johan 2004. "Veils and Ecstasy: Negotiating Shame in the Indonesian Borderlands", *Ethnos* 69 (4): 487–508.

Lisborg, Anders and Sine Plambech 2009. *Going Back, Moving On: A Synthesis Report of the Trends and Experiences of Returned Trafficking Victims in Thailand and the Philippines*. Thailand: ILO (International Labour Organisation).

Long, Lynellyn D. 2004. "Anthropological Perspectives on the Trafficking of Women for Sexual Exploitation", *International Migration* 42 (1): 5–31.

McIntyre, Donald 2002. "Base Instincts", *Time Magazine* (Asian Edition) 160 (5).

Mack, Jennifer 2004. "Inhabiting the Imaginary: Factory Women at Home on Batam Island, Indonesia", *Singapore Journal of Tropical Geography* 25 (2): 156–179.

McKay, Deidre and Carol Brandy 2005. "Practices of Place-making: Globalisation and Locality in the Philippines", *Asia Pacific Viewpoint* 46 (2): 89–103.

McLagan, Meg 2003. "Human Rights, Testimony, and Transnational Publicity", *Scholar and Feminist Online* 2 (1). Retrieved from http://sfonline.barnard.edu/ps/mclagan.htm.

McMichael, William H. 2002a. "MPs Watch Clubs Closely but Some Say Military Looks the Other Way", *Army Times*, August 19.

McMichael, William H. 2002b. "Sex Slaves: How Women Are Lured into South Korea's Flesh Trade, How Top U.S. Commanders Turn a Blind Eye Even as Troops are the Rackets Best Customers", *Army Times*, August 19, p. 14.

Mai, Nicola and Russell King 2009. "Love, Sexuality, and Migration: Mapping the Issue(s)", *Mobilities* 4 (3): 295–307.

Manzo, Kate 2008. "Imaging Humanitarianism: NGO Identity and the Iconography of Childhood", *Antipode* 40 (4): 632–657.

Marcus, George E. 2005. "The Anthropologist as Witness in Contemporary Regimes of Intervention", *Cultural Politics: An International Journal* 1 (1): 31–50.

Marten, Lisa 2005. "Commercial Sex Workers: Victims, Vectors or Fighters of the HIV Epidemic in Cambodia?" *Asia Pacific Viewpoint* 46 (1): 21–34.

Mendelson, Sarah 2005. *Barracks and Brothels: Peacekeepers and Human Trafficking in the Balkans*. CSIS Report. Washington, DC: Centre for Strategic and International Studies.

Miller, Elizabeth, Michele R. Decker, Jay G. Silverman and Anita Raj 2007. "Migration, Sexual Exploitation, and Women's Health: A Case Report from a Community Health Center", *Violence Against Women* 13 (5): 486–497.

Miller, Jody 2002. "Violence and Coercion in Sri Lanka's Commercial Sex Industry: Intersections of Gender, Sexuality, Culture, and the Law", *Violence Against Women* 8 (9): 1044–1073.

Ming, Kevin D. 2005. "Cross-border 'Traffic': Stories of Dangerous Victims, Pure Whores and HIV/AIDS in the Experiences of Mainland Female Sex Workers in Hong Kong", *Asia Pacific Viewpoint* 46 (1): 35–48.

Mohanty, Chandra T. 1987. "Under Western Eyes: Feminist Scholarship and Colonial Discourse". In Chandra T. Mohanty, Ann Russo and Lourdes Torres (eds.), *Third World Women and the Politics of Feminism*. Bloomington: Indiana University Press, pp. 51–80.

Montgomery, Heather 1998. "Children, Prostitution and Identity: A Case Study from a Tourist Resort in Thailand". In Kamala Kempadoo and Jo Doezema (eds.), *Global Sex Workers: Rights, Resistance and Redefinition*. New York and London: Routledge, pp. 139–150.

Moon, Katharine H.S. 1999. "South Korean Movements against Militarised Sexual Labour", *Asian Survey* 39 (2): 310–327.

Moon, Katharine H.S. 1998. *Sex among Allies*. New York: Columbia University Press.

Munshi, Shoma 2011. "Introduction". In S. Munshi (ed.), *Images of the "Modern Woman" in Asia: Global Media, Local Meaning*. Curzon, Richmond UK: Routledge, pp. 1–16.

Musto, J.L. 2008. "The NGO-ification of the Anti-Trafficking Movement in the United States: A Case Study of the Coalition to Abolish Slavery and Trafficking", *Wagadu* 5: 6–20.

Nagal, Joane 2003. *Race, Ethnicity, and Sexuality: Intimate Intersections, Forbidden Frontiers*. New York: Oxford University Press.

Nguyen, Thu-huong 2008. *The Ironies of Freedom: Sex, Culture, and Neo-liberal Governance in Vietnam*. Seattle and London: University of Washington Press.

Ong, Aihwa 1987. *Spirits of Resistance and Capitalist Discipline: Factory Women in Malaysia*. Albany: State University of New York.

Parrenas, Rhacel Salazar 2011. *Illicit Flirtations: Labour, Migration, and Sex Trafficking in Tokyo*. Stanford, CA: Stanford University Press.

Parrenas, Rhacel Salazar 2010. "Homeward Bound: The Circular Migration of Entertainers between Japan and the Philippines", *Global Networks* 10 (3): 301–323.

Parrenas, Rhacel Salazar 2006. "Trafficked? Filipino Hostesses in Tokyo's Nightlife Industry", *Yale Journal of Law and Feminism* 18: 145–180.

Parrenas, Rhacel Salazar 2005. "Mothering from a Distance: Emotions, Gender, and Intergenerational Relations in Filipino Transnational Families", *Feminist Studies* 27 (2): 361–390.

Parrenas, Rhacel Salazar 2001. *Servants of Globalisation: Women, Migration and Domestic Work*. Stanford, CA: Stanford University Press.

Peach, Lucinda Joy 2005. " 'Sex Slaves' or 'Sex Workers'? Cross-cultural and Comparative Religious Perspectives on Sexuality, Subjectivity, and Moral Identity in Anti-sex Trafficking Discourse", *Culture and Religion* 6 (1): 107–134.

Pearson, Elaine and Anne T. Gallagher 2008. "Detention of Trafficked Persons in Shelters: A Legal and Policy Analysis". Available at SSRN: http://ssrn.com/abstract=1239745 or http://dx.doi.org/10.2139/ssrn.1239745" \t "_blank.
Pile, Steve and Michael Keith 1997. *Geographies of Resistance*. London: Routledge.
Pratt, Geraldine 2000. "Research Performances", *Environment and Planning D: Society and Space* 18: 639–651.
Rabinoff, Jon 2010 "S Korea Prosecutors Drop Assault Charge against Soldier after Settlement Reached', *Stars and Stripes* (6 December).
Radcliffe, S., N. Laurie and R Andolina 2005. "Development with Identity: Social Capital and Culture". In R. Andolina, N. Laurie and S. Radcliffe (eds.), *Multi-ethnic Transnationalisms: Indigenous Development in the Andes*. Durham, NC: Duke University Press.
Rafael, V. 2000. *White Love and Other Events in Filipino History*. Durham, NC: Duke University Press.
Rafferty, Yvonne 2008. "The Impact of Trafficking on Children: Psychological and Social Policy Perspectives", *Child Development Perspectives* 2 (1): 13–18.
Raymond, Janice G., Donna Hughes and C. Gomez 2001. *Sex Trafficking of Women in the United States: International and Domestic Trends*. CATW. Retrieved December 12, 2010, from http://action.web.ca/home/catw/attach/sex_traff_us.pdf.
Reid, Bryonie 2007. "Creating Counterspaces: Identity and the Home in Ireland and Northern Ireland", *Environment and Planning D: Society and Space* 25: 933–950.
Richardson, Dianne, Meena Poudel and Nina Laurie 2009. "Sex Trafficking in Nepal: Constructing Citizenship and Livelihoods", *Gender, Place and Culture* 16 (3): 259–278.
Roces, Mina 2009. "Prostitution, Women's Movements and the Victim Narrative in the Philippines", *Women's Studies International Forum* 32 (4): 270–280.
Rodriguez, Robyn 2010. *How the Philippine State Brokers Labour to the World*. Minneapolis and London: University of Minnesota Press.
Saewoomt'uh 2002. *The Problems Facing Women and Children in Kijichon in Korea*. Seoul: Saewoomt'uh.
Saewoomt'uh 1998. *Kyunggi-do Province Human Trafficking Investigation and Policy Research Report* [*Kyunggi-do Giyok Sungmaemae Silt'ae Chosa mitch Chungch'aektae an Yungu*]. Seoul: Saewoomt'uh (in Korean).
Samarasinghe, Vidymali 2008. *Female Sex Trafficking in Asia: The Resilience of Patriarchy in a Changing World*. New York: Routledge.
Sandy, Larissa 2007. "Just Choices: Representations of Choice and Consent in Sex Work in Cambodia", *The Australian Journal of Anthropology* 18 (2): 194–206.
Santos, Aida F. 2002. *Women in the International Migration Process: Patterns, Profiles and Health Consequences of Sexual Exploitation. The Philippines Report*. Manila: Coalition Against Trafficking in Women.
Sariola, Salla 2010. *Gender and Sexuality in India: Selling Sex in Chennai*. London and New York: Routledge.
Sassen, Saskia 2002. Global Cities and Survival Circuits. Retrieved July 11, 2010, from http://portal.unesco.org/shs/en/files/7374/11090837201SaskiaSassen.pdf/Saskia Sassen.pdf.
Scott, James 1985. *Weapons of the Weak: Everyday Forms of Resistance*. New Haven, CT: Yale University Press.
Semyonov, Moshe and Anastasia Gorodzeisky 2005. "Labour Migration, Remittances and Household Income: A Comparison between Filipino and Filipina Overseas Workers", *International Migration Review* 39 (1): 45–68.

Shah, Svati 2006. "Producing the Spectacle of Kamathipura: The Politics of Red Light Visibility in Mumbai", *Cultural Dynamics* 18 (3): 269–292.
Shigekane, Rachel 2007. "Rehabilitation and Community Integration of Trafficking Survivors in the United States", *Human Rights Quarterly* 29: 112–136.
Sibley, David 1995. *Geographies of Exclusion: Society and Difference in the West.* London: Routledge.
Smith, C. 2002. Congressional-Executive Commission on China: Representative Christopher Smith. Retrieved June 15, 2011, from www.cecc.gov/smith.
Smith, Michael P. and Luis E. Guarzino 1998. *Transnationalism from Below.* New Brunswick, NJ: Transaction Publishers.
Soderland, Gretchen 2005. "Running from the Rescuers: New U.S. Campaigns against Sex Trafficking and the Rhetoric of Abolition", *NWSA Journal* 17 (3): 64–87.
Soh, Sarah 2001. "Prostitutes versus Sex Slaves: The Politics of Representing the 'Comfort Women' ". In Margaret Stetz and Bonnie B. C. Oh (eds.), *Legacies of the Comfort Women of World War II.* Armonk, NY: ME Sharpe, pp. 689–87.
Soh, Sarah 2000. "From Imperial Gifts to Sex Slaves: Theorising Symbolic Representations of the 'Comfort Women' ", *Social Science Japan Journal* 3 (1): 59–76.
Spivak, Gayatri 1988. "Can the Subaltern Speak?" In C. Nelson and L. Grossburg (eds.), *Marxism and the Interpretation of Culture.* Urbana: University of Illinois Press, pp. 271–313.
Steinfatt, Thomas M. 2002. *Working at the Bar: Sex Work and Health Communication in Thailand.* Westport, CT, and London: ABLEX Publishing.
Stoler, Ann Laura 1989. "Re-thinking Colonial Categories: European Communities and the Boundaries of Rule", *Comparative Studies in Society and History* 13 (1): 134–161.
Sturdevant, S. P. and B. Stolzfus 1993. *Let the Good Times Roll: Prostitution and the U.S. Military in Asia.* New York: The New Press.
Suzuki, N. 2004. "Inside the Home? Power and Negotiation in Filipina-Japanese Marriages", *Women's Studies* 33 (4): 481–506.
Suzuki, N. 2000a. "Between Two Shores: Transnational Projects and Filipina Wives in/from Japan", *Women's Studies International Forum* 23 (4): 431–44.
Suzuki, N. 2000b. "Gendered Surveillance and Sexual Violence in Filipina Pre-migration Experiences to Japan". In B. Yeoh, P. Teo and S. Huang (eds.), *Gender Politics in the Asia Pacific Region.* New York: Routledge, pp. 99–119.
Tadiar, N. 2004. *Fantasy-Production: Sexual Economies and Other Philippine Consequences of the New World Order.* Quezon City: University of the Philippines Press.
Tadiar, N. 1997. "Domestic Bodies of the Philippines", *Sojourn* 12 (2): 153–191.
Tyner, James A. 2009. *The Philippines: Mobilities, Identities and Globalisation.* London: Routledge Chapman and Hall.
Tyner, James A. 2004. *Made in the Philippines.* London: Routledge Curzon.
Tyner, James A. 2002. "Geographies of Identity: The Migrant Experiences of Filipinas in Northeast Ohio", *Asia Pacific Viewpoint* 43(3): 311–326.
United Nations 2000. *Protocol to Prevent, Suppress and Punish Trafficking in Persons, Especially Women and Children.* Geneva: United Nations Office of Drugs and Crime.
United Nations Inter Agency Project (UNI-IAP) 1998. *Training Manual for Combating Trafficking in Women and Children.* Bangkok.
United States Department of State (US DoS) 2000. *Annual Trafficking in Persons Report.* Washington D.C.: US DoS.
United States Department of State (US DoS) 2010. *Trafficking in Persons Report.* Retrieved September 19, 2010, from http://www.state.gov/g/tip/rls/tiprpt/2010.

United States Department of State (US DoS) 2006. *Trafficking in Persons Report.* Retrieved May 20, 2009, from http://www.state.gov/g/tip/rls/tiprpt/2006.

United States Department of State (US DoS) 2001. *Trafficking in Persons Report.* Retrieved March 5, 2011, from http://www.state.gov/g/tip/rls/tiprpt/2001.

Vertovec, S. and R. Cohen 2002. *Conceiving Cosmopolitan Theory, Context and Practices.* Oxford: Oxford University Press.

Wallace, Robert G. 2009. "Breeding Influenza: The Political Virology of Offshore Farming", *Antipode* 41 (5): 916–951.

Weitzer, Ronald 2005. "Flawed Theory and Method in Studies of Prostitution", *Violence Against Women* 11 (7): 934–949.

Yea, Sallie 2007. "*Kijich'on* as Transnational Space". In Tim Tangherlini and Sallie Yea (eds.), *Sitings: Critical Perspectives on Korean Geography.* Manoa: University of Hawaii Press.

Yea, Sallie 2005a. "Labour of Love: Filipina Entertainer's Narratives of Romance and Relationships with GIs in US Military Camp Town in Korea", *Women's Studies International Forum* 28 (6): 456–472.

Yea, Sallie 2005b. "When Push Comes to Shove: Violence, Family Dissolution and Personal Transformation in Trafficked Women's Migration Decisions", *Sojourn: Journal of Southeast Asian Studies* 20 (1): 67–95.

Yea, Sallie 2004a. "Challenges in Eliminating Sex Trafficking: Victim Control Mechanisms and Compensation", *Development Bulletin* (Special Issue on Human Trafficking, Human Security and Development), December.

Yea, Sallie 2004b. "Runaway Brides: Anxieties of Identity Among Trafficked Filipina Entertainers in South Korea", *Singapore Journal of Tropical Geography* 25 (2): 180–197.

Yeoh, Brenda S.A. and Shirlena Huang 2000. "'Home' and 'Away': Foreign Domestic Workers and Negotiations of Diasporic Identity in Singapore', *Women's Studies International Forum* 23 (4) 413–429.

Yeoh, B.S.A. and S. Huang 1999. "Spaces at the Margins: Migrant Domestic Workers and the Development of Civil Society in Singapore", *Environment and Planning A* 31: 1149–1167.

Yeoh, B.S.A. and S. Huang 1998. "Negotiating Public Space: Strategies and Styles of Migrant Female Domestic Workers", *Urban Studies* 35: 583–602.

Yuval-Davis, Nira 1998. "Women, Gender and Nationalism". In Rick Wilford and Robert L. Miller (eds.), *Ethnicity and Nationalism.* New York: Routledge, pp. 23–35.

Zelizer, Viviana 1997. *The Social Meaning of Money.* Princeton, NJ: Princeton University Press.

Zelizer, Viviana 2005. *The Purchase of Intimacy.* Princeton NJ: Princeton University Press.

Zhang, Sheldon 2010. "Beyond the 'Natasha' Story – A Review and Critique of Current Research on Sex Trafficking", *Global Crime* 10 (3): 178–195.

Zheng, Tiantian 2009. *Red Lights: The Lives of Sex Workers in Postsocialist China.* Minneapolis: University of Minnesota Press.

Zimelis, A. 2009. "Human Rights, the Sex Industry and Human Rights: Feminist Analyses of Nationalism in Japan, South Korea and the Philippines", *Cooperation and Conflict* 44: 71–91.

Zimmerman, C., K. Yun, I. Shavab, C. Watts, L. Trappolin, M. Treppete et al. 2003. *The Health Risks and Consequences of Trafficking in Women and Adolescents: Findings from a European Study.* London: London School of Health and Tropical Medicine.

Zontini, E. 2009. *Transnational Migration, Family and Gender: Moroccan and Filipina Women in Bologna and Barcelona.* Oxford: Berghahn Books.

Index

Note: page numbers with *f* indicate figures; those with *t* indicate tables.

abortions 83–5
Agathangelou, Anna M. 33
Agustin, Laura 8, 65
Air Force Times 101
Alma narrative 79–83
American Alley 20, 68, 86, 110–13
Andrijasevic, Rutvica 104
anthropologist as witness 10
Anti-Prostitution Law 27
anti-trafficking 130–47; the Centre and 132–5; local/religious third-sector organizations and, in Korea 135–40; by NGOs and entertainers 130–47; overview of 130–2; transnational support networks for 140–6
anti-trafficking framework 64
anxieties, of romance and club work 97–102; bar managers/club owners relationship and 98–9; decision to run away as 101–2; Filipinas and 97; fun boyfriends *vs.* good customers 97; relationships with GIs and 100; women with one serious boyfriend and 98
Aquino, Corry 23
Archdiocesan Pastoral Centre for Filipino Migrants 4
Article Six, Trafficking Protocol 73
Artist's Record Book (ARB) 42
Asia Times 30
Asis, M.M.B. 25
auditable victims 136

Bae-sook, Cho 27
balik bayan (homecoming) 156
bar fines 40, 50–3; Cherry-Lynn example of 94*t*, 95*f*; described 91; as possible romantic association site 89–93

bar managers/club owners relationship 98–9
Barracks and Brothels (Mendelson) 33
Battistella, G. 25
boundary work 49
Brandy, Carol 155, 156
Brennan, Denise 88, 140
Brunovskis, Anette 7, 8, 13, 15
buying time 93–6, 94*t*, 95*f*

Cabezas, Amalia L. 89
Camp Casey 1, 11, 19, 32, 102, 116
Caouette, T. 13
Capdevila, Gustavo 30
Castles, Stephen 41, 58
the Centre 4, 9; Cecile and 122–3; Filipino migrant community and 132–5; salary recovery and 63
Centre for Strategic and International Studies 33
Chang, Kimberley A. 118, 150, 156
Chapkis, Wendy 97
Cheng, Sealing 6, 27, 30, 46, 63, 131–2, 164
Cherry-Lyn vignette 38–40; bar fines and hostessing duties 50–3, 94*t*, 95*f*; boyfriends and 94, 96, 98–9; dance moves and 143; nights off and 57–8
Choi, Chungmoo 74
Coalition Against Trafficking of Women (CATW) 25, 30, 147
Coalition Against Trafficking of Women-Asia Pacific (CATW-AP) 33
Cohen, Erik 126
comfort women 29–32
Contagious Diseases Act 74
contract migration regimes 41–2
Cornwall, Andrea 87–8

Index

Correa, S. 87–8
Creswell, Tim 152
Cupples, Julie 11
customer-cum-boyfriend 9, 86, 97, 101–2, 104

debt bondage 163
Doezema, Jo 139
domestic trafficking 30
drink systems 49–50; *see also* bar fines; ladies drinks

emotional labour 97
Employment Permit System (EPS) 58
Enriquez, Jean 33–4
entertainer 14
E-6 visa 26, 39, 42, 59
Espiritu, Y. L. 138, 150
ethnography, human trafficking and 8–12

factory women, migrant entertainers as 119–24; Cecile's story 121–3; Charie's story 123–4; Jane's story 119–21; overview of 119
Faier, Lieba 6–7, 108, 113
failed heroines, women as 153–6
fallout geographies 27–8
Farley, Melissa 70, 85
Father Dong 130–1
Father Glenn *see* Jaron, Glenn
Female Sex Trafficking in Asia (Samarasinghe) 32–3
Ferguson, Kathy E. 151
Filipina entertainers 23; *see also* return migration, of Filipina entertainers; E-6 visa and 26; as gold diggers 115; health impacts of (*see* health in trafficking); return to Philippines of 148–60; in South Korea 19–21, 26
Filipinas in Prostitution around US Military Bases in Korea: A Recurring Nightmare (Enriquez) 33–4
Filipino labour migration 23–4; feminization of 24–5; Gulf War and 25
financial failure, prostitution stigma and 158–9
Foucault, Michel 79
Fox Television 28–9
Frederick, John 73
fun boyfriends *vs.* good customers 97
Furhman, James W. 32

Gabriella 147
Gaetano, Arianne 151

gijich'on 6, 8, 11; *see also* migrant entertainers, in Korea; romantic associations, as exit strategy; anti-trafficking support networks for 140–6; comfort women and 29–32; Fox Television and 28–9; masculinist-military formations and 32–4; overview of 19–21; peripheral Korea and 22–3; Philippines and 23–6; sex trafficking in Korea's 19–36; strategic intimacy concept and 89; US Department of Defense and 26–9; women as entertainers in 14
Giridharan, Beena 88–9
Glick-Schieller, Nina 108, 109
gold diggers, Filipina entertainers as 115
Grace vignette: boyfriends and 100; financial independence and 116–17; Pop Store Club and 63–6; return migration of 157–8; and Stuart 111–13
Gregory, Katherine 9
Groves, Julian McAllister 150, 156
Guevarra, Anna Romina 42
Gulcur, Leyla 104

Hae Mee vignette 19–20
Hangyure Sinmun (newspaper) 39
health in trafficking 68–86; Alma narrative 79–83; governance of 71–5; Korean women and 74–5; overview of 68–71; pregnancy/abortion and 83–5; profit *versus* 75–7; punishments against women and 77–9; US military CPs and 74–5; violence and 70–1
heulk in club 20
Hicks, George 31
Hildson, Anne-Marie 88–9
HIV/AIDS 71–3
Howell, Philip 74
Hughes, Donna 30
Human Rights Watch 71
human trafficking: categories of research on 5; constrained choices of women and 5–6; ethnography and 8–12; hidden populations of 7; research bias of 7–8; terminology 13–16; types of 30; United Nations definition of 14–15

Ilkkaracan, Pinar 104
illicit flirtation 47
indentured mobility 163
infidelity and trust 117–19
International Organisation for Migration (IOM) 30

Index

Japanese militarised prostitution 31
Jaron, Glenn 9–10, 40, 62–3, 103, 122, 130, 132–4, 142
Ji Eun-hee 27
Jolly, S. 87–8
juicy girl 89–90, 110

Kang Geum-sil 27
Kapur, Ratna 13, 36, 64
Kelly, Liz 105
Kelly, Patty 110
Kempadoo, Kamela 88
Kim, Elaine 74
Kim, Hyun Sook 30, 34
Kim Kang Ja 10
Koning, J. 151
Korea: fallout geographies and 27–8; *gijich'on and* 22–3; migration process to 38–66; Sex Trade Prevention Act 26–7
Korean Peninsula 2*f*
Korean Special Tourism Association 130

labour brokers 41
labour exploitation 6
labour trafficking, TVPA definition of 60–1
ladies drinks: GI expectations for 90–1; as possible romantic association site 89–93; as symbolic act 89–90; women's customer preference for 91–2
Lainez, Nicolas 4
Law, Lisa 10, 70, 144
Limoncelli, Stephanie 74
Lindquist, Johan 136, 150
Ling, L. H. M. 33
Lisa vignette 48, 49, 51, 53, 69; boyfriends and 93, 96, 99; circulating support 142; and David story 113–14, 116–17; health and 75, 76; money conflicts 114–16; pregnancy and 83, 86; running away and 125–6; trust issues 117–18
Lisborg, Anders 13, 153, 159
living accommodations 57
local/religious third-sector organizations, anti-trafficking and 135–40
Long, Lynellyn D. 7–8
long time sex performance 2

Macapagal-Arroyo, Gloria 23
Magdalena, Mary 150
mama-san 3
Manzo, Kate 35
Marcus, George E. 10
Markle, Kenneth 32

marriage for visas 124–7
masculinist-military formations 32–4
McAllister Groves, Julian 118
McKay, Deidre 155, 156
M Club 1, 46, 51–2, 85–6
Mendelson, Sarah 33
Merriman, Tom 28, 29
migrant entertainers, in Korea 38–66; auditions of 42–3; bar fines and 50–3; Cherry-Lyn vignette 38–40; club rules and punishments 57–8; contracts for women 53–6, 54–5*f*; debt and salaries of 44–6, 45*f*; described 41–7; drink systems and 49–50; living accommodations 57; pimping of 58; post-exit trajectories of 107–29; respect and, claiming 61–4; sexual and intimate labour 47–9; TIP reports and 58–61; VIP rooms and 51–2; *Walang pera* (no money) and 47–9
Migrant Workers Act 23, 42
mobility, negotiations of 108; *see also* post-exit trajectories, migrant entertainers
Mohanty, Chandra 144
money conflict 114–16
Montgomery, Heather 10–11
Moon, Katharine H. S. 34, 74
Musto, Jennifer Lynne 140, 145

National Campaign for the Eradication of Crime by the US Troops in Korea 22
NBC Club 1
Nguyen, Thu-huong 72
normative disruptions 13

Olympia Club 38
Ong, Aiwha 79
Overseas Filipinos Act 23, 42
Overseas Investment Fund Act 23
overtime pay 54, 56

Parrenas, Rhacel Salazar 6, 13, 14, 16, 23, 47, 49, 123, 163
Philippine Migrants Rights Watch (PMRW) 46
Philippine Overseas Employment Administration (POEA) 23, 46
Philippines; *see also* migrant entertainers, in Korea: Labor Code 23; political-economic positioning of 23–6; second tiger status of 23; US bases in 25
Plambech, Sine 13, 153, 159
Polaris Project 30

post-exit trajectories, migrant entertainers 107–29; dependence and boredom issues with 116–17; as factory women 119–24; infidelity and trust issues with 117–19; marriage for visas and 124–7; money conflict and 114–16; overview of 107–9; runaway brides 109–14; stigma of club women and 114–19
pregnancy 83–5
promotion agencies 46
prostitute body, governance of 71–5; HIV/AIDS and 71–3; sex trafficking and 73–5; STIs and 71–3
prostitution stigma, financial failure and 158–9
prostitution vs. trafficking 156–8
Protocol to Prevent, Protect and Suppress Trafficking in Persons, Especially Women and Children 14–15

Rafael, V. 138
recruitment agencies 41
rescue industry 65
return migration, of Filipina entertainers 148–60; characteristics of 152–3; financial failure combined with prostitution stigma 158–9; moral tropes of 149–52; overview of 148–9; prostitution vs. trafficking and 156–8; women as failed heroines 153–6
Rodriguez, Robyn 43
romantic associations, as exit strategy 87–106; anxieties about club work and 97–102; boyfriends as financial support and 96; breakups and scarring from 102–4; buying time and 93–6, 94t, 95f; ladies drinks/bar fines and 89–93; overview of 87–8; strategic intimacy and 88–9
Rosie vignette 1–5; boyfriends of 4–5, 93, 96; the Centre and 4; health of 76; migration to Korea 1; points system and 3; punishments imposed upon 3–4; Time Magazine report of 4–5; as trafficked person 1; Y Club requirements of 2–3, 56
Rumsfeld, Donald 28, 29, 33
runaway agency 108, 109
runaway brides 109–14; described 9; Grace and Stuart 111–13; Lisa and David 113–14; overview of 109–10; Valerie and Chris 111

Saito, Y. 13
Samarasinghe, Vidymali 32–3

Santos, Aida F. 92
Sariola, Salla 75
Sassen, Saskia 146
selection effects 8
Seoul-Kyunggi-Incheon Migrant Workers Trade Union 58
sex performance, long time 2
Sex Trade Prevention Act 26–7
sex trafficking 14
sexual and intimate labour 47–9
Shah, Svati 21
Shigekane, Rachel 149
short time sex performance 1–2
Smith, Chris 28, 29, 59
Soderland, Gretchen 65
Soh, Sarah 34
Songtan 2f, 8; anti-trafficking performance in 10; Cherry-Lyn vignette 38–40; trafficking of sex slaves in 9–10
Soo, Kim Kyung 47–8
South Korea: anti-trafficking paradigm in 130–47; exit strategies of entertainers in 87–106; Filipina entertainers in 19–21, 26; health impacts of trafficking in (see health in trafficking); political-economic positioning of 22–6; US military presence in 22, 26–9
Status of Forces Agreement (SOFA) 29
stigma, of club women 114–19
Stoler, Ann 74
strategic intimacy 17, 88–9
Surtees, Rebecca 7, 8, 13, 15
Suzuki, N. 118, 150

Tabitha's House 19–20
tactical sex 89
Tadiar, N. 138, 150
TDC see Tongducheon (TDC)
Time Magazine 4–5
Tongducheon (TDC) 1; Camp Casey in 11; changing dynamics of 20–1; clubs in 19–20; Fox Television in 28–9; freedom of movement in 57; health issues in 68–9, 76–7; introduction to 8–10; pimping of migrant entertainers in 58; Rosie in 4–5; sex trafficking in 19–21; Tabitha's House in 19–20; violence involving GIs in 32
Top Hat Club 38
trafficked person 1, 13
Trafficking in Persons (TIP) report 26–7; migrant entertainers and 58–61
transnational trafficking 30

trust issues 117–19
Tyner, James A. 150

United Nations (UN), human trafficking definition of 14–15
US Department of State (US DoS): *gijich'on* trafficking and 26–9; Trafficking in Persons (TIP) report 26–7
US Forces Korea (USFK) 29
US military: in Philippines 25; South Korea and 22–3
United States Trafficking Victims Protection Act 60–1; labour trafficking definition of 60–1

Valerie and Chris story 111
victim, usage of term 15–16
victim of trafficking 13
the 'victim staged' 4, 5
violence, health in sex trafficking and 70–1; club profits and 75–7; penalties/ punishments and 77–9

wives troika 27
woman employment contract 54–5*f*
women: comfort 29–32; contracts for 53–6, 54–5*f*; as entertainers in *gijich'on* 14; factory, migrant entertainers as 119–24; as failed heroines 153–6; with one serious boyfriend 98; punishments against 77–9; stigma of club 114–19

yanggongju (foreign princess) 31, 34
Y Club 51, 56; labour relations in 6; points system at 3; punishments imposed by 3–4; sex performances at 1–2
Yes Club 38
Yoon Geun Mi 32
Yun Won-ho 27

Zelizer, Viviana 63–4, 88
zero tolerance policy 29
Zheng, Tiantian 49, 104
Zimelis, A. 34
Zimmermann, C. 70